Manra
Starbuck
Eiao
Tokelau
Islands (NZ)
Penrhyn
Nukuhiva
Rakahanga
Manihiki
Vostok
Caroline Island
Pukapuka
Nassau
Flint
FRENCH
Suwarrow
Apia
Tutuila
AMERICAN
SAMOA
Makemo
Anaa
Palmerston
Alofi
NIUE
Duke of Gloucester
Islands
Rurutu
Tubuai
Raevavae
AUSTRAL ISLANDS
POLYNESIA
Rapa
Marotiri
NORTH
0
250
500 km

South Pacific Islands

Joan Beard

Little Hills Press

Cover by NB Design

Printed in Singapore

ISBN 1 86315 103 6

Little Hills Press Pty Ltd
37-43 Alexander Street
Crows Nest NSW 2065
Australia

Moorlands Publishing Company
Moor Farm Road, Airfield Estate, Ashbourne
Derbyshire, DE6 1HD
England

(ISBN 0 86190 649 7 - UK only)

DISCLAIMER
Whilst all care has been taken by the publisher and author to ensure that the information is accurate and up to date, the publisher does not take responsibility for the information published herein. The recommendations are those of the author, and as things get better or worse, places close and others open, some elements in the book may be inaccurate when you get there. Please write to our Australian address and tell us about it so we can update in subsequent editions.

Facing Title Page: Tahitian Scene.

CONTENTS

THE COOK ISLANDS

The 15 islands that form the Cook Islands Group are scattered over 2 million sq km of the Pacific Ocean. They lie virtually in the centre of the Polynesian Triangle of the South Pacific, and are flanked in the west by the Kingdom of Tonga and the Samoas, and to the east by Tahiti and the islands of French Polynesia.

The Cook islands are in the same time zone as Hawaii and are the same distance south of the equator as Hawaii is north. They cover a land area of 241 sq km.

The main island of Rarotonga, has a mountainous interior rising to 652m. The capital Avarua is located here.

Other islands accessible by plane are Aitutaki, Mangaia, Atiu, Pukapuka, Mauke, Penrhyn, Mitiaro, Rakahhnga, Manihiki, Nassau, Palmerston and Suwarrow.

Fruit, copra and mother-of-pearl are the main exports.

History

The first settlers in the Cook Islands were Polynesians who arrived about 800AD during the Great Polynesian Migration, which had begun in 1500BC.

In the 11th century a chief named Toi built a road called Ara Mewtua. He built it inland, of pavers, across swamps, and it is still the second main road of Rarotonga. Where the chief came from or where he went is a mystery.

Two centuries later the great chiefs Tangiia from Tahiti and Karika from Samoa, met at sea and joined forces to conquer the earlier inhabitants.

The Spanish explorer Alvaro de Mendana reported sighting Pukapuka on August 20 1595. Pedro Fernandez de Quiros, the Portuguese navigator, saw Rakahanga on March 2 1606.

It was over 160 years later that another European sailed into the area, Captain James Cook. He saw Manuaia atoll (Hervey Island) in 1773. In 1777 he discovered Palmerston, Takutea, Mangaia and Atiu. The islands were subsequently named after him.

Captain William Bligh found Aitutaki in 1789 and the same year, after the mutiny on the *Bounty*, Fletcher Christian discovered Rarotonga.

Officially, the discovery of Rarotonga is credited to Captain Philip Goodenough in the *Cumberland*, while he was looking for sandalwood in 1814.

In 1888 the Cook Islands became a British Protectorate, then in 1901, part of New Zealand. In 1965 the islands gained self-government as a dependency of New Zealand.

Members of parliament are elected by the people. There is also a group of main chiefs of the islands, called The Home of Ariki. These chiefs advise the government on legislation concerning customs and traditions. For more information about the history of the islands, we suggest a visit to the library in Avarua.

Climate

The Cook islands enjoy a pleasantly warm and sunny climate all year round. June-August are the cooler months; November-March are the hottest months with some heavy rain. The drier months, April-November, have an average maximum temperature of about 26C. During the warmer, humid, damp months December-March, the temperature range is 22C-28C. October has the most sunshine.

Population

The total population of the islands is 18,552, of which Rarotonga has 10,198. The Polynesian people are delightful. It is this friendly community who make a holiday in the Cook Islands so enjoyable.

Language

The official language is Cook Islands Maori, but everyone speaks English. Here are a few words so you can have a taste of the native language.

Kia Orana................All purpose term of greeting
Kia Manuia ....Good luck (a toast)
Meitaki ....Very good, and used to say thank you.
Aere ra ....Goodbye
Maori ....Polynesian person; local language
Papa'a ....European or Caucasian person; English language.
Pareu.........................Local wrap-around sarong type garment.

Public Holidays

January 1 ....New Year's Day
March/April...........Good Friday/Easter Monday
June ....Queen's Birthday
August 4..................Constitution Day
October 26...............Gospel Day
December 25...........Christmas Day
December 26...........Boxing Day

Festivals

Arts Exhibition: features original paintings in oils and watercolour, wood and shell carvings and coral-stone sculptures. Second week in February.

Dancer of the Year: elaborate original costume designs and unique dance movements are two points for winning when dancers grace the floor to compete for the coveted title. Each is representative of his or her island, group or school. Late April.

Constitution Celebrations: the Cook Islands biggest celebration observed during a two week period. It commemorates the attainment of self government on August 4 1965, and is filled with fun, colour and excitement. This is a time to renew friendships and to review each island's culture. The strength of the warriors and the grace of the dancers is expressed in song and dance. The planter's best harvest, and the small farmer's best beast compete for prizes in the Agricultural Show. Handicrafts by the island women are displayed, and cause a great deal of curiosity and attention. For the sports minded there is rugby, netball and a host of traditional sports form part of the activities. Begins on the last Friday in July.

Cultural Festival Week: is run in conjunction with the Constitution celebrations. Throughout the islands you will see examples of the various influences that have moulded each island throughout their long history. You will see Cook Islands heritage at its best. First week in August.

Round Rarotonga Road Race: the 32km RRRR is extremely popular in Rarotonga and many international runners compete. The event looks for the best in four divisions: individual, Cook Islands residents, veterans and teams. First Saturday in October.

Gospel Day: the pageant commemorates the arrival of Christianity in 1823. It is performed in the open air and each display depicts a story from the Bible. Splendid costuming enhances great acting performances, and the pageant ends with the singing of hymns. October 26.

Food Festival: this is a treat for food lovers. It offers possibilities for discovering new exotic tastes and creativity in cooking. A chance to sample true Cook Islands fare. November.

Tiare (Floral) Week: The natural beauty of the Cook Islands is acknowledged during Tiare Week. Shop fronts are decorated, and offices replenish fresh arrangements each day. Colourful displays of island blooms compete for admiration and prizes. Tiare Week ends with a glamorous parade of flower-covered floats and the Miss Tiare Pageant. Fourth week in November.

Entry Regulations

New Zealand citizens do not require passports for stays of up to 31 days. However, they must produce their passports upon re-entry into New

Zealand. All other visitors must have a current passport.A bona-fide visitor does not require an entry permit provided he or she possesses an onward ticket and does not intend staying more than 31 days. Pre-booked accommodation is essential. Extensions of stays may be granted on a monthly basis for up to 3 months, and are available on application to the local Immigration Department 14 days prior to expiration of permit.

Customs

There is no duty on clothing or personal effects including sporting equipment. The Duty Free allowance is 200 cigarettes or up to 250gm of tobacco or 50 cigars, 2 litres of spirits or wine or 4.5 litres of beer. Goods up to the value of NZ$250 (US$173) do not attract duty, goods over NZ$250 are liable for duty.

Departure Tax

There is a departure tax of NZ$25 (US$17) for adults, and NZ$10 (US$7) for children 2-11, payable in NZ dollars.

Embassies

Australia: No resident representative. Refer to High Commission in Wellington, NZ, ph 64 (4) 736 411.
New Zealand: Philatelic Bureau Building, Takuvaine, Avarua, ph 22 201.
US: No resident representative. Refer to Embassy in Wellington, NZ, ph 64 (4) 722 068.
UK: No resident representative. Refer to High Commission in Wellington, NZ, ph 64 (4) 726 049.
Canada: No resident representative. Refer to High Commission in Wellington, NZ, ph 64 (4) 739 577.

Money

The Cook Islands unit of currency is the New Zealand dollar, but there are a few notes and coinage minted for local use. The dollar coin bearing the symbol of the God Tangaroa is popular with coin collectors.
Approximate exchange rates are:

A$	=	NZ$1.11
Can$	=	NZ$1.07
S$	=	NZ$1.05
UK£	=	NZ$2.29
US$	=	NZ$1.48

Communications

Mail and telegrams are available from the post office. Airmail is despatched from Rarotonga twice a week. The post office also has a Postshop with all the materials needed to wrap and post parcels. Almost next door is the Philatelic Bureau, where collector sets of colourful local stamps are available.

International telex, telephone and fax services are available from Telecom Cook Islands (TCI). International calls can be dialled direct or through the operator on 015. For calls to the Cook Islands, the country code is 682.

Calls can be made from most hotels and motels or from cardphones. Telecom phone cards are available in $10 (US$7) and $20 (US$15) units. They make attractive souvenirs, and are also a world wide collector's item. TCI has a 24hr service, 7 days a week.

There is a small newspaper with local news.

Miscellaneous

Time

Local time is GMT - 10. 'Cook Islands Time' means that everything takes a little longer than at home. Sit back and relax and enjoy the slow pace.

Business Hours

Banks	-	Westpac and ANZ in Avarua are open	
		Mon-Fri	9am-3pm.
Post Office	-	Mon-Fri	8am-4pm.
Shops	-	Mon-Fri	8am-4pm,
		Sat	8am-midday.

Some village shops, that sell mainly food, may open in the evening and Sundays.

Electricity

Supply is 230 DC/50 cycle, the same as Australia and New Zealand. A 2-pin plug may be needed so take one with you. Some hotels and motels have provision for 110V electric shavers.

Credit Cards

Major hotels, duty free shops and restaurants accept major credit cards.

Tipping

No tipping or bargaining is permitted.

Dress

Although dress should be informal, brief attire must not be worn when visiting town or villages. A respectable standard of dress is required when attending church services. Nude or topless sunbathing is offensive to the locals.

Health

Medical and dental services are available 24hrs a day. Rarotonga's hospital is well-equipped, with overseas trained staff. There is a pharmacy, and many doctors in private practices.

There are no poisonous animals or insects in the Cook Islands, but non-malarial mosquitoes can be annoying in inland areas. The usual repellents provide protection.

Typical South Pacific scene

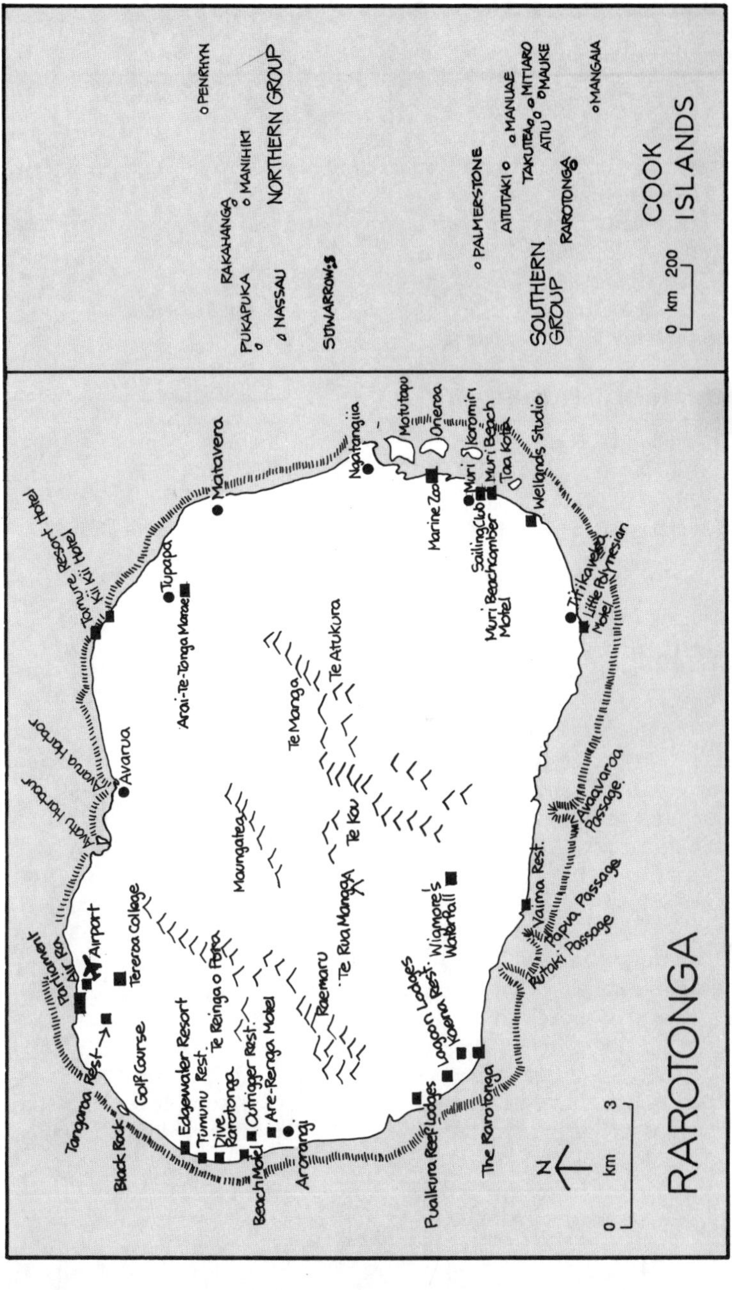
RAROTONGA
0 km 3
N
Black Rock
Tangaroa Rest.
Parliament
Pacific Rim
Airport
Tereora College
Golf Course
Edgewater Resort
Tumunu Rest.
Dive Rarotonga
Beach Motel
Outrigger Rest.
Are-Renga Motel
Arorangi
Te Reinga o Pora
Raemaru
Te Rua Manga
Maungatea
Te Kou
Te Manga
Te Atukura
Arai-Te-Tonga Marae
Avarua
Avatiu Harbour
Avarua Harbor
Tamure Resort Hotel
Kii Kii Hotel
Tupapa
Matavera
Ngatangiia
Motutapu
Oneroa
Koromiri
Taakoka
Muri
Muri Beach
Marine Zoo
Sailing Club
Muri Beachcomber Motel
Wellands Studio
Titikaveka
Little Polynesian Motel
Avaavaroa Passage
Vaima Rest.
Papua Passage
Rutaki Passage
Wigmore's Waterfall
Lagoon Lodges
Kaena Rest.
The Rarotongan
Pualkura Reef Lodges
COOK ISLANDS
NORTHERN GROUP
PENRHYN
MANIHIKI
RAKAHANGA
PUKAPUKA
NASSAU
SUWARROW
SOUTHERN GROUP
PALMERSTONE
AITUTAKI
MANUAE
TAKUTEA
ATIU
MITIARO
MAUKE
RAROTONGA
MANGAIA
0 km 200

Travel Information

How to get there

By Air

Air New Zealand has regular flights from New Zealand, Tahiti, Hawaii, Los Angeles and Fiji.

Regular services are operated by *Polynesian Airlines* from Western Samoa, Tahiti and New Zealand.

The Airport is 4.5km from the town centre.

Domestic flights to all islands with airport facilities are made on a regular basis by *Air Rarotonga.*

Tourist Information

Cook Islands Tourist Authority is on the main road in downtown Avarua. It is open Mon-Fri 8am-4pm, Sat 9am-12noon.

Accommodation

Following is a selection of available accommodation, with prices for a double room per night, which should be used as a guide only.

Rarotonga

Rarotonga Resort Hotel, PO Box 103, Rarotonga, ph 25 800, fax 25 799. Set on a white sandy beach in tropical gardens. 151 rooms including 4 suites and 3 room categories - Paradise, Beachfront and Garden, all connected by covered walkway. Most have A/C, and all have private facilities, fans, phone, tea/coffee making, mini-bar, fridge, free paper, balcony. Bars, restaurants, pool, conference facilities. Water sports, beach volley ball, fish feeding, nature/reef walks. tennis and more. Culture shows, island night, Sunday brunch with the locals, fishmarket and Asian banquet. Price NZ$150 (US$82).

Edgewater Resort, PO Box 121, Rarotonga, ph 25 435, fax 25 475, is 5 minutes from airport. 180 rooms and 9 VIP honeymoon suits, A/C, spa. Right on beach in garden setting. All rooms with ensuite, air cooling, fridge, tea/coffee making, patios or balconies, phone, TV/Video. Room service, telex, fax and baby sitting. Restaurants, bars, convention facilities, 4 floodlit tennis courts, 4 squash courts, table tennis, pool tables, island walks. Sunday night BBQ. Activities director. Price NZ$105-170 (US$57-92).

Manuia Beach Resort, PO Box 700, Rarotonga, ph 22 461, fax 22 464, is a Polynesian inspired cottage colony of 20 duplex bungalows with thatched roofs and tropical interiors. Refrigerated mini-bars, hairdryers, screened windows, fans, tea/coffee making, verandahs. Restaurants, bars, beach, lagoon, spa pool, freshwater pool, tropical gardens. Snorkelling, canoeing, skiffs on site. Complimentary tropical breakfasts, gifts, golf, tennis, sailing/windsurfing (on or off site). No children accepted. Resort is for the romantics with top of the range accommodation and natural Polynesian service. Price NZ$250-325 (US$136-177).

Moana Sands Hotel, PO Box 1007, Rarotonga, ph 26 189, fax 22 189. Medium grade, small personable hotel with fun atmosphere. On beach with deep water swimming. Rooms have kitchenettes, covered patios facing lagoon. Dinner party style dining on beach or in the dining room. Complimentary snorkelling, canoeing and sailing off beach. Price NZ$175 US$95).

Pacific Resort, PO Box 790, Rarotonga, ph 20 427, fax 21 427, set on Muri Beach and lagoon. Units with lounge, kitchen, bedroom, patio, air circulation, hair dryers, daily service. Laundry, vehicle rental, pool, beach activities, lagoon viewing craft, area for private parties. Bar, restaurant, theme nights, entertainment. Two stores close for provisions and tours, game fishing, scuba diving, bowling, tennis, golf, flightseeing, outer island travel. Price NZ$230-315 (US$125-171).

Tamure Resort, PO Box 483, Rarotonga, ph 22 445, fax 22 415, 2.3km from town on lagoon. 35 rooms with private bath, fridge, tea/coffee making, fans. single/double only. 24hr reception, daily tours, tennis, car, scooter and bike rentals. Pool, children's pool, pool bar, cocktail bar, restaurant, laundry. Island night Wednesday with Polynesian buffet, entertainment and dancing. Price NZ$85 (US$46).

Puaikura Reef Lodges, PO Box 397, Rarotonga, ph 23 537, fax 21 537, studio or 1 bed units. Kitchen, bath, lounge/dining, verandah. Pool, 25m from beach and snorkelling lagoon. Laundry, BBQ area, vehicle rental. Price NZ$85 (US$46).

Muri Beachcomber, PO Box 379, Rarotonga, ph 21 022, fax 21 323, on Muri beach. 10 condo-style units all self-contained and serviced. Complimentary fruit on arrival, tea, coffee daily. Vehicles for hire, BBQ area. pool, laundry. Water sports equipment may be hired next door, grocery store near. Restaurants close, bus at door. Tours arranged. Price NZ$125 (US$65).

Lagoon Lodges, PO Box 45, Rarotonga, ph 22 020, fax 22 021. 2 and 3 bedroom units with kitchen, insect screens, fans, private bath, dining/lounge, patio. Serviced daily. Pool, BBQ, tennis, children's play equipment, sports equipment, sandy beach. A store and restaurant close. Tours, vehicle rental arranged. Price NZ$100 (US$54).

The Little Polynesian, PO Box 366, Rarotonga, ph 24 280, fax 21 585 - 9 beachfront studios self-contained, serviced daily except Sunday and some Public Holidays. Tour desk, snorkelling equipment, pool, trampoline, dinghy, BBQ. Scooter and bicycle rental. On beach and lagoon. Ideal for honeymooners. Price NZ$120 (US$65). Weddings can be arranged and take place on the beach.

Kii Kii Motel, PO Box 68, Rarotonga, ph 21 937, fax 22 937, 2km from town. 24 rooms with kitchen, TV and phone. Pool, BBQ, recreation room. Holiday cottages available. Price NZ$54 (US$29).

Palm Grove Lodges, PO Box 23, Rarotonga, ph 20 002, fax 21 998 - 6 studio units, 2 family units. All separate with cooking facilities. Pool, BBQ. Small shops near. Bus service. vehicle rental. Tour desk arranges restaurant bookings and leisure activities. Price NZ$130-175 (US$71-95).

Paradise Inn, PO Box 674, Rarotonga, ph 20 544, fax 22 544. Renovated historic Maruajiai dance hall in Avarua. Bar, recreation area, outdoor terrace, elevated sun deck, lounge, view of Pacific. Self-contained rooms particularly suitable for adults. Close to shops and restaurants. Price NZ$55 (US$36).

Budget

Ati's Bungalows, PO Box 693, Rarotonga, ph 21 546, fax 26 174. In Arorangi village on sandy beach. 5 garden, 4 beachfront self-contained bungalows with kitchens, serviced, bathrooms, fan, phone, TV, lounge, library, ironing and washing machines. BBQ area, bar, Transfers, close to shops and restaurants. 10 minutes to town. Price on request.

Are Renga Motel, ph 20 050, fax 26 174. 20 units, 6km from the airport in Arorangi village. Fully self-contained units. Price Share NZ$15, single NZ$25, double NZ$40.

Airport Lodge, ph 20 050, fax 26 174. 6 self-contained units 2km from the airport. Price share NZ$15, single NZ$25, double NZ$40.

Backpackers International Hostel, PO Box 878, Rarotonga, ph/fax 21 847. Ask for Bill Bates at the airport for free pick-up service.

Matareka Hostel and Tourist Apartments, PO Box 587, Rarotonga ph 23 670 fax 23 672. 15 minutes walk from Tere's Bar close to town centre. Sea views in tropical bush setting. Double and triple units with private bath, lounge, cooking facilities, laundromat. Volleyball. Bike hire. Price Share NZ$15, NZ$25 share twin or double.

Aitutaki

Aitutaki Lagoon Hotel, PO Box 99, Aitutaki, ph 31 201, fax 31 202. On sandy beach and lagoon. 9 beachfront, 15 garden bungalows. Restaurant, bar, pool, gift shop, laundry. Lagoon cruises, picnics, snorkelling, outrigger canoes. Island tours can be arranged. Twice weekly island night with floor show. Weekly BBQ. Price NZ$145 (US$79).

Aitutaki Lodges, ph 31 334, fax 31 333, on lagoon. 6 bungalows, cooking facilities, fridge, mini bar, fans, balcony. Bar, dining room. Lagoon cruises, fishing, snorkelling and scuba, bush and village walks. Added are room service, on site shop, hire motor scooters, cars, taxi service. Price NZ$145 (US$79).

Rapae Cottage Hotel, PO Box 4, Aitutaki, ph 31 320, fax 31 321, on beachfront close to town. 12 standard double/twin units. Coffee/tea making, bath with shower. One family unit 6 beds. Bar, restaurant. Weekly island feast. Price NZ$75 (US$45).

Budget

Paradise Cove, PO Box 64, Aitutaki, ph 31 218, fax 31 456, and Toms Beach Cottage, ph 31 051, fax 21 409, offer budget accommodation with communal kitchen.

Atiu Island

Atiu Motel, Atiu, ph 33 777, fax 33 775. Atiu is not an atoll nor mountain peaks, but it offers something completely different. Contact Air Rarotonga for bookings.

Mauke

Tiare Holiday Cottages. 3 bungalows 3km from the village. Share facilities, meals available. Contact Air Rarotonga for bookings.

Cove Lodge, large guest house with 3 separate bedrooms. Self-catering. Private facilities. Contact Air Rarotonga for bookings.

Mitiaro

Mitiaro Guest House. Nane Pokoati has turned her property into a guest house for visitors. Tariff includes 3 meals. Contact Air Rarotonga for bookings.

Mangaia

Mangaia Lodge, a large house with 3 guest rooms. Separate facilities. Tariff includes 3 meals. Contact Air Rarotonga for bookings.

Other Islands

Local-type accommodation can be arranged for islands in the northern group. Contact Air Rarotonga for details.

Local Transport

Air

Air Rarotonga, PO Box 79, Rarotonga, ph 22 888, fax 20 979, has flights to the outer islands. They also have a day tour to Aitutaki, departing at 8am returning 6.30pm. It includes an island tour, a lagoon cruise, hotel transfers, air fares, BBQ lunch. Price adult NZ$299 (US$208), children under 12 NZ$149.50 (US$104).

A Stopover and Paradise Island Pass, which includes accommodation packages, is available to visitors who travel to 2 or more islands in 30 days. Bookings for Air Rarotonga can be made through Air New Zealand.

Scenic flights over Rarotonga are also available. A 20-minute round-the-island scenic flight operates every day from the airport, ph 682 22888. Price NZ$49 (US$34) per person.

Sea

Local cargo boats operate an inter-island service. Most are to the southern islands but a less regular service goes to the northern group. Timetables are not confirmed until a few days before sailing. Enquire at Avatiu Wharf.

Bus

The Island Bus has a round-the-island service that leaves from Cooks Corner shopping centre every half hour Mon-Fri 7am-4.30pm, Sat 8am-12noon. There is also a night time service six evenings a week for diners and night clubbers. No midnight bus on Saturdays. Tuesday night only if required at Edgewater Resort, bus circles back at 10.40pm.

The bus stops at all hotels and motels but you can catch it anywhere by signalling the driver. Cost NZ$2 one way, night return NZ$4, day pass, hop on and off as much as you like, NZ$5. Family Pass 2 adults 2 kids NZ$12. Concession and family tickets can be purchased at most hotels and motels.

Courtesy Transport. Some restaurants offer low cost or free transport for their diners. Check when booking for evening meals or refer to the night bus timetable.

Taxi

Fares are government controlled and displayed in each car. The charges are approximately NZ$3 minimum fare plus $1 per kilometre. Taxis are generally available 6am-10pm only.

Car, motorcycle or scooter

Most hotels and motels have car hire. There are also car hire companies: Rarotonga Rentals, ph 22 326; Avis, ph 22 833; Tipani Rentals, ph 21 617; Budget, ph 20 895; Rental Cars Cook Islands, ph 24 442; TPAS Rental cars, ph 20 611.

It is not economical to hire a car for one person.

Driving is on the **left-hand** side of the road. Drivers of all vehicles must have a Cook Islands driving licence obtainable from the Police Station in Avarua, on presentation of your own current licence, for NZ$10.

The speed limit is 40kph in town and 50kph outside. The roads are narrow and not built for speed.

Blow-holes of Tongatapu, Tonga

Games in the South Pacific

Bicycle

Bicycles can also be hired from your hotel/motel or from *Polynesian Bike Hire*, ph 20 895. Insurance is included in the rate. Damage excess is NZ$300 (US$209).

Eating Out

There are so many restaurants in all categories that it would be impossible to try even half unless you intend staying for months. Rarotonga offers a little of everything, from first class to friendly 'island' style cafe, and some offer courtesy transport or transfers at a nominal charge. Arrange this when you phone to make your reservation.

Old favourites like Chinese, Italian, seafood and steaks are available, and all restaurants are licensed.

Try some traditional food like Ika Mata (marinated fish with coconut sauce); eke (octopus); taro (tuber vegetable); poke (pawpaw pudding); and if you can find a local who makes them, breadfruit chips are delicious.

Sundays are a day of rest, but the restaurants at the resorts are open. The *Rarotonga* has a lunch-time fashion show on the patio. Bars are closed and drinks can only be served with meals.

Friday night is the late night; on Saturday restaurants, bars and night clubs close at midnight.

Here are a few restaurants you might like to try:

Tumunu, ph 20 501 - seafood specialties. Value for money. *Tamure Resort*, 2km from downtown Avarua. Open daily for breakfast, lunch, dinner, BBQs, Polynesian buffets, island nights Wednesday and Friday. Rage until late.

Ronnies BYO in Avarua, ph 20 823 - open 6 days for lunch and dinner.

Edgewater Resort, ph 25 435. Spit Roast and BBQ Sunday with fashion parade. Carvery Friday, Island Feast Tuesday and Saturday, a la carte dining Wednesday and Thursday. Bar open from 9am.

Sails, at Rarotonga Sailing Club, Muri Beach, ph 27 350. Casual dining on the broadwalk. Open 7 days lunches, dinners cocktails. Free transport.

Barefoot Bar Pacific Resort, Muri Beach, ph 20 427 or 21 156. A bar on the edge of the lagoon. Great lunches and snacks.

The Flame Tree, Rarotonga's most exotic restaurant, ph 25 123 - open Monday-Saturday for dinner from 6.30pm. Special 3 course menu $24.50.

Trader Jacks, ph 26 464. Open lunch, dinner. Blackboard specials.

Spaghetti House, near Edgewater Resort, ph 25 441. Authentic Italian cooking. Pizzas, cappuccino.

Portofino, 1km from town centre, ph 26 480 - Italian - everything from quick snacks to innovative specials. Open Mon-Sat.

Rarotonga, ph 25 800. Reservations essential. Monday fitness evening;

Tuesday fish market; Wednesday and Saturday island night; Thursday Italian; Friday Asian; Sunday brunch and BBQ.

The Jam Hut, Titikaveka. Coffee bar, licensed restaurant open 7 days for brunch, lunch, dinner, snacks.

Sandals Pacific Resort, ph 20 427. Open every day. Breakfast all you can eat 8am-10.30am. Wednesday island night, Friday feast, Sunday carvery.

Oasis Village, 10 minutes from town centre. Steakhouse. Metua's, European and local food, ph 20 850. Hamburgers, fish and chips, take away. Open Mon-Sat 7.30am-late. BBQ Friday night with live music, Main meals from $10.50.

Kaena, 50m from Rarotonga Hotel, ph 25 433. Seafood and steaks.

Liana's, 200m from Sheraton Hotel, ph 26 123 - Chinese and European cuisine. Realistic prices. Open 6-10pm, closed Friday.

PJ's Arorangi, ph 20 367. European, Chinese and Mongolian. Open lunch, dinner. Happy hour Mon-Sat noon-6pm. Live entertainment and jukebox.

Mama's Cafe, next to Foodlands. Open Mon-Fri 8am-4.30pm Sat 8am-noon. Croissants, hot and cold snacks, ice creams, soft drinks.

Southern Fried Chicken, downtown Avarua, ph 24 142. Island food, drinks, ice cream, Chinese food. Open Mon-Thurs 8am-10pm Fri 8am-3am. Sat 8am-midnight.

Priscilla's, next to the Beachcomber, ph 23 530. Indian. Open for lunch noon-3pm, dinner 6-11pm.

Whatever you do, don't miss an Island Night or two. They have traditional 'umukai' feasts with succulent food cooked in an underground oven. They also feature very good song and dance troupes.

Visit the *Banana Court*. This is a sprawling bar in the middle of the town centre. Here you will meet everyone, locals and visitors alike. The editor of the local newspaper sits here hoping to find news for his paper. It can be quite a trap as sessions go on for hours and the stimulating company makes you lose track of time. Friday nights they have dancing, live bands on the other nights. The TAB (Totalisator Betting Agency) is here for bets on NZ races, and there are discos for the real late nighters.

Aitutaki

The Crusher Bar, ph 31 283. Fish and steaks $9.50 including salad. Saturday night Roast Sucking Pig $15 (US$10), Sunday night Roast Dinner $12.50 (US$9). Live entertainment nightly.

Ralphie's Bar & Grill, ph 31 418. Steak and salad, pasta, Chinese, chicken, pork. Open 7 days. 10am-midnight Sundays 6pm-10pm.

Aitutaki Resort, ph 31 201. A la carte/buffet/island style.

Rapae Hotel, ph 31 320. Island night Fridays from 7pm.

Shopping

The main shopping area is located in downtown Avarua. There are some small shops dotted around the island but they mostly sell food.

There is no bargaining. Duty Free goods are available at competitive and fixed prices.

Look for traditional handicrafts especially from the Outer Islands. Each island specialises in various products, e.g finely woven mats from Pukapuka in the northern group.

Local carvings in wood and pearl shell are good examples of the Cook Islands, and Cook Islands stamps are popular souvenirs.

Art lovers will find local artists produce distinctive paintings and pottery.

Every visitor should buy a pareu. It is easily worn by men and women and ideal for casual wear. Other good buys are fashion wear and stationery.

Cook Island natural pearls and black pearls are very popular. When buying pearls look at the Pearl Guide membership certificate as a guarantee of quality and value. Don't overlook the natural pearls found on Penrthyn. They are predominantly golden but with all colours of the rainbow occurring.

Pearl Guide members are: Beachcomber, Island Craft Ltd, June's Pearls, Poe Manea, The Pearl Hut, The Pearl Shop, The Pearl Trader.

There is also a shopping centre at Tangaroa behind the airport.

Outlets in Cooks Corner are:

Kirsty & Kendrick, manufacturers and importers of ladies and men's fashions.

Capricorn Music for all island music.

Body Boutique for lingerie.

Pacific Gifts for souvenirs.

The Kenwell Gallery - island art and artists supplies. *Tuki's Pareu* for pareus, shirts, ties, kids' clothing, swimwear.

Island Craft for everything Polynesian.

T-Shirt Factory - also has other clothing and shoes.

Odds & Ends Warehouse, opposite the market.

The Perfume Factory has perfumes and liqueurs. Taste before you buy. (The liqueur not the perfume!)

Paradise Hair and Beauty.

Cook Islands Trading Corp, a big department store. *South Seas International* and *Vanwil's* have everything from duty free to knick knacks and electronic equipment.

The Salon for Hair and Beauty.

Bounty Bookshop and Toys has everything a kid could want.

Other outlets worth checking out are:

Higan's at Arorangi for petrol.

CITC Duty Free.

Tattslotto for Photos.

Treasure Chest for all gifts and souvenirs.

Black Pearl Perfume, next to Banana Court.
Jillian Sobieska for original paintings.
Erita has dolls, needlecraft and gifts.
Shells & Craft on main road at Muri beach.

Food
Foodlands Supermarket, The Market Place, near the main port. Foodstalls, traditional produce and the island's latest gossip!
Mai-Hina's, airport shopping concourse. Duty Free. European imports.

Liquor Supplies
Cook Islands Liquor Supplies, Main Road, Avatiu. Open Mon-Fri 10am-4pm, Sat 9am-noon.
Most small stores have a limited supply.
Rarotonga's own brewery where you can sample the beer.
Tangaroa is a local liqueur, sold in a porcelain bottle. It makes a very good souvenir.

Sightseeing

Whether you walk, bus or drive, don't miss the key points of interest. The island is only 32km in circumference so places of interest are not far apart.

Start from the Cook Islands Tourist Authority and head uptown.
CICC Church Yard is built from coral and lime, and stands as a symbol of the faith the people have in God. Around the church are graveyards, including that of the late Prime Minister Hon Albert Royle Henry.

At the **Library and Historical Society Museum** visitors can take out books and pay a deposit of $25 (US$17), refundable when you return the books before leaving, and a monthly fee of $10 (US$7). Open Mon-Thurs 12 noon-4.30pm Fri 9am-4pm Sat 9am-11am.

Takaamoa Theological College is the headquarters of the island's Christian church and training centre.

National Culture Centre is a superb venue for cultural events, as is the Library and Museum. Open 9am-3pm.
Walk back towards the sea to:

The **Old Sunday School** ruins. Built by the London Missionary Society as a Sunday school. Now the Beachcomber Gallery.

The Wreck of the Maitai. The SS *Maitai* was wrecked December 24, 1916. This 3393 ton vessel was owned by the Union Steamship Co and traded between the Cook Islands and Tahiti. No lives were lost.

Wreck of the Yankee. The world famous 94ft (29m) brig *Yankee* ran aground on July 24, 1964, while on a world cruise. No lives were lost.
It doesn't matter which way around the island you take. There are only two roads, so you can branch off the main coastal road to see the

interior at any point. The following route is from east to west.

Inland Drive. This scenic drive into Takuvaine/Avatiu Valleys provides an opportunity to see the lush tropical vegetation.

Arai-Te-Tonga. These stone structures form the Koutu, the royal court of a reigning Ariki (High Chief), where offerings to the ancient gods were assembled prior to going to the Marae (meeting place). Investitures, annual tribal feasts and the presentation of first fruits were held here. The outstanding surviving feature of the Arai-Te-Tonga is a rectangular platform 4m long, 2.2m wide and 20cm high. Offset from the central long axis of the platform is the Investiture Pillar a large upright of natural squared basalt standing over 2m above ground level.

NB Marae are sacred sites and visitors are requested not to walk on them.

Ara Metua - The Great Road of Toi. Almost circling the island is an inland road known as the Great Road of Toi. When the first Europeans came to the Cook Islands, the Ara Metua already existed, made of paved stones laid through the swamps to create an all-weather road. Where Toi came from or why he built the road is not known, but archaeologists claim the work took place over 1000 years ago.

Pokata Paepaer (meeting place) is a T-shaped site in the district of Takitumu.

Pa's Palace. The palace of Pa (Takitumu's high chief) was built of coral and lime, indicting the central place of the village. The people of Takitumu lived inland and it was not until the missionaries built the churches that people moved to the coast.

The **Court House.** This was the site of the first court house built in Rarotonga.

Kainuku's Marae was a typical Marae with basaltic rock used as seats.

CICC Church Ngatangiia is a superb church of coral and lime. These churches are the main centre of villages for followers of Cook Islands Christianity.

Ngatangiia Harbour - Departure Point. According to Cook Islands legend, the great migration of Maori Canoes departed from here for New Zealand in 1350. The Takitumu District was named after one of the seven canoes.

Cook Islands Cultural Centre has demonstrations of Maori medicine, history, weaving, carving, coconut husking and much more. There is also dancing and singing, and lunch is available. Open Mon-Fri 10am-1.30pm. Entrance fee, including lunch, is from NZ$34 (US$24) per person.

Highland Paradise is a unique historical and scenic attraction, but can only be visited by 4WD vehicles.

The Tinomana Palace. This is the second palace built on this site. The name of the palace is Au Maru meaning 'The Peace Brought by Christianity'. The palace was built during the time of Enuarurutini.

Black Rock. The original name of this place was Tuoro meaning 'welcome'. According to ancient belief this is the jumping off point of souls. From here, the souls of the departed commenced their journey back to the fatherland Avaiki. It is now a popular swimming place.

The Stadium was constructed for the 1985 South Pacific Mini Games. It is the international sports centre for the Cook Islands. Situated at Tereora College.

Papua (Wigmore's) Waterfall is the only waterfall on the island, and is at Vaimaanga.

Rarotonga Breweries. You can enjoy a brewery tour absolutely free and taste the local product, Mon-Fri at 2pm.

Piri Purruto gives tree climbing and fire-making shows around the island.

Take an **Air Rarotonga Skydive Tandem** and see the sights as you fall from 2440m! Phone 22 888 for reservations.

Sport, Treks and Sailing

For the sports minded Rarotonga offers mini-putt golf, lawn bowls, golf, tennis, squash, sailing, horse-riding, snorkelling, scuba diving, windsurfing, game fishing and even jogging, and a gymnasium for those who want to keep fit.

Team Sports

These are highly competitive. Ask your hosts where to see rugby, netball, tennis, league, soccer, cricket, touch, seven-a-side and even boxing.

Watersports

Muri beach is the centre for windsurfing and sailing whether you are experienced or want to learn.

The Sailing Club, is the water sports centre, with lagoon and snorkelling cruises, and scuba diving for beginners. Catamarans and windsurfers are available for hire. Personal tuition in sailing and windsurfing is also available.

Captain Tama's Sportz is at nearby Pacific Resort. Modern glass bottom coral cruiser for a fun day on Muri lagoon, the only large area of water inside Rarotonga's encircling reef suitable for sailing and cruises. The cruise consist of swimming, snorkelling, viewing fish in the coral gardens and relaxing on Motu Koromiri beach. Have an Island BBQ lunch, walk it off on a culture walk and a visit to the Marae. A pareu tying and coconut husking show is also provided. Take along swimmers, sun tan oil, towel and family. Snorkel gear is provided. Departs Mon-Sat 11am. Price adult NZ$35 (US$24), children NZ$20 (US$17). Snorkel only NZ$25 (US$18) includes return transfers from any hotel or motel. Bookings ph 24 427 or 20 810 A/H.

Aroa Pony Trek

Whether you've never been on a horse before or are an experienced rider, you'll enjoy this 2hr excursion. Riding trails take you through tropical plantations, up to Wigmore's Waterfall for a swim, then canter (optional) along the white beaches, ph 21 415 or 20 048. Price adult NZ$30 (US$21), children under 14 NZ$20 (US$17).

Hash House Harriers meet every Monday at 5.30pm at various points for a 'fun run'. Visitors of any age are welcome, ph David Lobb on 22 000 (business) for information.

Tennis

The Rarotonga Resort and the Edgewater Resort have courts. Professional coaching is available, and equipment can be hired. Ask your host about any other tennis courts.

Squash

Edgewater Resort has courts which can be reserved. All gear is available for hire.

Mini-golf

Take a break from the sun and sea and have a round or two of mini-golf in Arorangi. People of all ages can play and it can be as relaxed or as competitive as you like.

Golf

Rarotonga Golf Club has a 9-hole course. Hire of a half set of clubs NZ$10 (US$7), green fees for either 9 or 18 holes are NZ$5. Trundlers (buggy) NZ$1 (US$0.70c) a round, ph 27 360. Make sure you stay for a 'cold one' after your game. Saturdays are club days. No play Sundays.

Bowls

The Rarotonga Bowling Club boasts an international bowling green. Visitors welcome at the Saturday roll up starting times 10am and 1pm. Creams/whites please on club day. Mon-Fri 4pm multi-dress. Closed Sunday. Hire of bowls NZ$1 (US$0.70c) green fee, NZ$1 (US$0.70c). Bar open from 4 pm.

Treks

If you are keen on exploring and tramping there are plenty of options from gentle valley walks to tough mountain climbs. As there are no poisonous snakes, insects or wild animals, inland exploring is relaxing and enjoyable. You can see birds, butterflies and exotic plants, and islanders working on their plantations.

A good family walk starts at Ngatangiia Harbour and follows the Avana Stream inland to a pleasant picnic spot.
Coming from downtown, turn inland immediately after crossing Avana Stream Bridge, just along from the Ngatangiia harbour entrance.

For more adventurous walks, take a guided tour.

Tours

Cultural Village and Circle Island Historic Tour -
These tours can be taken separately but there is a discount for taking them in one day. Price from NZ$34 (US$24) per person.

Starts with Cultural Village open Mon-Fri 9.45am. and finishing the show at 1.30pm, lunch included. The historic cultural tour starts after the show and ends at 5pm. Price from NZ$24 (US$17) per person.

Bookings essential for Cultural Village, ph 21 314.
Circle Island Tour - 9.30am Mon-Fri. Nite-life tours 9pm every Thurs and Sat. High Henry ph 25 320/25 321.
Piri's Umukai Picnic - 10.30am every Sunday. Includes lunch (chicken, lamb, fish, vegetables) and Piri's show. Bookings essential, ph 20 309. Price NZ$30.
Pa's Mountain Walk with the most experienced guide. Lunch and transfers provided. Take swimwear and mosquito repellent. Nature Walk 4hrs, Across island 5hrs. Mon-Fri, ph 21 079.
Highland Paradise Botanical Gardens & 183m high mountain vantage. Mon-Fri 9.30am-4pm ph 20 610/20 611. Bookings essential. A 2hr tour NZ$20 (US$17) including refreshments and fruit.
Across Island Adventure takes you up to the Needle (413m), then down via Wigmore's Waterfall, a swim to the other side of the island and lunch on the beach. Tues, Fri, Sat, Sun 9am, adult NZ$25 (US$18), child NZ$12 (US$8) including transport and lunch.

Other Treks

Te Kou Trek - 5 hours return. Steep very slippery when wet, fine views.
Ikurangi Trek - 4 hours. The most spectacular walk of all. A 4m rock face climb near the summit.
Te Manga Trek - 6 hours, for durable climbers only. A rope is useful to avoid plant damage near the summit.
Raemaru Trek - 2 hours return. Starts opposite Sam Rere, Panelbeaters. A serious cliff just before the summit. Take a 10m rope.
Maungatea Bluff - 3 hours return. Some scrambling required near the top but worth it. Beautiful views over Avarua.

NB A detailed pamphlet on Rarotongan walks is available from Cook Islands Conservation Service. Visitors are advised not to take treks in the late afternoon as it is difficult to find your way back after sundown.

Diving and Fishing

If you are not already a diver, now is the time to learn. The tuition is professional, fees are probably the lowest in the world, and your international qualification will enable you to dive anywhere.

Canyons, caves and varieties of coral - including plate, shelving, mushroom and brain - make it a most unusual terrain. Visibility is usually superb ranging from 30 to 61m, depending on wind and weather.

The most memorable diving is on the drop-off which starts at 24-30m and descends vertically for hundreds of metres.

Dive Rarotonga, ph 21 873, for all dive trips.

PADI, ph 21 873, for dive training.

Pacific Divers, phone Warren on 22 450 for daily dive trips.

For advice, talk to Ken at the Dive shop in Avarua.

BECO Game Fishing Charters, ph 21 525 or 24 125 - 30 years experience.

Pacific Marine Charters, ph 21 237, for experts or beginners. Lunch and light refreshments included.

MV *Seafari* (10m), ph 20 328 Canadian built. All fishing and safety gear.

Fisher's Fishing Tours. The *Corey Anne* is an 8m catamaran in Polynesian style. Approx 3hr trips.

Cook Islands Game Fishing Club, ph 21 419. Visitors welcome. Open 4pm.

Tour Operators

Tipani Tours, Cooks Corner, Avarua, ph 25 266.

Stars Travel, downtown, ph 23 669 - Outer islands.

Island Hopper, ph 22 036

Hugh Henry, ph 25 320

Baker's Cross Island Adventures, ph 20 019.

Cook Islands Visitors Centre will have all the information.

Package Tours

Since you have to pre-book accommodation, it is well worth considering a package deal. For 5 nights including economy airfares, accommodation and transfers, a package staying at Ati's Beach Bungalows would be from A$999 (US$730). Ati includes free BBQ, 1 day motor scooter hire and a free Cultural Village Tour if staying 10 nights. Top of the range staying in a resort would cost around A$1688 (US$1232).

Ask your Travel Agent which package is the best value for money.

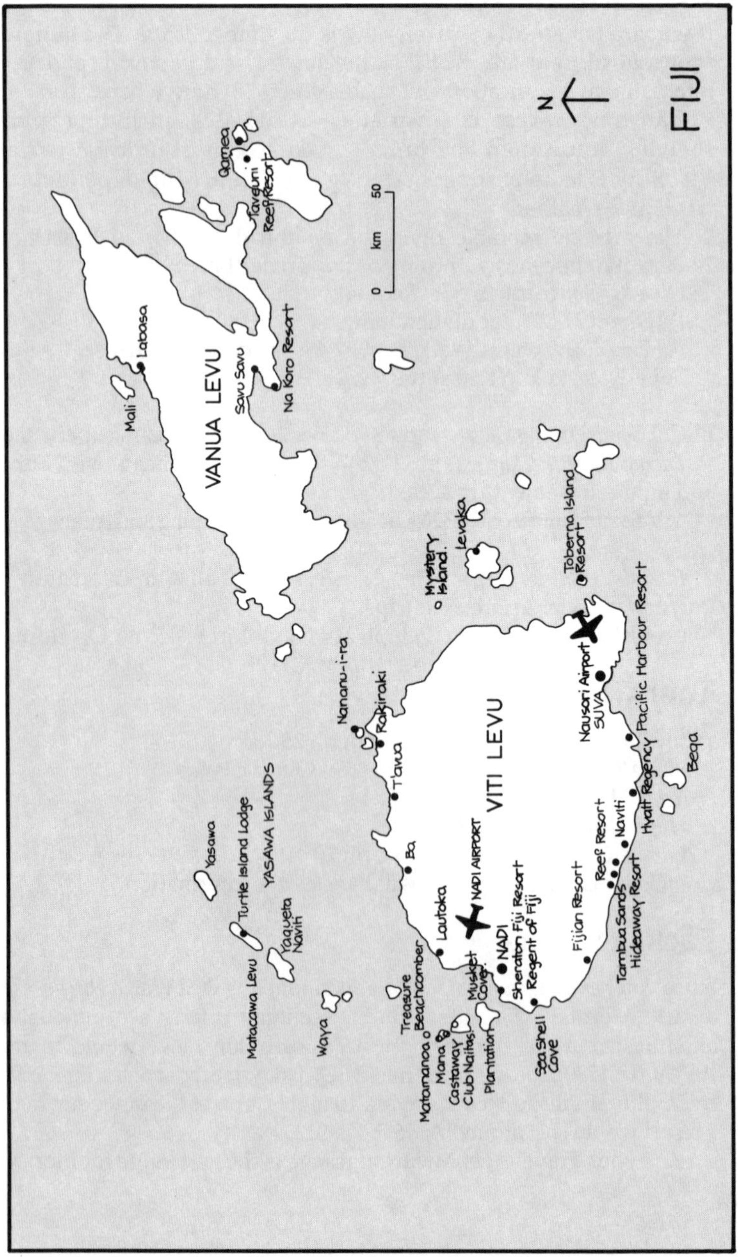
FIJI
N
0 km 50
VANUA LEVU
Labasa
Mali
Savu Savu
Na Koro Resort
Qamea
Taveuni
Reef Resort
VITI LEVU
NADI AIRPORT
NADI
Lautoka
Ba
T'avua
Rakiraki
Nananu-i-ra
Nausori Airport
SUVA
Pacific Harbour Resort
Beqa
Hyatt Regency
Naviti
Reef Resort
Tambua Sands
Hideaway Resort
Fijian Resort
Sheraton Fiji Resort
Regent of Fiji
Musket Cove
Sea Shell Cove
Plantation
Castaway
Club Naitasi
Mana
Matamanoa
Treasure
Beachcomber
Waya
Matacawa Levu
Yaqueta
Naviti
Turtle Island Lodge
Yasawa
YASAWA ISLANDS
Mystery Island
Levuka
Toberua Island Resort

REPUBLIC OF FIJI

The Fijian archipelago includes more than 300 islands scattered across some 230,000 sq km in the south-west Pacific Ocean. Over 100 of these islands are inhabited.

Nadi International Airport is 1710km north-east of Sydney; 1164km north of Auckland; 2756km south-west of Honolulu; and 3851km south-east of Tokyo.

The two main islands of the group, Viti Levu and Vanua Levu, comprise 85% of the total land mass. Some of the islands are surrounded wholly or in part by coral reefs that form natural harbours and deep lagoons. The larger islands are primarily volcanic in origin with high rugged peaks that typify this type of formation. The smaller islands are mainly coral or limestone. The chief products are: coconuts, forest products, sugar, beer, cement and cigarettes.

The capital of the republic is Suva.

History

Archaeologists have found pottery in Fiji that suggests the islands may have been settled by Polynesians around 1500BC. Other discoveries suggest that the Melanesian people joined them about 500BC. Whatever their origins, the people engaged in continual warfare, and were extremely barbaric and cruel. They were cannibals, but even more. If they captured a particularly hated person they would chop off an ear, nose or hand, maybe cook it is front of him, and then offer him first bite. Small wonder Fiji was once known as the 'Cannibal Isles'.

European Discovery

The Dutch explorer Abel Tasman sighted the eastern islands in 1643, but did not land. Captain Cook, the famous British navigator and explorer, visited Vatoa (Turtle Island), one of the southern islands, in 1774. The first European to see the main islands was Captain William Bligh. In 1789 he passed through them after the *Bounty* mutiny on his open-boat voyage to Timor, and made the first chart of the area. He and his crew were chased by canoe-loads of cannibals in a stretch of water now known as Bligh Sea.

Early explorers all stressed the danger of Fiji. Warring tribes, cannibals, and the reefs surrounding the islands made sailors wary of exploration. In 1804 a survivor from a shipwreck realised that sandalwood grew along the coast of Vanua Levu. This caused a rush of traders and adventurers who stripped the forests bare. Later, others came for *bêche-de-mer*, a sea slug considered to be a delicacy in Asia, and whalers called in for provisions.

Missionaries

The first Christian missionaries, two Protestant Tahitians, arrived at Lakeba in 1830, followed by two Wesleyan Europeans in 1835. The missionaries made little headway until they settled near the small island of Bau off the south-west corner of Viti Levu in 1839. Bau was the headquarters of a chief named Cakobau who had much influence over the coastal villages of Viti Levu and many of the islands to the east. By 1850 he was commonly known as *Tui Viti*, King of Fiji. Later some of his people revolted against him, and he thought that if he embraced Christianity, peace would be restored. He was right. Much of the fighting ceased and cannibalism was abandoned.

European Settlers

Cakobau faced debts arising from claims by a former American Consul, John B. Williams. When W.T. Pritchard arrived as the first British Consul in 1858, Cakobau offered to cede his islands to Britain if they would pay his debts. Pritchard went to London to put the case before the government who sent two investigators to examine the country's potential.

Rumours that Fiji would become a British colony brought many Europeans to settle. These pioneers made numerous attempts to establish a stable government under Cakobau's authority, but they failed. On October 10 1874, Britain accepted a second offer of cession and Fiji became a Crown Colony with the capital at Levuka. It was moved to Suva in 1882.

When the first British Governor, Sir Arthur Gordon, arrived, the economy was stagnant. He thought growing sugar was the best way to revive the economy, but feared that large scale employment of Fijians as labourers would disrupt their traditional way of life, so he authorised the importation of Indians to work the sugar plantations. The first Indians arrived in 1879 under an indenture system that lasted until 1916. Many stayed on after their contracts expired, and by 1946 the Indians outnumbered the Fijians.

Fiji became independent on October 10 1970. Ratu Sir Ksamises Mara, a Fijian chief, led a multi-racial Fijian dominated government until 1987. In the fifth election since independence he was defeated by Timoci Bavadra, the Fijian leader of an Indian dominated coalition. In May 1987, the army led by Colonel Sitiveni Rambuka overthrew the government, and a second coup in September 1987 consolidated Rambuka's hold. Fiji then became a republic, and the government promised to ensure democracy, but many of the Indian population left the country. The 1992 elections resulted in a coalition victory with Rambuka as Prime Minister. The new constitution prevents the army from taking control.

Climate

With a warm and pleasant climate throughout the year, Fiji is an ideal holiday destination. It has a subtropical climate without extremes of hot and cold. The best time to visit is April to October when it is mild and dry with temperatures ranging from 23C to 30C. The warm wet season is November to March with temperatures from 20C to 36C. There is a possibility of cyclones.

Population

The total population is 781,000, made up of 50% Fijians, 46% Indians and the remainder are Chinese, Rotuman (from the small island of Rotuma, north of Fiji) and European.

Religion

Christianity, Hinduism and Islam are practised. About 50% are Christians, 10% Muslims.

Language

English, Fijian and Hindi are the official languages. The only Fijian word you need to know is 'bula', the word of greeting, and you will get to use it quite often.

Public Holidays

January 1 ....New Year's Day
March 11 ....National Youth Day
March/April..........................Good Friday\Easter Monday
May 30 ....Rafu Sukuna Day
June 13 ....Queen's Birthday
July 25 ....Constitution Day
August 15 ....Mohammed's Birthday
October 10 ....Fiji Day
October\November ....Diwali
December 25 ....Christmas Day
December 26 ....Boxing day.

Festivals

Sugar Festival - in September. The sugar city of Lautoka comes alive with the annual festival.

Bula festival - in July. Nadi town has its annual Bula festival.

Diwali Festival - Held in the first half of the Hindu month of Kartika (October\November) this is the Festival of Lights, commonly called Diwali. Hindu homes are elaborately decorated with lights.

Hibiscus Festival -Fiji's carnival of the year. Held in Suva during August to coincide with school holidays. Lasts one week.

Traditions-Legends

Firewalking

The unsolved mystery of how Fijians from the island of Beqa can walk on white hot rocks is seen in the spectacular ritual of firewalking. The firewalkers attribute their power to the God Veli. The Hindu ritual of firewalking is also carried out in Fiji.

The Tabua

Originally the tabuas were highly polished pieces of wood from the bua tree. When the whalers first visited Fiji, they brought whales teeth to use for trading. The Fijians were struck by the similarity of the whale's teeth to their wooden Bua-ta. The whalers named them Tabua, from the word 'tabu' meaning sacred.

The Tabua is highly valued in tradition. To be presented with one is a great honour. It is not permitted to take a Tabua out of Fiji without an export licence from the Ministry of Fijian Affairs.

Calling of the Turtles

On the island of Kadavu, the maidens of the village of Namuana sing a strange chant which brings the large sea turtles to the surface to listen to the music. This unusual phenomenon does take place and is based on an ancient legend.

Red Prawns

Legend has it that these red prawns were once a gift to the daughter of the chief of Vatulele. The daughter was so disgusted with the gift that she had the prawns thrown from the cliffs. Today, these sacred prawns can be found in pools under the cliffs.

Entry Regulations

A passport valid for at least three months beyond the length of stay is required and a ticket for onward travel. Visas for 30 days are issued to Commonwealth visitors on arrival. Other nationals should check with their travel agent before leaving their home country. Vaccinations are not required unless entering from a designated infected area.

Duty Free Allowance

Travellers over the age of 18 are allowed to import the following free of duty:

500 cigarettes or 500gm of cigars or 500gm of tobacco or a combination of all three provided the total does not exceed 500gm.

2 litres of liquor or 4 litres of wine or 4 litres of beer. Up to F$400 (US$267) per passenger of any duty assessed goods.

Departure Tax

There is a departure tax of F$20 (about US$15) levied on all travellers over 12 years of age. It is payable in local currency.

Embassies

Australia: Dominion House, Thomson Street, Suva, ph 312 844.
Canada: Honorary Consul, 7th Floor, L.I.C.I Building, Butt Street, Suva, ph 300 589
New Zealand: Reserve Bank Building, Pratt Street, Suva, ph 311 422.
USA: 31 Loftus Street, Suva, ph 314 466.
UK: 47 Gladstone Road, Suva, ph 311 033.

Money

The basic unit of currency is the Fijian dollar. Notes come in denominations of $1, $2, $5, $10, $20, $50, and coins are 1c, 2c, 5c, 10c, 20c, 50c, $1. Approximate rates of exchange are:

A$	=	F$1.06
Can$	=	F$1.02
NZ$	=	F$0.95
UK£	=	F$2.12
US$	=	F$1.38

As the rate of exchange varies, check before changing money. Most major credit cards are accepted by hotels. Please note that most hotels require an imprint of a credit card on check-in or a substantial cash deposit to cover incidentals over and above your accommodation charges.

There is a 10% goods and service tax - VAT.

Banks

ANZ, Westpac, NBF, Bank of Baroda, Habib Bank and the Bank of Hawaii are all represented in Suva and Nadi. There are also agencies throughout Fiji.

Communications

International Direct Dialling is available and the country code is 679. No area code is required, simply dial the Fiji number. Outer islands in the Fiji group not on direct dialling, are serviced by a radio telephone system.

Fax and telex services are available through FINTEL (Fiji's telecommunications operator), 158 Victoria Parade, Suva, open Mon-Sat 8am-10pm. Facilities are available in most major hotels.

Public telephones take 10c coins for local calls and can be found at all post offices. Phone cards are available.

There are two English language daily newspapers, the *Fiji Times* and *Fiji Sun*. Fijian and Hindi language newspapers are published weekly.

TV programs are from Australia and New Zealand. There is a local radio station.

Miscellaneous

Time

Local time is GMT + 12.

Business Hours

Banks:	Mon-Thurs	9.30am-3pm,
	Friday	9.30am-4pm.
	There is a 24hr service at Nadi Airport.	
Post Offices:	Mon-Fri	8am-4.30pm,
	Sat	8am-11am.
Government Offices:		
	Mon-Thurs	8am-4.30pm,
	Fri	8am-4pm. Closed for lunch.

Commercial outlets, including vegetable and handicraft markets are open five days a week and half day Saturday. There is little open on Sundays and Public Holidays.

Electricity

Supply is 240V AC 50 HZ, and three-pin plugs, as used in Australia and New Zealand, are found in hotels. If your appliances are 110V you will need a converter.

Fijian lad fishing (opposite)

Credit Cards

Major cards are accepted by hotels and businesses. American Express Suva, can replace lost credit cards and travellers cheques. Diners Club, Visa, JCB and Mastercard are represented in Suva.

Tipping

Tipping is not expected nor encouraged. All hotels have a staff Christmas Fund and contributions may be made to this fund for exceptional service.

Health

Fiji is free from most tropical diseases including malaria. No vaccinations are required unless coming from an infected area. Hospitals are located in Suva, Sigatoka, Lautoka, Savusavu and Nadi. Most towns have a government clinic staffed by a District Nurse. There is a reasonable charge for patients who are not citizens of Fiji. Private medical services are also available.

Drinking water is safe in all cities, resorts and urban areas but it is advisable to buy bottled water in outlying districts.

Insurance

It is advisable to take out full travel insurance, especially medical.

Emergency Telephone Numbers

Fire, Police, Ambulance - 000.

Weights and Measures

Fiji uses the metric system.

Etiquette

Clothing should be suitable for a warm climate but modest. Always carry a sulu to cover bathing togs, shorts and halter tops.

Do not wear a hat in a village as it is considered to be an insult to the chief.

Do not wear shoes in people's houses.

It is considered an insult to touch someone's head.

When visiting a village it is customary to present a gift of Yaqona. Half-a-kilo costs about A$10 (US$7).

Observing the Fijian customs will make you a welcome guest in their homes and enhance your holiday.

Members of the Fijian Police Force (opposite)

Photography

Most locals do not object to having their photo taken. The main problem is that they want to pose so candid shots are hard to take. The latest photographic equipment is available as is same day processing.

Street scene, Suva.

Travel Information

How to get there

By Air

Air Pacific has regular flights from Sydney, Brisbane, Melbourne, Christchurch, Honiara, Tonga, Apia, Tokyo and Port Vila to Nadi and from Tonga and Apia to Suva.
Qantas flights all arrive at Nadi from Australia, Honolulu, San Francisco, Los Angeles and Vancouver.

Air New Zealand, Air Vanuatu, Air Nauru, Air Caledonie, Air India, Singapore Airlines and *Solomon Airlines* have regular flights to Fiji.
Domestic Airlines.
Air Fiji Ltd, Sunflower Airlines and *Turtle Airways* have flights to the outer islands.

By Sea

Many cruise ships call at Suva and Lautoka.

Tourist Information

Fiji Visitors Bureau has an office in Thomson Street, Suva, ph 302 622, and one at Nadi Airport, ph 722 433. Up to date tourist information is distributed free through hotels.

Accommodation

There is no shortage of accommodation in Fiji, the only problem is making up your mind what type of accommodation to choose - international standard resort, large town hotel, island resort or bure (Fijian native house) accommodation. Following are some examples of what's available, with prices for a night's stay, which should be used as a guide only.

Nadi

Moderate Class
Tana Apartments, PO Box 9203, Nadi Airport, ph 723 685. 3 minutes from Nadi Airport and 10 minutes from Nadi town. Set on a hillside with view of Nadi Bay, but not near beach. 23 self-contained serviced apartments 1-2 bedrooms. Continental breakfast included, use of all facilities at Tanoa International (free shuttle). Ideal base for larger families. Price A$69 (US$48) per apartment single A$138 (US$97) + 10% VAT.

Tanoa International, PO Box 9203, Nadi Airport, ph 720 277, fax 720 191. 3 minutes from Nadi Airport and 10 minutes from Nadi town. Not near beach. 114 rooms with 1 double bed, 1 sofa bed. Daytime child-minding, babysitting, children's playground and pool. Refurbished and suitable for long or short stays. Price twin A$59 (US$41), single A$118 (US$83), child 2-15 free. Return coach transfers: adult A$12 (US$6), child A$6 (US$4) + 10% VAT.

Fiji Mocambo, PO Box 9195, Nadi Airport, ph 722 000, fax 720 324. 3 minutes from Nadi Airport, 10 minutes from Nadi town. Nice view, but not near beach. 124 rooms with one queen size bed. Babysitting, child menus, high chairs, cots. 9-hole golf course, restaurants, bars, lively night-time atmosphere. Price twin share A$60 (US$42), single A$120 (US$84), child 2-15 free. Return coach transfers: adult A$12 (US$6), child A$6 (US$4) + 10% VAT.

Tokatoka Resort, PO Box 9305, Nadi Airport, ph 720 22, fax 720 400. 2 minutes from Nadi Airport and 10 minutes from Nadi town. Not near beach. 20 Villa, apartments, 20 Villa studios, plus apartment suites and apartment studios. Playground/pool complex. All rooms have cooking facilities, supermarket on-site. Good value for families. Price twin share A$61-117 (US$43-82), single A$122-234 (US$85-164), child 2-15 free. Return coach transfers from airport: adult A$12 (US$6), child A$6 (US$4) + 10% VAT.

Standard Class

Fiji Club, Wailoaloa Beach, Nadi Bay, ph 702 189, fax 702 324. 15 minute drive from Nadi Airport, 10 minutes from Nadi town. 254 timber thatched bures all facing beach, with one queen bed and one single divan. Family bures, baby sitting, highchairs and cots. Windsurfing, paddle boards, waterskiing, scuba diving, horseriding, sailing, excursions. Well run resort with good food. Suit budget-conscious looking for beach location. Price twin share A$41 (US29) single A$82 (US57), child 2-15 free + 10% VAT.

Skylodge, PO Box 9222, Nadi Airport, ph 722 200, fax 720 212. 5 minutes from Nadi Airport, and midway between airport and Nadi town. Not near beach. 49 rooms with one double and one single bed. Baby sitting, cots, playground, kids under 13 eat free. Set in 4.45 hectares of garden. Well suited for those on a budget and families. Ideal base for day tours and excursions. Price twin share A$40 (US28) single A$80 (US$56) child 2-15 free. Return coach transfers from airport: adult A$12 (US8), child A$6 (US4) + 10% VAT.

Raffles Gateway, PO Box 9891, Nadi Airport, ph 722 444, fax 720 620. Opposite Nadi Airport, 10 minutes from Nadi town. 22 standard rooms and 5 suites with one queen and one single bed. Baby sitting, video hire, highchairs, cots, playground. Ideal for early starts or late

arrivals. Bar, restaurant, swimming pool. Twin share A$49 (US34), single A$98 (US69), child free + 10% VAT.
Dominion International, PO Box 9178, Nadi Airport, ph 660 219, fax 720 187. 10 minutes from Nadi Airport, 5 minutes from Nadi town. Not near beach. 38 rooms with one double and one single bed. 38 deluxe rooms with one queen and one single bed. Babysitting, cots, children's pool, kids activities, tennis, playground. A popular and convenient hotel close to all activities. Price twin share A$50 (US$35), single A$93, child 2-15 free. Return coach transfers: adult A$12 (US$8), child (US$4) + 10% VAT.

Budget
New Westgate, PO Box 10097, Nadi Airport, ph 720 044, fax 720 071. 10 minutes from Nadi Airport, 5 minutes from Nadi town. Not near beach. 35 rooms with double and single bed. Baby sitting, cots, high chairs, children's menus, video. 'Jessica's' nightclub is one of Nadi's hottest night spots. Recommended for overnight or short stays. Price twin share A$44 (US$30), single A$88 (US$62), child 2-15 free + 10% VAT.
Coconut Inn, 37 Vunavau Road, ph 701 011. In centre of Nadi town. 22 rooms air-conditioning, fans, tea and coffee making facilities. Restaurant, bar. Tours and cruises available. Price A$25-$45 (US$18-32) + 10% VAT.
Horizon Beach Resort, PO Box 1401, Nadi, ph 722 832. A few minutes from Nadi Beach, 4 minutes from 18-hole golf course, free green fee. Close to Nadi airport and town. Activities include volleyball, diving, fishing, horseback riding, tours and cruises. Restaurant, bar, TV lounge, courtesy transport. Single and double air-conditioned rooms Price A$45-$50 (US$32-35) + 10% VAT.

Melanesian Hotel, PO Box 9242, Nadi, ph 722 438. Five minutes from airport, beach and golf course. All rooms with private facilities, tea and coffee making, phones and baby-sitting. Pool, meet flights, handy to tours and cruises. Price A$28-$40 (US$20-28) + 10% VAT.
Sandalwood Inn, PO Box 9454, Nadi Airport, ph 722 044. 25 rooms and 12 lodge rooms with kitchenette. Courtesy airport transfers. Air-conditioned or fans with private facilities, tea/coffee making, fridge. ISD dialling from lodge and A/C rooms. Bar, restaurant, pool, tour desk. Pick up for all cruises and tours Nadi/Lautoka. Price A$22-$60 (US$15-42) plus 10% VAT.
Nadi Sunseekers Hotel, Narewa Road, ph 700 400. Includes a Youth Hostel. Coffee shop, pool, gift shop, restaurant, bar, tour desk. Dormitory rates include free continental breakfast. Other rooms self-contained with fan or A/C. Price single with fan A$20 (US$14), double with fan A$25 (US$18), A/C A$35-$40 (US$25-28), dorm A$6 (US$4) + 10% VAT.
Whitehouse Inn, PO Box 2150, Nadi, ph 700 022. For budget travellers. Cooking facilities, tea and coffee making, laundry, ironing, pool, A/C

or fan cooled rooms fully serviced. Tour desk. Near golf course, 5 minutes from Nadi shopping. Courtesy transport to and from airport. Price A$20-38 (US$14-27), dorm $8 (US$6) + 10% VAT.

Sonaisali Island

Sonaisali Island Resort, PO Box 2544, Nadi, ph/fax 720 411. 10km south of Nadi Airport, 10 minutes from Nadi town. Built on a large island 150m from mainland with sheltered lagoon and water sports. 32 rooms and 6 bures. Rooms have one king or 2 queen beds. Bures have 2 bedrooms (1 air-conditioned) 1 queen, 1 double sofa, 2 single beds. Child menus, babysitting, playground, kids pool. Stay 7 nights pay for 6 and receive free jungle cruise per person. Meal Guide: 3 meals a day should cost A$50 (US$35) per adult. Superior resort with good facilities yet accessible to Nadi town and attractions. Price suite twin share A$82 (US$57), single A$163 (US$114), child 2-15 free. Bure $A111 (US$78), single A$222 (US$155) + 10% VAT.

Suva

Moderate

Suva Travelodge, PO Box 1357, ph 301 600, fax 300 251. On waterfront close to all activities. 131 rooms with one queen and one single bed. All facilities expected of a Travelodge. Close to shops and restaurants. Price twin share A$77 (US$54), single A$100 (US$70), child 2-15 free + 10% VAT.

Standard

Raffles Tradewinds, PO Box 3371, Lami, Suva, ph 362 450, fax 362 455. 10 minutes from Suva overlooking 'Bay of Islands' at Lami. 108 rooms with queen or king size beds. New York deli/brasserie and floating chargrill restaurant. Price twin share A$61 (US$43), single A$115 (US$80), child 2-15 free + 10% VAT.

Suva Peninsular Hotel, PO Box 888, Suva, ph 313 711, 313 574. 40 A/C units with kitchen only 5 minutes from GPO. Lounge/bar, restaurant, lift, pool, parking, conference room, function hall. Price double/twin A$75 (US$53), single A$55 (US$39) + 10% VAT.

Budget

South Seas Private Hotel, PO Box 888, Government Buildings, Suva, ph 312 296. All rooms have fans and insect screens. Communal bathroom and kitchen. Washing facilities. Security. Short walk to city. Price double/twin A$8 (US$6) per person, singles A$10 (US$7), family units A$23 (US$16) plus 10% VAT.

Lautoka

Waterfront, Volivoli Road, ph 694 433, fax 694 499. On the waterfront 30 minutes from Nadi. Standard class. 41 rooms with one double and one single bed. Convenient to Blue Lagoon Cruise departures, adjacent to Lautoka shops and business centre. Price twin share A$50 (US$35), single A$100 (US$70), child 2-15 free + 10% VAT.

Budget

Cathay Hotel, PO Box 239, Lautoka, ph 660 566. 46 rooms with fridge, tea/coffee making and phone. Licensed dining room, lounge, pool. Function room. Off street parking. Security. Price A/C suite, sleeps 3, A$60 (US$42), A/C double and twins, private facilities A$37 (US$26), A/C single with private bath A$30 (US$21), doubles and twins with fans and bath A$30 (US$21), singles with fans and private baths A$23 (US$16), dormitory with bath and fans A$9 (US$6) per person. All plus 10% VAT.

Saweni Beach Hotel, PO Box 239, Lautoka, ph 661 777. 14 self-contained beachfront apartments that sleep 3. All have fans and verandah, A$35-$40 (US$25-28). Licensed lounge and bar, mini market, pool, parking. Dormitory with fans A$10 pp (US$7) Campsite A$4 pp (US$3) plus 10% VAT.

Raki

Standard

Raki Hotel, PO Box 31, Rakiraki, ph 694 101, fax 694 545. On the north-east side of Viti Levu, 2½ hour drive from Nadi. 36 refurbished rooms with one double and one single bed. In part of Fiji not usually seen by tourists. Colonial style hotel set in garden. Lawn bowls. Quaint charming atmosphere. Price twin share A$44 (US$31), single A$88 (US$6) child 2-15 free + 10% VAT.

Coral Coast

First Class

The Shangri-la's Fijian Resort. Private Mil Bag Nadi, ph 520 155, fax 500 402. 84 rooms on Ocean, 48 on Reef, 101 Lagoon Superior, 44 Coral superior, 22 Coral family rooms, 48 Golden Cowrie, 66 Lagoon deluxe, 7 studios, 20 suites and 4 beach bures. 2 restaurants, pool, cocktail bars, disco. Free accommodation for up to 3 children under 18 years sharing parents room. $12.50 (US$9) meal plan for children up to 11 years, daily movies, safe swimming beach, children's pool, daily children's programs, free child care centre for 1-6, baby sitting. Meal Guides: 5 day meal plan F$212 (US$148) per person over 12 years and F$100 (US$77) food and beverage credit. Plenty of activities for singles. Free

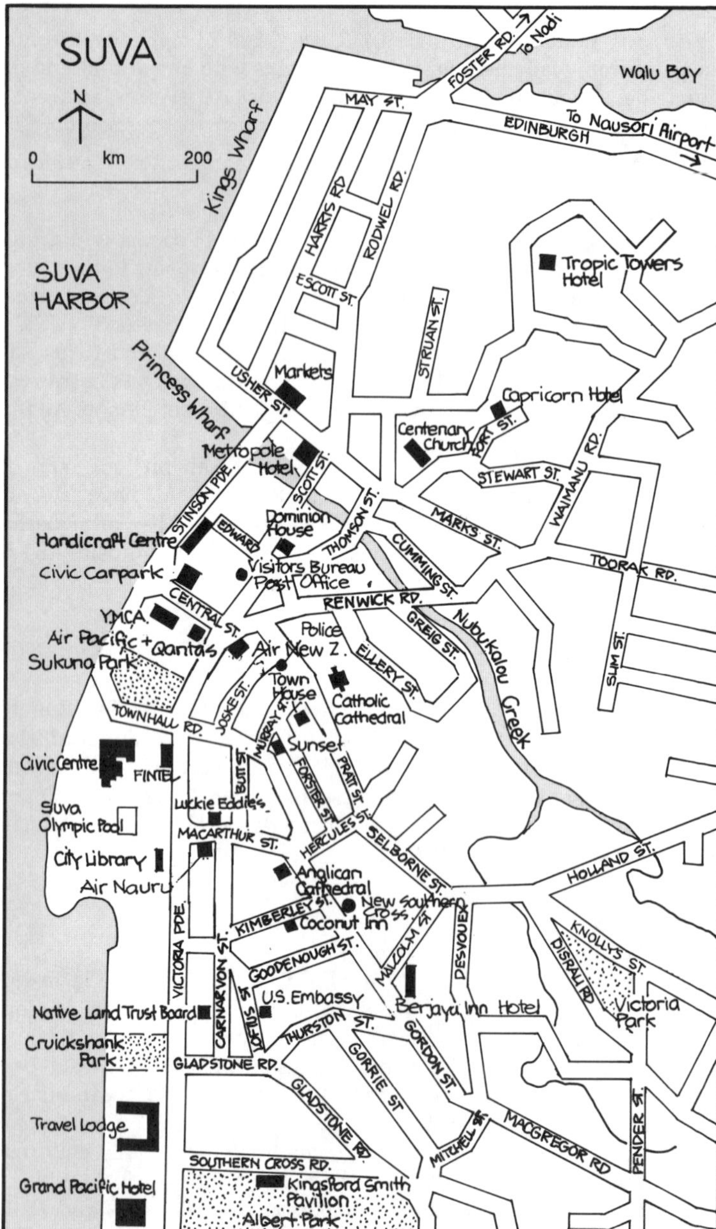
SUVA
N
0 km 200
SUVA HARBOR
Kings Wharf
Princess Wharf
Walu Bay
FOSTER RD.
To Nadi
To Nausori Airport
EDINBURGH
MAY ST.
HARRIS RD
RODWEL RD.
ESCOTT ST.
STRUAN ST.
Tropic Towers Hotel
Markets
USHER ST.
Capricorn Hotel
Centenary Church
FORT ST.
WAIMANU RD.
STEWART ST.
Metropole Hotel
SCOTT ST.
STINSON PDE.
EDWARD
Dominion House
THOMSON ST.
MARKS ST.
TOORAK RD.
Handicraft Centre
Civic Carpark
Visitors Bureau
Post Office
RENWICK RD.
CUMMING ST.
CENTRAL ST.
Y.M.C.A.
Air Pacific + Qantas
Air New Z.
Police
GREIG ST.
ELLERY ST.
Nubukalou Creek
SLIM ST.
Sukuna Park
Town House
Catholic Cathedral
TOWNHALL RD.
JOSKE ST.
MURRAY ST.
Sunset
Civic Centre
FINTEL
BUTT ST.
FORSTER ST.
PRATT ST.
Suva Olympic Pool
Luckie Eddie's
MACARTHUR ST.
HERCULES ST.
SELBORNE ST.
HOLLAND ST.
City Library
Air Nauru
Anglican Cathedral
New Southern Cross
KIMBERLEY ST.
Coconut Inn
VICTORIA PDE.
GOODENOUGH ST.
MALCOLM ST.
DESVOUEX
KNOLLYS ST.
DISRAELI RD.
Victoria Park
CARNARVON ST.
U.S. Embassy
Berjaya Inn Hotel
Native Land Trust Board
LOFTUS ST.
THURSTON ST.
Cruickshank Park
GLADSTONE RD.
GORRIE ST.
GORDON ST.
Travel Lodge
MITCHELL ST.
MACGREGOR RD
PENDER ST.
SOUTHERN CROSS RD.
Grand Pacific Hotel
Kingsford Smith Pavilion
Albert Park

activities: 9-hole golf course, 32 par executive golf course, 5 tennis courts, lawn bowls, handline fishing competition, sailing dinghies, canoeing, snorkelling gear, windsurfing, croquet, aerobics, volleyball, badminton, indoor games, in-house movies. Other activities: scuba diving, deep-sea fishing, snorkelling safari, private golf and tennis lessons, firewalking, waterskiing. Free: traditional Meke, Kava drinking, torch lighting ceremony. There is also a full range of day trips and excursions available from the tour desk. Price: twin share A$100-174 (US$77-122), single A$200-348 (US$140-244) + 10% VAT. Coach transfers, return airport-hotel: adult A$42 (US$29), child A$22 (US$15). Private car one-way A$70 (US$49) per car, maximum 4 people.

Moderate

The Warwick, PO Box 100, Korolevu, ph 530 5555, fax 530 010. On the beach, 2½ hours Nadi Airport by coach, 1½ hours by car. Set on leafy gardens on a long white beach. 217 mountain and ocean view rooms, 23 Warwick Club rooms, 10 suites, each with one double and one sofa bed. Children's menus, playground and activities, indoor games and amusement machines, babysitting, child care centre. Free activities: windsurfing, canoes, snorkelling, kayaks, 6 hole pitch'n'putt golf, volleyball, scuba lesson, live entertainment and lots more. Extra activities, scuba diving, horseback riding, coral viewing, deep sea fishing, squash, waterfall hikes, firewalking, day tours and excursions, floodlit tennis. Well established popular hotel. You can use the facilities of The Naviti Hotel. Price twin share A$66-112 (US$46-78), single A$132-223 (US$92-156), child 2-15 free. Return coach transfers: adult A$48 (US$34), child A$24 (US$17); private car A$82 (US$57) per car + 10% VAT.

The Naviti, PO Box 29, Korolevu, ph 530 444, fax 530 343. On a sandy lagoon 2½ hours by coach 1½ hours by car from Nadi Airport. Set in large open grounds surrounded by hills. 32 mountain view, 108 ocean view rooms, 4 suites with one queen bed, plus rollaway if required. Children's menu and meal sittings, activities and donkey rides, babysitting, children's pool, playground and nanny service. Free activities: snorkel gear, windsurfing, canoes, tennis, golf, paddle skis, scuba diving lesson, volley ball, village tour, evening entertainment, games room, TV room. Extra activities: horseback riding, coral viewing, snorkelling, fishing trips, firewalking. Price twin share A$63-170 (US$44-124), single A$126-340 (US$88-238), child 2-15 free. Bonus: for A$110 (US$ 77) per person one extra night free, 6 full American breakfasts, 6 lunches, and one day car hire, weekends only. Must stay 7 consecutive nights. Minimum 2 adults. All prices + 10% VAT.

Standard

The Reef Resort, PO Box 173, Sigatoka, ph 500 044, fax 520 074. On the beach in the heart of the Coral Coast 1½ hours by coach, 70 minutes by car from Nadi Airport. 67 rooms, 5 family rooms with one queen bed and one single. Babysitting, cots, highchairs, children's menu and meal times, kids pool, playground, supervised kids activities. Price adult twin share A$62 (US$43), single A$124 (US$87). Family room A$70 (US$50), child 2-15 free. Meal guide: for a minimum of 7 nights you can purchase a 'Reef Feast' meal package for A$86 (US$60) per adult, A$59 (US$41) per child under 12. Free activities: tennis, games room, horseriding, bicycles, canoes, fishing, reef walking, snorkelling, one scuba dive lesson. Near Sigatoka for shopping. Tour desk has tours + 10% VAT.

Hideaway Resort, PO Box 233, Sigatoka, ph 500 177, fax 520 025. On sandy beach 2hrs by coach from Nadi Airport, 70 minutes by car. Ocean swimming at high tide only. Leafy gardens. 56 bures with one queen and one single bed; and 4 x 2-bedroom bures with one queen and three single beds. Baby sitters, cots, highchairs, children's pool, playground, supervised activities, bumper boats and Le Mans raceway. Price twin share A$55 (US$39), single A$110 (US$77), family bure $75 (US$53), child 2-15 free. Meal guide: Hideaway's 'Magic Pass' includes five cooked breakfasts and five special lunches, plus one day unlimited kilometre car hire (category A) for A$110 (US$77) each. Free activities: windsurfing, snorkelling, tennis, volleyball, bicycles, golf driving range, archery, mini golf, nightly entertainment, one scuba diving lesson. Caters for the 'young at heart'. All prices + 10% VAT.

Pacific Harbour Resort, PO Box 144, Deuba, ph 450 022, fax 450 262. On long sandy beach 3½ hours by coach, 2½ hours by car from Nadi Airport. 84 rooms with twin or double bed plus up to 2 rollaways. Babysitters, high chairs, cots, children's menus, playground facilities, children's pool. Price twin share A$72 (US$50), single A$143 (US$100), child 2-15 free. Meal Guide: 3 meals a day should average A$55 (US$39) per adult + 10% VAT. Free activities: canoes, tennis, turtle feeding, volleyball, snorkelling, games room. Extra activities: golf, deep-sea fishing, sailing, scuba diving, windsurfing, waterskiing, fire walking (Tuesday/Saturday) horseriding. Only 30 minutes from Suva, near a Robert Trent-designed 18-hole golf course.

Budget

Vakaviti Resort, PO Box 5, Sigatoka, ph 500 526. 5 self-contained lagoon-side bures in tropical garden. Walking distance to restaurants and entertainment. Snorkelling, scuba diving. Restful holiday. Price single A$45 (US$32), double/twin A$55 (US$39), dormitory A$12 (US$8) + 10% VAT.

Den Erau Beach

Deluxe

Sheraton Fiji Resort, PO Box 9761, Nadi Airport, ph 750 777, fax 750 818. On Denerau Beach, 20 minutes from Nadi Airport, 10 minutes from Nadi town, near departure point for daily launch to Mamanuca Islands and the Island Hopper Helipad. 300 rooms all with ocean views. Daily children's activities, pool, creche, babysitting, children's menu, evening BBQ. Meal guide: 3 meals a day should average A$80 adult. 4 restaurants, bars. Free activities: windsurfing, catamarans, laser cars, volleyball, aerobics, daytime tennis. Other activities: Golf, waterskiing, new health club, scuba diving, snorkelling trips, sunset cruise, night tennis, deep-sea fishing, local and off-shore excursions. Cultural activities: woodcarving, storytelling, garden walk tour, Kava and torch lighting ceremony, Meke and firewalking show, fashion shows. Price twin share A$144-246 (US$101-172), single A$288-492 (US$201-344). Return coach transfers: adult A$20 (US$14) child 2-15 years A$10 (US$7). Car A$22 (US$15) per person. All prices + 10% VAT.

Regent of Fiji, PO Box 9081, Nadi Airport, ph 750 000, fax 750 259. Next door to the *Sheraton* and the facilities of both hotels can be used. 284 rooms, 3 handicapped rooms, 6 suites. Children's menus, children's playground, activities, babysitting, pool. Meal guide: 3 meals a day around A$80 (US$56) with a choice of 4 restaurants and bars. Free activities: daytime court use at tennis club, hobbie cats, windsurfing, paddle boats, lawn bowls, archery, mini golf, aerobics, volleyball, games bure. Other activities: golf, tennis lessons, waterskiing, parasailing, scuba diving, snorkelling expeditions, deep-sea fishing, daily full and half day tours and cruises, sunset cruise. Cultural activities: Denarau Village - living arts complex with carving, weaving, pottery and garland making, traditional meke, firewalking. Price twin share A$117-149 (US$82-104), single A$233-298 (US$163-208). Return coach transfers: adult A$20 (US$14), child A$10 (US6). Car A$22 (US$15) per car + 10% VAT.

Mamanuca Island (pronounced Mamanutha)

These islands off Nadi have been transformed into holiday resorts. Wherever you stay the mood is the same. Don't worry about packing a lot of clothes, buy a Fijian sulu, their version of a sarong. Wear shoes for coral reefs. Swim, sail snorkel, watch the brightly coloured fish, look at coral through a glass-bottomed boat. Take a day cruise to another island. Prices range from twin share A$70 (US$49), single A$140 (US$98) at standard Plantation Island; to twin share A$130 (US$91), single A$260 (US$182) at moderate class Castaway Island. All cater for children, all have meal plans, and the activities are similar. Accommodation is in bures.

Unique Hideaways

Vanua Lavu

Kontiki Resort, Private Mail Bag, Savusavu, ph 880 333, fax 880 334. 15 minutes from Savusavu airport on Vanua Lavu. 60.7 hectares of copra, bananas, pineapples, pawpaws, across the road from the beach. Budget class. 13 bures, 1 family bure, 1 suite, 1 honeymoon bure. Babysitting, children's playground. Meal guide: 3 meals a day adult A$60 (US$42), children under 15 A$30 (US$21). Free activities: golf, tennis, snorkelling, reef walks, bush hikes, volleyball, croquet. Other activities: scuba diving, fishing. Price twin share A$63 (US$45), single A$84 (US$59) + 10% VAT.

Taveuni

Taveuni, the Garden Isle of Fiji, is a 1½ hour flight from Nadi by Sunflower Airlines. It is a combination of a romantic past and an unspoilt present. Breathtaking excursions are available: 4WD to Tagimoucia Crater Lake, bird watching, 40m Bouma Cascade waterfall, and world-renowned dive sites.

First Class

Qamea (pronounced Gum-ayuh) Beach Club, PO Matei, Taveuni, ph 880 220, fax 880 092. Off the island of Taveuni. 1½ hours by Sunflower Airlines from Nadito Taveuni Airport then 30 minutes by taxi and boat to the island. First class right on the beach. 11 luxurious Fijian bures. Children under 13 not accepted. 3 meals a day cost about F$83. This is compulsory and paid on arrival. Free activities: windsurfing, village tours, outriggers, snorkelling, dinghies. An upmarket resort well away from the tourist run. Price twin share A$155 (US$109), single A$265 (US$186) + 10% VAT. Return vehicle/boat transfers from Taveuni Airport included.

Moderate

Maravu Plantation Resort. On the island of Taveuni, 150m from beach in a copra plantation. 3 honeymoon, 7 deluxe bures. Babysitting, cots, children's meals. 3 meals a day will cost adult A$55 (US$39), children under 15 A$30 (US$21). Price twin share A$91 (US$64), single A$152 (US$106) + 10% VAT. Return transfers from Taveuni Airport are included.

Dive Taveuni Resort, PO Matei, Taveuni, ph 880 441, fax 880 466. On the island of Taveuni, 5 minutes from the airport. Perched on a clifftop with views across the Somo Somo Straits. Hectares of landscaped gardens running down to a white sandy beach. 6 bures. Children under 15 not accepted. All meals included in the tariff. Especially recommended for divers. Closed 18 Jan-28 Mar. Price twin share A$179 (US$125), single A$179 (US$125) + 10% VAT. Transfers from Taveuni airport included.

Nanunu-I-Ra

Mokusigas Island Resort, 130km north-east of Nadi Airport on the island of Nananu-i-ra, just off the coast of Raki Raki. 2 hours by car or coach from Nadi to Raki Raki, then 10 minutes by launch to the 870 acre island with 7 white sandy beaches surrounded by clear water and reefs. Moderate class. 14 Laguna Vista and 6 Ocean Panorama bures. Recommended as an adult resort but children over 16 years can be catered for. Meal Guide: A$49 (US$34) per adult for 3 meals a day. Free activities: snorkelling, windsurfing, gymnasium, tennis, volleyball, surf skis, nature walks. Price twin share A$103 (US$72), single A$206 (US$144). Return coach and launch transfers from Nadi: adult A$110 (US$77), child A$50 (US$35) + 10% VAT. Launch free.

Viti Levu

Naigani Island Resort, GPO Box 12359, Suva, ph 312 069, fax 302 058. Off the north-east coast of Viti Levu. A one hour scenic drive through villages from Suva then a 30 minute cruise to the 218.52ha beach fringed island of Naigani. Moderate class. 9 large deluxe 2 bedroom villas and 3 three bedroom deluxe villas. Each sleep 6-8 people. Children's activities, special meals, babysitting. A compulsory meal plan must be purchased on arrival and paid for in local currency, adult F$38.50 (US$27), child up to 11 years F$19,25 (US$13) for 3 meals a day. Two meals adult F$25.30 (US$17), child F$13 (US$9) + 10% VAT. Free activities: snorkelling, windsurfing, canoeing, hand-line fishing, bush walks. Formerly Mystery Island, Naigani is steeped in history. Nearby Levuka, Fiji's old capital, can be reached by boat. Ideal for families. Price twin share A$85 (US$60), single A$170 (US$119). Vehicle and boat transfers from Suva Airport to Naigani: adult A$37, A$19 (US$13) child + 10% VAT.

Toberua Island (pronounced Tom-berua)

The 1.6ha island is off the east coast of Viti Levu about 1 hour by car and launch from Suva. The resort is of first class standard. 14 large bures. Children's menus, cots, highchairs, babysitting. Three meals a day cost about F$81 (US$54). Breakfast and dinner or lunch compulsory F$68 (US$45) payable on arrival in local currency. Free activities: windsurfing, paddle-boats, sailing, canoes, water-skiing, snorkelling, table tennis, reef golf. Very up-market and member of Select Hotel Group. Recommended for the most discerning. Price twin share A$157 (US$110), single A$285 (US$200) + 10% VAT. Car and Launch transfers from Suva Airport provided.

Budget
Leleuvia Island Resort, PO Box 50, Levu Ovalau, ph 313 366. Situated on a 17ha island off Ovalau. 3 dormitories, 15 bures, canteen, dining hall, volleyball, snorkelling, scuba diving and fishing. Close to Levuka. For backpackers. Price bungalows A$26 (US$18), bure A$21 (US$15), dorm A$18 (US$13), tent A$15 (US$11) + 10% VAT. All prices include 3 meals. For accommodation in Levuka, try Old Capital Inn 1 or 11 for a cheap visit.

Local Transport

Coach transfers to Suva hotels from Suva Airport: adult A$40 (US$28), child A$20 (US$14).

To Lautoka from Nadi Airport: adult A$34 (US$24), child A$18 (US$13).

To Raki Raki from Nadi Airport: adult A$110 (US$77), child $50 (US$35).

Private car transfers are available on request.

Bus

There are plenty of local buses especially around the towns. The charges are reasonable, ranging around 35c-55c. They buses can usually be waved down on the road. Air-conditioned coaches also take tourists on excursions. Passengers on package deals are met at the airport by their hotel or tour operator.

Taxis

Most towns have taxi services. All taxis are metered and the fares are reasonable, 50c flag fall plus 10c per kilometre. If making a longer trip by taxi, agree a price before you start.

Car

Overseas driving licences and international permits are recognised for six months after arrival. The minimum age limit for driving is 21 and the maximum 65. Driving is on the **left** hand side of the road, although in the small towns and villages the locals tend to drive in the middle of the road, and it seems they also consider the most important part of a car to be the horn, which they use frequently.

All major car rental firms operate in Fiji and can be booked before you leave, at the airport or from your hotel. Avis, Hertz, Central, Khan's, Budget, Thrifty, Sharma's Dove and Letz.

Sea

There are a number of small boats which plough between the islands of the Pacific. Bookings would have to be made when you arrive.

Eating Out

The resort hotels have a good variety of meals, usually with European, Fijian, Chinese and Indian cuisines being available. There are small cafes and restaurants in all major towns, for example, *Chefs*, Sangatam Road, Nadi, ph 703 131 - open Mon-Sat for lunch 10am-2pm, candlelight dinner 6-10pm. Indian curry houses are plentiful. Chinese, Italian, French, European, Japanese and Fijian cuisine can be found depending on the region.

On the outer islands, your resort or hotel may be the only restaurant available. There are licensed restaurants, clubs and hotels throughout Fiji offering local beer, wines and spirits. At hotels and resorts the prices are from: breakfast F$12(US$8); lunch F$16 (US$11); dinner F$25 (US$17). bottle of wine F$9 (US$6); glass of beer F$3 (US$2); cocktails from F$5 (US$3). At restaurants and pubs: dinner from F$5 (US$3); glass of beer F$2 (US$1.30) + 10% VAT, all payable in local currency.

Entertainment

The larger towns have cinemas, nightclubs, and at weekends, dances. Ask your hotel what's on or check the local papers. Movie tickets cost F$1.50 (US$0.99) (A$1.42); Fijian Village entertainment F$24 (US$16) (A$23); Hotel Island Night F$30 (US$20) (A$29). Don't forget the 10% VAT.

Lovo

The 'lovo' is a Fijian feast in which food is wrapped in banana leaves and cooked slowly in an earth oven over smouldering stones. The food has a faintly smoked taste. Vegetables, meat, fish are placed in the earth oven. The centre piece is often a whole pig. This is a must.

Yaqona (Kava)

Throughout Fiji and in most Polynesian countries the drinking of Yaqona (pronounced Yanggona) or Kava is a common social custom. Yaqona is made from the root of the pepper plant, *Piper methysticum*. It is pounded in a pestle and mortar and after the water is added, strained through the shredded bark of the Vau tree. You can attend a Yaqona ceremony which is usually held at night. The Kava is served in a coconut bowl and the correct thing to do is clap twice when you are offered the drink and drink it all at once. It looks and tastes like dirty water and the locals more often than not have a beer chaser. It is supposed to give you pleasant dreams.

Shopping

Fiji is a major duty free shopping island. Duty free shops can be found in all towns and hotels. Check the local paper or the Fiji Visitors Bureau for a list. Everything from electrical goods to accessories can be found at reasonable prices. Resort wear and local fashions can be purchased in shops and resorts. These include sulus, bula shorts for men and swimwear. Tailors make quality men's and women's fashions in a few days. Dress lengths are an excellent buy. Bargaining is still conducted even in duty free shops. Fijian handicrafts are well made. Tapa, the name given to Fijian bark cloth, mats made from leaves, pottery, baskets and wood carving are all good buys.

Sightseeing

The Fiji Islands are a tropical paradise of white sandy beaches, coconut palms, clear blue water, and lagoons fringed with coral reefs. Larger islands have volcanic mountains, tropical rainforests, clear streams and waterfalls. Birds and turtles prefer the smaller islands. Water sports, cruises and coral viewing from glass bottom boats are the main interests for visitors. The majority of resorts are found on Viti Levu the principle island where Suva is situated. The resorts have everything anyone could need and there is no reason to leave them unless you particularly want to take a trip, which they will arrange.

Viti Levu

Nadi (pronounced Nandee), on the west coast of Viti Levu, is the main point of entry at the International Airport. Apart from the many duty free shops, Nadi has nothing to offer the tourist. It is, however, accessible to the resorts and offshore islands. You can take a tour for a day or longer to anywhere in the islands from Nadi.

Suva,

The capital of Fiji, is in the south-eastern corner of Viti Levu. It is very much a multi-racial town. It also has good duty free shopping but the Handicraft Centre on Stinson Parade, where the locals shop, has better

Suva Markets (opposite)

apples

bargains but you will have to do some hard haggling to get a good deal. Beware of touts who will even try to physically drag you into a shop. Never tell them your name or you will find yourself presented with a piece of wood or some other useless item with your name scratched on it and be expected to pay a ridiculous price for it. This can turn nasty so ignore whatever they say.

Suva became the capital in 1882 replacing Levuka on the island of Ovalau. Its rapid growth through the establishment of trading companies, missionary churches and colonial government has left many buildings from the turn of the century. They are all protected under the Suva City Town Planning Scheme.

A one hour walk from the heart of the city along Victoria Parade, following the foreshores will reveal a variety of Fiji's most important buildings.

Burns Philp, built in 1930, on Marks Road, was the first building in Suva to have a lift. Its large imposing design with central tower has been copied throughout the Pacific.

Morris Hedstrom, originally Henry Marks, of the present Morris Hedstrom Supermarket and Department store chain, erected the building in 1918. It is situated on land once owned by large business concerns Brown & Joskie and Jung King Loon at the turn of the century. The arcaded verandah gives the building a Venetian appearance.

The **Fiji Visitors Bureau** in Thomson Street, occupies a Victorian Building, erected in 1912 as a savings bank and telephone exchange.

Close by, **Sichuan Pavilion** restaurant and the **Garrick Hotel** date from 1920. Formally the Pier Hotel, built by the Costello family, it retains its original post supported verandah and elaborate second story balcony.

Continue along Thomson Street to the **G.B. Hari**, on a corner, built around the start of World War 1; it was formally the Universal Picture Theatre. It is one of the few double storey wood and corrugated iron buildings remaining. It has several of shops on the ground floor and offices above.

The **Catholic Cathedral** is in Pratt Street. Father Rosier designed the crypt and nave in 1893. It was the initiative of Bishop Julian Vidal, Australian Bishop of Fiji. The pyrmont stones came from Hunters Hill, Sydney, and were carried in ships as ballast. The timber flooring came from Quebec, Canada.

Prouds Building on the corner of Thomson Street and Renwick Road was built by chemist Mitchelmore in 1929/31. This impressive three storey building faces the triangular park that was once the site of the original Suva market.

Fintel, on Victoria Parade, was built in 1926. The first radio broadcasts were made from a room in this building. It retains its cable and wireless function to this day.

A short distance along is the **Old Town Hall**, built in 1904 as a memorial to Queen Victoria on her Diamond Jubilee. With its cast iron

Fijian Cultural Entertainment (opposite)

lacework it is one of Suva's finest example of colonial architecture. In earlier times it was used by dance companies and bazaars.

Suva City Library, formally Carnegie Library, was built in 1909 with a grant from Andrew Carnegie.

St Andrew's Presbyterian Church in Gordon Street was built through the generosity of Mr William Kerr Thomson who donated £100 and the site. Built in 1883, it had just been finished when it was demolished by a hurricane. The present wooden church was erected in 1896.

Government Building, built in 1939 on Victoria Parade, houses major government departments

Grand Pacific Hotel on Victoria Parade was designed to look like a ship, and opened in May 1914. All rooms were protected from the sun by wide verandahs and balconies. At present the building is being refurbished.

Botanic Gardens Clock Tower, further along Victoria Parade, was built in 1918 by Henry Marks & Co in memory of their director G.J. Mark, the first mayor of Suva. The tower is located in the Thurston Gardens, formerly called the Botanical Gardens. Close by is **Government House**. The original house, which was built on the site of an old Fijian village, Nakorobaoa, was destroyed by fire in March 1921. The new building was completed in 1928.

The **Suva Museum**, also in Thurston Gardens, is open Mon-Thurs 8am-4.30pm, Fri 8am-4pm, Saturday 9am-4pm, and admission is F$3.30. It houses the most comprehensive collection of Fijian artifacts, and also offers tours on the Tabu Tabu-Soro, a traditional double-hulled canoe.

For those who do not wish to walk there is a bus tour of Suva and surrounds, and enquiries can be made at the information office or your hotel.

Pacific Harbour

A 40 minute drive from Suva, on the Coral Coast, is this luxurious resort. Home of the mythical sharkgod, Qaraniqio, it is guarded by two female spirits. They had to be appeased before the swamps could be drained and the project commenced.

It has everything including a golf course and a five mile beach. Visit the Cultural Centre which is also the home of the Fiji Dance Theatre. Craftsmen, musicians and artists can be seen at work. Pacific Harbour can also be reached on a day tour from Nadi.

Sigatoka

Sigatoka lies at the mouth of the Sigatoka River, Fiji's second longest river, in a fertile valley known as 'the salad bowl of Fiji'. It is a small town with a good market and duty free shops. It is much more pleasant for shopping than Suva or Nadi. It can be reached by bus from Nadi or by Coral Coast Railway in a c.1911 steam train.

Sigatoka Sand Dunes, ph 315944. A small, arid desert amidst the surrounding tropical vegetation. Important archaeological relics have been found here establishing that Fiji was settled about 3500 years ago. They begin at the mouth of the Sigatoka River and can be reached off the main Queen's Highway. Do not remove or 'souvenir' anything. Admission is free.

Tavuni Hill Fort, radio ph RP 3740. Situated 4km off the main highway at Sigatoka, the Tavuni Hill fortification is an example of bygone eras. The site was manned by Tongan warriors whose descendants live in a village nearby and provide the guides to explain the history. Lookout points offer spectacular views. There is a reception bure with a display by the Fiji Museum. Refreshments, gift shop and toilets. Admission is F$6.

Lautoka

Situated 19km north of Nadi, Lautoka is famous for its sugar mill (conducted tours June-December). Most of the cruise lines include Lautoka in their itineraries but the prices at the local markets go sky high when a ship comes into port.

The town is the departure point for *Blue Lagoon Cruises* and *Island in the Sun Cruises*.

Although Lautoka has its fair share of duty free shops, it is more interested in sugar than tourism, and for that reason alone it is worth a visit.

Vanua Levu

The country's second largest island is north of Viti Levu. Once the centre of the sandalwood trade, its present economy depends on sugar and copra. Its main port is Savusavu. The principle urban centre is Labasa which has the island's main airport and a small port.

You can visit a copra plantation, a citrus orchard or take a full day tour to Labasa and surroundings. This is sugar cane country. There are plenty of cruises and all water sports are available.

Taveuni

Known as the Garden island, Taveuni is the third largest island of the Fijian group. It boasts lush green vegetation, waterfalls, sandy beaches and the country's national flower, Tagimoucia. Although copra is its principal money earner, tourism is dominant. Taveuni is easily reached by air.

Lomaiviti

This group of islands includes Ovalau and the private island of Wakaya which is famous for its wild deer. Found east of Viti Levu it attracts few tourists. There are airfields at Koro and Gau and a private landing strip at Wakaya.

Ovalau

Situated off the eastern side of Viti Levu, this is the home of the old capital, Levuka. This was the site of the Deed of Cession in 1874, and the waterfront looks much as it did a century ago. It is the centre of Fiji's fishing industry complete with canning factory. There is a road around the island linking villages with the airport at Bureta and the town of Levuka. Tours are available.

Kandavu

This island is accessible by boat and air and has the finest scuba diving locations in the world, the great Astrolabe.

Lau Group

These islands form the eastern section of Fiji. Hardly any tourists visit although there is guest house accommodation. There are airports on Lakeba, Vanuabalavu, Moala, Cicia and Ono-i-Lau. Yachts wishing to call at Lau must receive permission from the Secretary of Fijian Affairs, Suva.

The Yasawas

The westernmost islands of the Fijian chain, the Yasawas remain only slightly influenced by the outside world. They have become known because *Blue Lagoon Cruises* make 4-7 day trips through the islands. The mountain scenery is magnificent, the beaches isolated and the limestone caves at Sawa-i-Lau have ancient writings on the wall. Well worth a visit.

The Mamanucas

A chain of islands visible from Nadi, The Mamanucas have often been called the Mecca of Fiji. Many island resorts can be found here. They are considered to be among the most scenic islands in the country.

Bau

A small island off Viti Levu, Bau lies a few kilometres south of Suva. It is the home of the Paramount Chief of Fiji, and also of the former

Governor General Ratu Sir George Cakobau, whose grandfather ceded the Fiji Islands to Great Britain.

Organised Tours

There are plenty of package tours to Fiji. All travel agents have brochures. The package deal will be better for the budget traveller and families. An 8 day/7 night tour of Fiji's 'big island' will cover most of the sights. It departs on Tuesdays from Nadi.

Itinerary

Day 1: Check into your hotel. Your tour escort will brief you over a drink at 7-7.30pm.

Day 2: Travel by air-conditioned car or coach to South Sea Orchid Gardens. Visit the local market at the port of Lautoka, then giant mango trees line the King's Road which takes you to Ba for lunch. Drive through Yagara Cattle Ranch and pass salt farms on the way to Raki for the night.

Day 3: Raki-Naigani Island. Drive through countryside dotted with farms to Wailotau Snake-God cave for lunch. From Natovi Jetty transfer by boat to Naigani Island resort for the night. Day 4: Naigani-Levuka-Naigani. Travel by boat to Levuka. Enjoy a scenic round island trip. Lunch Levuka town. Transfer to boat back to Nauigani Island.

Day 5: Naigani-Suva. Travel by boat to Natovi Landing then by coach to Suva. On the way pass Wainibuka Gorge and the Rewa River. Rest of day at leisure.

Day 6: Suva-Coral Coast. Drive to your hotel and enjoy its activities.

Day 7: Head up the river to Namuamua Village for a traditional Fijian feast and entertainment. Return to your hotel.

Day 8: Coral Coast-Nadi. After breakfast take a scenic drive to Nadi where your tour ends. Price adult twin share A$1270 (US$889), triple share A$1146 (US$802), single A$1735 (US$1214).

Fiji Outback Adventure 10 days/9 nights.

Leaves from Nadi on Tuesdays. The first five days are the same as the 'big island' trip except you fly to Savusavu.

Day 6: Discover Savusavu. See the early colonial buildings, hot springs, hill forts and colonial plantations.

Day 7: After breakfast fly to Taveuni the 'Garden Isle' for two days.

Day 8: Visit the natural wonders of the island. Walking along forest trails to diving spots and early Catholic missions.

Day 9: Transfer to Matei Airport for your flight to Nausori. Time to shop in Suva then to the Coral Coast for the night.

Day 10: Drive to Nadi where tour ends. Price twin share A$2157 (US$1510), triple share A$2080 (US$1400, single A$2980 (US$2086). VAT is usually included in all package deal prices.
The average price of a half day tour by motorcoach is F$29 (US$22), (A$30). Full day by motorcoach F$60 (US$46), (A$63).

Cruises

Blue Lagoon Cruises, PO Box 54, Lautoka, ph 661 622, cruise the Yasawas islands. Duration: 4 days/3 nights and 7days/6 nights.

Beachcomber Cruises, Lautoka, ph 661 500, cruise to Beachcomber Island daily.

Tropic Cruises, Lautoka, ph 661 622, *South Sea Cruises,* Nadi, ph 722 988, *Captain Cook,* Nadi, ph 701 823, *Oceanic,* Nadi, ph 723 590, *Bay Cruises,* Nadi, ph 722 696, *Bounty Cruises,* Sigatoka, ph 500 963, all cruise around the islands. *Moorings Rainbow,* Nadi, ph 666 710, has charter yachts.

A Day Tour to an island costs F$55-150 (US$37-100), (A$52-142).

Day Tours

No matter where you are staying half day and full day excursions can be arranged through your hotel. Pick up a brochure from the Fiji Visitor's Bureau at the airport when you arrive. Some suggestions:

Pacific Harbour Cultural Centre, ph 450177, featuring Fijian life of former times in an attractive island setting. One hour entertainment, sacred firewalking ritual Tuesday and Saturday 3pm. Home of the Dance Theatre of Fiji, Treetop restaurant, shopping complex and an 18-hole golf course.

Orchid Island Cultural Centre, PO Box 1018, Suva, ph 361 128. A unique cultural attraction. Authentic Fijian cultural centre with Fijian village, bure kalou (pagan temple), chief's bure, handicraft demonstrations, traditional traps and mini museum. See Fiji's flora and fauna in attractive bush setting. Rare banded iguana, flying foxes, boa constrictors, birds and other animals. Phone for operating hours and admission fees.

Shotover Jet Fiji, ph 750 400, the world's most exciting jet boat ride. Departures 7 days a week, every 30 minutes from Denarau Island Marina. Complimentary transfers from Nadi and Denarau Island resorts. Booking essential from your hotel tour desk. Price A$55 (US$39) adult, 15 years and under A$24 (US$17) and family specials.

Navua River Tour, Coral Coast, ph 722811, cruises 20km up the river past villages, waterfalls and untouched jungle. Village lunch. Price A$54 (US$38) adult, under 12 A$33 (US$23).

Rafting Navua River with a scenic drive to the upper reaches and raft trip down the river with stops for swimming. BBQ lunch. Price A$65 (US$46).

Abaca (Ambatha) Hiking & Sightseeing, ph 664047. Thirty minutes from Lautoka a trekker's paradise through black volcanic mountains, forests and open grassland. A 20-minute walk from the car park offers spectacular views of the Yasawa and Mamanuca Islands. Cliff faces for rock climbers. Admission F$5. In Abaca village there is a lodge with 12 beds and BBQ, and swimming in the river and authentic handicrafts. Bed per night F$18.

Outer Islands

Bouma Forest Park on the island of Taveuni. Colourful tropical vegetation, clear fresh mountain stream and Bouma Falls. Offers peace and tranquillity in beautiful bush. Swimming and BBQ facilities at Tevoro Falls. Admission F$4, F$10 with guide.

Lavena Coastal Walk on Taveuni Island, ph 880 453. The wild south-east coast of Taveuni offers nature lovers a wealth of scenic attractions. White coral and black sand beaches give way to forests rich in bird life. A well-formed 5km path starts from Lavena Village. Unique rock pedestals are found near the half-way mark. A guide describes the history of the area and the use of various plants. The trail ends at Wainibau falls where there is a pool and a pause for lunch. Allow about 3hrs round trip. Admission F$5, with guide F$10.

Tour Operators

Adventure and Endless Holidays PO Box 9241, Nadi Airport ph 720 066, fax 720 072.

Rosie the Travel Service, PO Box 9268, Nadi Airport, ph 722 755, fax 722 607.

Sun Tours Fiji, PO Box 9403, Nadi Airport, ph 722 666, fax 722 607.

Tapa International Ltd, PO Box 654, Suva, ph 302 333, fax 302 048.

United Touring Fiji Ltd, PO Box 9172, Nadi Airport, ph 722 811, fax 720 389.

Fiji Tours, PO Box 74, Nadi, ph 700 922, fax 702 090. *Japan Travel Bureau (NZ) Ltd*, PO Box 9433, Nadi Airport, ph 702 755, fax 702 708.

Murray's Coaches, PO Box 10260, Nadi Airport, ph 721 344, fax 721 341.

Ovalau Tours & Transport, PO Box 249, Levuka, ph 440 611, fax 440 405.

South Pacific Tour Planners, PO Box 9306, Nadi Airport, ph 722 911, fax 720 363.

A Fijian ceremony

Sports

Facilities for aquatic sports are found at all resorts. Some also have para-flying. On-shore sports include tennis, volleyball (the staff and locals will join in with gusto), bowling, golf, archery, horse riding, aerobics, swimming and jogging.

Team sports are cricket, soccer and rugby, and your hotel can arrange for you to watch an event.

Dive Operators

Aqua-Trek Ocean Sports Adventure. Diving on Mana Island. Price A$50-450 (US$35-315). Gear for sale, instructors available.

Dive Kadava Matana Resort. 3 dives daily and night dives. Dive shop, equipment rental. 10 dive package US$300 (A$428).

Other operators with prices on request: *Beqa Divers Fiji*, ph 361 088; *Captain Cook Cruises*, ph 701 823; *Nai'a Cruises*, Lami, ph 450 382; *Sea Fiji Travel*, Savusavu, ph 850345; *The Wakaya Club*, Suva, ph 440 128.

Golf - *18-hole courses*

Denarau Golf and Racquet Club; Kontiki Resort; Nadi Airport Golf Club; Pacific Harbour Golf Club; Fiji Golf Club Suva.

- 9-hole courses

Ba Golf Club; Fiji Mocambo; Labasa Golf Club; Lautoka Golf Club; Raki Raki Golf Club; Reef Resort Golf Club; Fijian Shangri-la; The Naviti Golf Club; Vatukoula Golf Club.

Pitch'n'Putt

Warwick of Fiji; Sheraton Vomo; Regent of Fiji; Toberua Island Resort (only at low tide).

Sports events usually cost F$10

NOTES

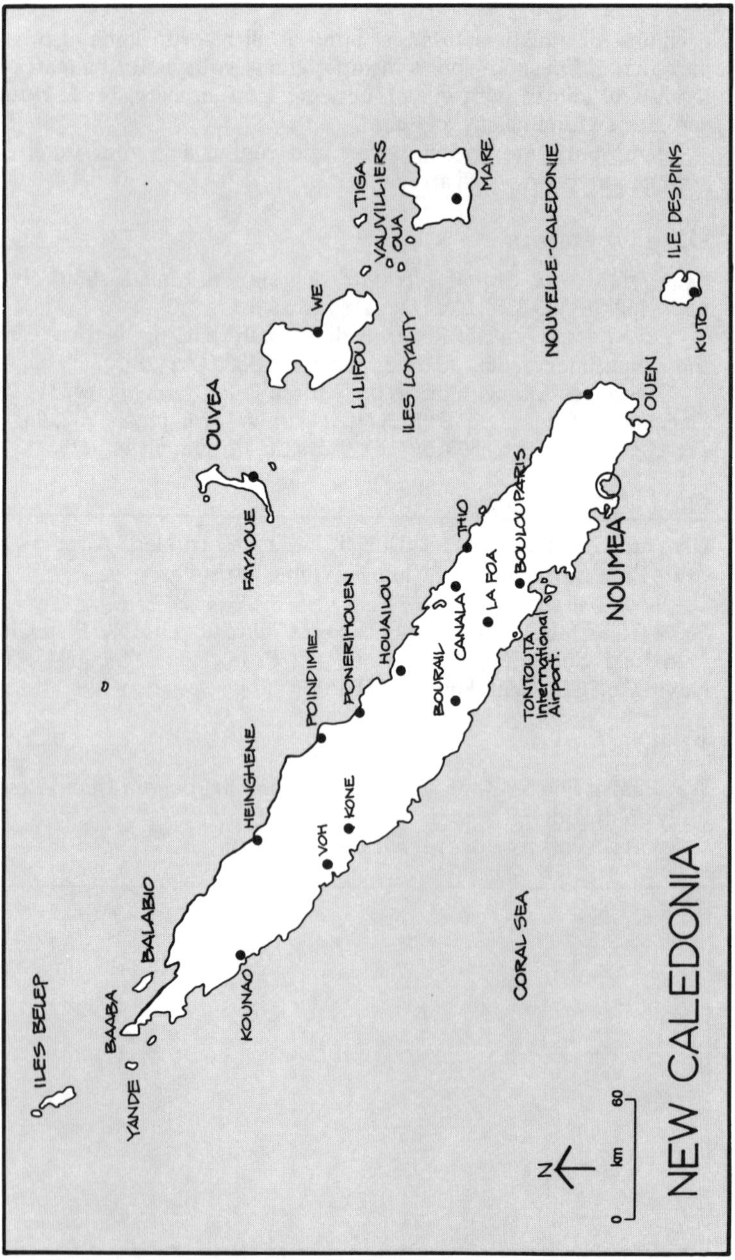
NEW CALEDONIA
0 km 60
N
ILES BELEP
YANDE
BAABA
BALABIO
KOUNAO
HEINGHENE
VOH
KONE
POINDIMIE
PONERIHOUEN
HOUAILOU
BOURAIL
CANALA
LA FOA
THIO
BOULOUPARIS
TONTOUTA International Airport.
NOUMEA
OUEN
CORAL SEA
FAYAOUE
OUVEA
WE
LILIFOU
ILES LOYALTY
TIGA
VAUVILLIERS
OUA
MARE
NOUVELLE-CALEDONIE
ILE DES PINS
KUTO

NEW CALEDONIA

New Caledonia (French name Nouvelle Caledonie), is situated in the south-west Pacific Ocean between Australia and Fiji. It is a French overseas territory. New Caledonia covers an area of 19,103 sq km including dependencies.

New Caledonia is made up of:
The Mainland.
Ouen Island and the Isle of Pines in the south.
The Loyalty Islands (Mare, Lifou, Ouvea, Beautemps-Beaupre and Tiga) to the east.

The main island is an elongated shape about 50km wide by 400km long. It is surrounded by over 800km of barrier reef enclosing one of the most beautiful lagoons in the world.

A central chain of mountains extends the length of the mainland, the highest peaks rising to 1200m and 1600m. This mountainous backbone creates a natural division between two distinct regions.

The east coast is narrow, with night rainfall and fresh trade winds. The coastline has varied tropical vegetation. There are large coconut plantations at the foot of waterfalls or enclosed in valleys through which rivers pass on their way to the sea.

The west coast is on the leeward side of the island. It is broad and ideally suited to cattle farming and agriculture. Covered mostly by gum-trees it has many interesting areas for tourists.

The main industries are nickel mining and processing and meat preserving. Nickel, coffee and copra are exported.

The capital of New Caledonia is Noumea.

History

Captain James Cook first discovered these island on September 4, 1774. He named them New Caledonia because the mountains in the Balade area where he anchored, reminded him of Scotland (Latin name Caledonia).

The country was inhabited by Melanesians, later called Kanaks, which in the Polynesian language means 'man'.

After a short stay at Balade, Cook sailed his ship *Resolution* to Amere Island near the Isle of Pines, without sighting the Loyalty Islands.

In 1792 the Frenchman Bruni d'Entrecasteaux, while searching for missing navigator La Pérouse, stopped at Balade and the Isle of Pines.

The Loyalty Isles were finally discovered and Protestant

missionaries settled there. The first Catholic Missionaries settled at Balade in 1843.

Admiral Febvrier-Despointes officially took possession of New Caledonia on September 24, 1853 on the orders of Napoleon 111.

In 1862 Admiral Guillain became the first Governor. Two years later New Caledonia was established as a penal settlement receiving thousands of convicts and political prisoners (in particular those from the uprising of the Paris Commune between 1872 and 1878).

In 1863 nickel was discovered and a rush of European settlers with their families commenced. With the arrival of Governor Feillet, free colonisation grew and in 1897 transportation of convicts ceased.

New Caledonia developed slowly and with some difficulties until World War II. In 1940 it was one of the first French colonies to join General De Gaulle's Free French. From 1942-45 the territory became an important American military base, an exposure that led the country into modern-day development.

In 1951 the government abolished the indentured labour system under which about 13,000 Chinese, Indonesian and Vietnamese had worked in New Caledonia. In the 1960s these people were returned to their homeland.

Since 1982 the Melanesians, realising that they were to be outnumbered by the French settlers, agitated, sometimes violently, for independence. The 1985 elections resulted in control of most regions by Kanaks but not the majority of seats. The push for independence continued and in 1987 a referendum was held. The result was that New Caledonia remained French. In 1989 the leader of the Socialist National Liberation Front, Jean-Marie Tjibaou, was murdered.

The French Government appoints a High Commissioner, who has considerable powers, as its representative in New Caledonia. An elective territorial assembly of 36 members debates and approves the budget submitted by the administration. The assembly may also express its desires on policy matters outside the jurisdiction controlled by Paris. The Governor meets, as executive, with the Consell de Gouvernment, of which he is President. Other members are elected by the territorial assembly. New Caledonia has two representatives in the French parliament.

Climate

Known as 'The Land of Eternal Spring', New Caledonia is blessed with a semi-tropical climate all year round. September-March is the warm season with temperatures averaging 25C; June-August it is around 20C. Rainfall is more prevalent December-March.

Population

At the last census the population was 165,368 although the latest estimate is over 220,000. Around 74,000 are Melanesians, 55,000 Europeans, 19,000 Tahitians and Wallisians, and about 16,000 are of other origins.

Language

The official language is French, although there are about 30 Melanesian dialects. English is taught in schools and most people in the tourist industry speak and understand English.

It is courteous and appreciated if you at least try to say a few words in French.

Hello ....Bonjour
Goodbye..................Au revoir
See you soon...........A bientot
How are you? ....Comment allez vous? Comment ca va bien?
Please.......................S'il vous plait.
Thank you. ....Merci.
The bill please.........L'addition s'il vous plait.
How much is it? .....Combien ca coute?
How do I get to? ....Comment puis je me rendre à/au...?
Where is the...? ....Ou est le/la...?
I'm lost can you help me?...............Je me suit égaré pouvez vous m'aider?
Do you accept credit cards/travellers cheques?
Acceptez vous les cartes de credit/les cheques de voyage?
Does anyone speak English? .. Est-ce que quelqu'un parle anglais?
What sizes do you have?.............Quelles tailles avez vous?
Could I try this on? ....Est-ce que je peux essayer cela?
You have been kind......................Vous avez été très gentil.
Sandwich Half a long loaf of French bread stick with filling.
Croque monsieur is a toasted ham and cheese sandwich.
Croque madame is a toasted ham, cheese and egg sandwich.
Ham ....Jambon
Chicken....................Poulet
Meat ....Viande
Open ....Ouvert
Shut ....Fermé
Exit ....Sortie
A Coffee ....Un café

Public Holidays

January 1 ....New Years Day
March/April..........Easter Good Friday/Easter Monday
May 1 ....Labour Day

May 8 .... Ascension Day
July 14 .... Bastille Day
August 15 .... Assumption Day
September 24 .... New Caledonia Day
November 1 .... All Saints Day
November 11 .... Armistice Day
December 25 .... Christmas Day

Entry Regulations

If travelling on a valid EEC, New Zealand, Japanese or USA passport, no visa is required but you must have a return ticket. Australians need a visa which is issued free of charge.

Noumea

Customs

Duty Free allowance: 1 litre of spirits, 200 cigarettes.
Animals, plants, seeds, etc cannot be imported.
There is no departure tax.

Consulates

Australian: 19-21 Ave Maréchal Foch, ph 27 2414.
New Zealand: 4 Boulevard Vauban, ph 27 2543.

Money

The currency is the French Pacific franc. Notes are in denominations of CFP 500, 1000, 5000 and 10,000. Coins are CFP 1, 2, 5, 10, 20, 50 and 100.

Approximate rates of exchange are:

A$	=	CFP69.48
Can$	=	CFP64.95
NZ$	=	CFP62.02
S$	=	CFP65.05
UK£	=	CFP139.07
US$	=	CFP90.76

Communications

The daily newspaper is in French, but some newspapers and magazines in English can be found.

There are two TV channels and six radio stations. RRB broadcasts news in English at 8.30am every day except Sunday.

The main post office is near the Museum on Baie de la Moselle, corner Avenue Maréchal Foch. It is open Mon-Fri 7.45am-11.15am, 12.15pm-3.30pm, Sat 7.30am-11am.

Phone cards are available from the post office, tobacconists, newsagents, supermarkets and major hotels.

Most hotels have direct dialling phones, and there is a public facility at the post office. The country code is 687. To make a call from Australia dial 0011 687 then the number. From New Zealand 00687 then the number.

Emergency telephone numbers: medical 15, police 17.

Miscellaneous

Time

Local time is GMT + 11.

Business Hours

Most shops and offices open at 7am and close at 6pm with lunch 11.30am-1.30pm. On Wed and Fri shops in the central business district stay open until 8pm.

Some shops are open on Saturday and in the main, supermarkets stay open Saturday and Sunday.

Banks and smaller post offices stay open for lunch but close around 3.45pm.

Electricity

Supply is 220 volts AC 50, and plugs have 2 round prongs. Take an adaptor and converter with you.

Credit Cards

Major credit cards are widely accepted.

Tipping

Do not tip.

Tax

There is a hotel tax which is already included in package deals. It depends on the classification of the hotel as to how much tax has to be paid.

Medical Facilities

The main hospital is Hospital Gaston Bourret,ph 27 2121. There are also a number of private hospitals.

Doctors, dentists, hospitals and pharmacies are all available. The hotel can contact a doctor for guests.

Good medical centres and dispensaries can be found inland and on the islands.

No vaccinations are required unless travelling from an infected area, although protection against typhoid is recommended. New Caledonia is free from malaria.

Insurance

It is advisable to have full medical insurance as well as cover for other emergencies.

Dress

The warm climate warrants comfortable and cool clothing. Cotton dresses, T-shirts and shorts are perfect for day. Something a little warmer for evening. Dressing up is not uncommon for the evening, especially if dining out.

Water

To be on the safe side, It is advisable to drink only boiled water or mineral water, which can be purchased in any supermarket.

Etiquette

To enter a Melanesian village, unless by invitation from one of the villagers, permission must be sought from the High Chief or a village elder. At all times visitors must accept and respect Melanesian tradition and culture.

Tip

New Caledonia can be very expensive. It is advisable to take a package tour to the island so that the prices for sightseeing tours, etc, will be known beforehand. The city of Noumea is not a place to linger, but it is worth a quick look at the sights and shops.

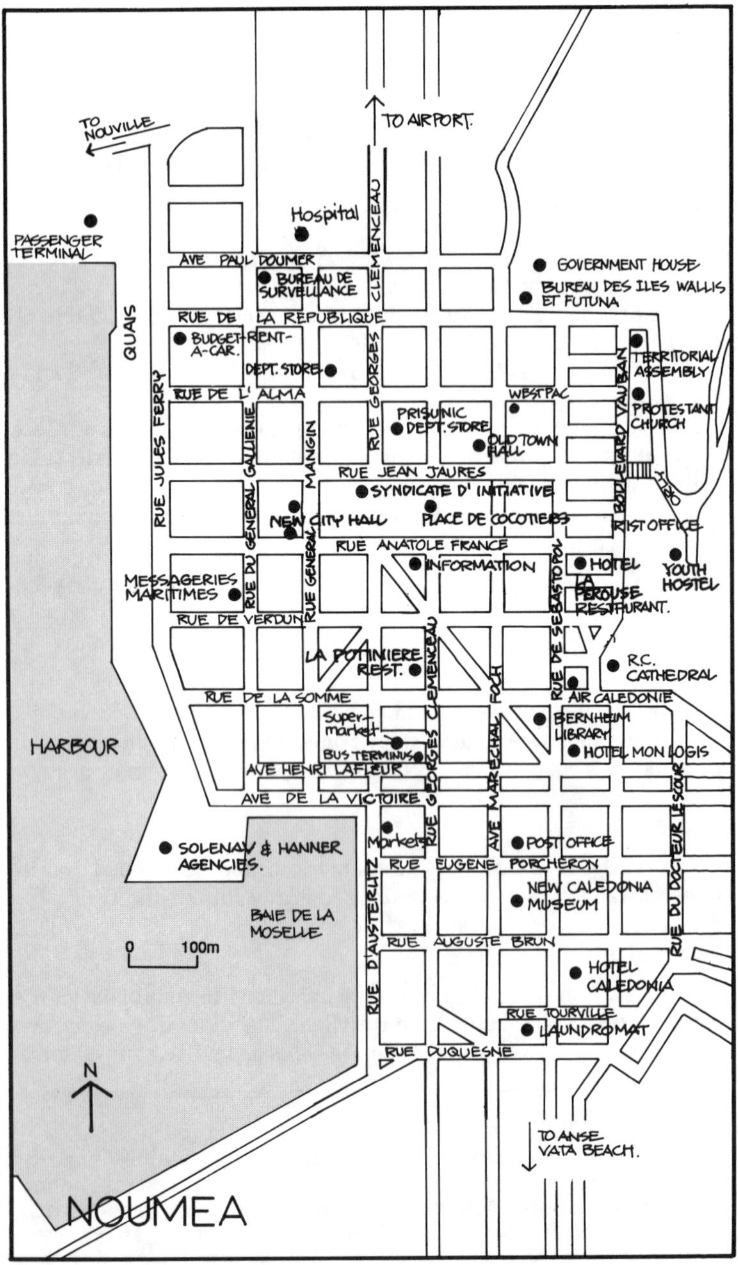
TO NOUVILLE
TO AIRPORT.
PASSENGER TERMINAL
Hospital
AVE PAUL DOUMER
BUREAU DE SURVEILLANCE
CLEMENCEAU
GOVERNMENT HOUSE
BUREAU DES ILES WALLIS ET FUTUNA
RUE DE LA REPUBLIQUE
QUAIS
BUDGET-RENT-A-CAR.
DEPT. STORE
TERRITORIAL ASSEMBLY
RUE DE L' ALMA
WESTPAC
PROTESTANT CHURCH
PRISUNIC DEPT. STORE
OLD TOWN HALL
RUE GEORGES
BOULEVARD VAUBAN
RUE JULES FERRY
RUE DU GENERAL GALLIENIE
RUE GENERAL MANGIN
RUE JEAN JAURES
SYNDICATE D' INITIATIVE
NEW CITY HALL
PLACE DE COCOTIERS
POST OFFICE
RUE ANATOLE FRANCE
INFORMATION
HOTEL LA PEROUSE
RESTAURANT.
YOUTH HOSTEL
MESSAGERIES MARITIMES
RUE DE VERDUN
RUE DE SEBASTOPOL
LA POTINIERE REST.
R.C. CATHEDRAL
RUE GEORGES CLEMENCEAU
FOCH
RUE DE LA SOMME
AIR CALEDONIE
Super-market
BERNHEIM LIBRARY
HARBOUR
BUS TERMINUS
HOTEL MON LOGIS
AVE HENRI LAFLEUR
AVE DE LA VICTOIRE
AVE MARECHAL
Market
SOLENAV & HANNER AGENCIES.
POST OFFICE
RUE EUGENE PORCHERON
NEW CALEDONIA MUSEUM
RUE DU DOCTEUR LESCOUR
BAIE DE LA MOSELLE
0 100m
RUE AUGUSTE BRUN
RUE D'AUSTERLITZ
HOTEL CALEDONIA
RUE TOURVILLE
LAUNDROMAT
RUE DUQUESNE
N
TO ANSE VATA BEACH.
NOUMEA

Travel Information

How to get there

By Air

Air Calédonie International flies to Noumea from New Zealand and Australia.
Qantas flies from Sydney.
Air New Zealand and *Air Nauru* also have services to Noumea.
Air France flies from France via Sydney.

By Sea

Cruise ships make regular calls at Noumea. P&O and CTC are the main visitors.

Tourist Information

Noumea Tourist Office, 24 rue Anatole France BP 2828 Noumea, ph (687) 28 7580.
Northern Province Tourist Bureau, Le Manhattan Building, 39 rue de Verdun BP C5 Noumea, ph (687) 27 7805.
Major hotels can provide brochures on available tours.

Accommodation

Following is a selection of available accommodation, with prices for a room per night, which should be used as a guide only.

Noumea

Club Mediterranée Chateau Royal, Ouen Toro BP 515 Noumea, ph 26 1200, fax 26 20.71. 280 rooms, conference facilities, sports activities, disco, shows, pool, beach, restaurant, bar, shops, bank. Price on request.

Deluxe

Le Méridien Pointe Magnin, BP 1915 Noumea, ph 26 5000, fax 26 5100. 240 rooms, 10 jnr suites 2 diplomatic suites, 1 presidential suite. 4 restaurants, pool, sports, business centre, beach, conference facilities, shops, lobby and pool bar, boutique, concierge. Price CFP23,000, 38,000, 56,000, 92,000. (US$267-1068).
Nouvata Parkroyal, 123 Prom R Laroque Avenue, Anse Vata BP137 Noumea, ph 26 2200, fax 26 1677. Built on the site of the old Nouvata. 101 rooms, villas, suite. A/C, restaurant, lounge, bar, TV tea and coffee making, phone, mini bar, fridge. Business facilities, parking. Price per room CFP21,000 (US$243), villa CFP18,000 (US$209), suite CFP44,000 (US$510).

First Class

Escapade Resort, Ilot Maitre, BP 4918 Noumea, ph/fax 28 5320. First class. 44 rooms 2 suites. Bar, restaurant, beach, pool, shop, water activities. Price per room CFP15,900 (US$185), suites CFP25,000 (US$290).

Le Stanley, rue de la Riviéra, Ouémo, BP 1617 Noumea, ph 26 3277, fax 25 2656. 44 rooms, 12 superior, 2 suites, studio apartments. Bar, restaurant, TV, A/C, phone, pool, coffee, room service, conference facilities. Fully equipped units, sea view. Price per room CFP12,000 (US$139), superior CFP14,000 (US$163), suite CFP19,000 (US$220), apartments CFP34,650/7 days (US$402).

Budget

Caledonia, 10 R.A. Brun, Quartier Latin, BP 2168 Noumea, ph 27 3821, fax 27 8145. 9 double rooms, 11 with shared facilities, 6 studios. Bar, restaurant, A/C, TV and video to rent. Boutique, snack bar. Price room with bath CFP4,500 (US$52), without bath CFP4,000 (US$46), studio CFP5,000 (US$58).

Le Lapérouse, 33 rue de Sébastopol, BP 1915 Noumea, ph 27 2251, fax 27 1187. 18 rooms with facilities, 11 share bath. TV lounge, fans, A/C, bar, restaurant, snack bar, room service for breakfast. Price room with facilities CFP5,600 (US$65), share facilities CFP5,190 (US$60).

Le Paris, 45 rue de Sébastopol, BP 2226 Noumea, ph 28 1700, fax 27 6080. 48 rooms, bar, snack bar, restaurant, TV, A/C, coffee shop, laundry, night club, lounge, video. Price CFP5,820 (US$68), CFP29,200/7 nights (US$339), CFP57,000/14 nights (US$661).

Youth Hostel, 51 rue Bis Olry, Noumea (PO Box 767), ph 27 5879. 88 beds, kitchen, laundry, TV room. Price 2 bed share CFP2,600/2,800 (US$30-33) per room. 4 bed share 1,000/1,100 (US$12-13) per person.

West Coast

Paillotes de la Quenghi, BP 56 Boulouparis, ph 35 1735. 15 rooms. Restaurant, pool, tennis, river activities golf, horse riding. Price CFP6,500 (US$75).

Hotel Banu, BP 57 La Foa, ph 44 3119, fax 44 3550. 9 rooms, A/C, restaurant, bar, pool. Price twin CFP4,200 (US$49), single CFP3,200 (US$37), A/C CFP5,600 (US$62).

Evasion, 130 Sarraméa, BP La Foa, ph 44 3235. Restaurant, pool, bar, horse riding, walks, excursions. Price CFP4,000 (US$66).

Le Nera, RTI Bourail, ph 44 1644, fax 44 1831. 8 rooms, 1 suite. Restaurant, bar, A/C, TV, pool, tea and coffee making, laundry, jet boat, tours, picnic, hunting, visit to cattle ranches. Price CFP4,800 (US$56), suite CFP7,200 (US$84).

El Kantara La Roche Perceé, BP 244 Bourail, ph 44 1322, fax 44 2033. 20

rooms with bath. Restaurant, bar, A/C pool, tennis, canoe, sea excursion. Price CFP4,500 (US$52), superior room + CFP500 (US$6).
Poe Beach, BP 481 Bourail, ph 44 1850, fax 44 1070. Bungalows A/C, 24 rooms, 6 bungalows, with fans, extra rollout bed. Restaurant, bar. pool, tennis, horse riding, TV, volleyball, canoe, city tour, glass bottom boat, kids playground. Price CFP8,500 2 pers. Twin share CFP6,600 (US$77), sup bed CFP600 (US$7) extra.
Le Bougainville, RTI BP 78, Pourmout, ph 35 5255/35 5060, fax 35 5984. 6 bungalows, 7 rooms. Restaurant, bar, A/C, pool laundry. Price bungalow CFP5,800 (US$67), rooms CFP5,500 (US$64).
Gite Le Tamaon, BP 46 Pouemout, ph 35 5726. 13km from village in cattle station. 1 bungalow, 1 unit with kitchen, 2 with shared bathroom. Restaurant, traditional meals, horse riding, cattle station, VTT (video TV transmission), trekking. Price CFP3,000 (US$35), shared facilities CFP1,000 (US$17) per person.
Hotel Koniambo, RTI BP 35 Kone, ph 35 5186, fax 35 5303. 13 rooms, 12 bungalows. Restaurant, bar, TV, A/C, pool, tennis, horse riding, ping pong, Pétanque, VTT (video TV transmission) rental, archery, badminton, canoe. Camping possible. Price CFP5,500 (US$64) twin share, A/C +CFP500 (US$6). Weekend DBLB CFP5,600 (US$65).
Monitel L'Hibiscus, RTI BP 45 Kone, ph 35 5261, fax 35 5535. 20 rooms A/C, TV, bar, restaurant, room service, pool, spa, laundry, fax, car rental, conference room, horse riding. Price CFP7,000, CFP6,500, CFP5,000 supplement CFP500 per person (US$81, US$75, US$58. sup US$6).
L'Escale De Kone, BP 25 Kone, ph 35 5109. 15 rooms, restaurant. Price CFP3,200 (US$37) twin share, CFP2,800 (US$33) single.
Gite D'Ateou, Tribu d'Atéou, Kone, ph 35 5613. 1 hut. Restaurant, camping. Price CFP1,500 (US$17).
Monitel, RTI BP 75, Koumac, ph 35 6666, fax 35 6285. 29 rooms. Restaurant, laundry, bar, A/C, horse riding, excursions, VTT (video TV transmission) rental, pool. Price CFP6,500 (US$75).
Le Grand Cerf, RTI BP 58, Koumac, ph 35 6131, fax 35 6016. 9 bungalows. Restaurant, pool, A/C, TV, bar, excursions (group). Price CFP5,000 (US$58) twin share.
Passiflore, RTI, Koumac, ph 35 6210. 5 twin rooms 6 single rooms. Restaurant, bar, A/C, visits to nickel mines and caves. Price CFP4,500 (US$52) twin, CFP3,500 (US$41) single.
Malabou Beach, Baie de la Neéhoué, BP 4 Poum, ph 35 6060, fax 35 6070. 37 bungalows, 3 suites. TV, Video room, A/C, pool, bar, restaurant, tennis, volleyball, excursions, beach games, windsurfing, golf practice, diving centre, archery, car rental possible. Price CFP9,300-10,600 (US$108-123) bungalow, CFP16,000-18,500 (US$185-214) suites.
Gite Poingam, Pointe Nariah, ph 88 2420. Far north of mainland above

Poum. 7 bungalows. Restaurant, tennis, sea trips, camping, walks, canoe. Price CFP5,500 (US$63) twin.

East Coast

Le Normandon, Route Principale, Ouegoa, ph 35 6828. 8 rooms, restaurant. Price CFP2,000 (US$23) twin.
Camping Col D'Amos, Ouegoa. Camping CFP1,000 (US$12) tent.
Villa Club Mediterraneé, Koulnoué Village, BP 63 Hienghene, ph 42 8166, fax 42 8175. 50 bungalows. TV, Video room, restaurant, bar, A/C, pool, mini-bar, shop, VTT (video TV transmission) rental, diving, excursions, golf practice, tennis, horse riding, volleyball, table tennis, canoe, kayak, archery, mini golf. Price low season CFP9,300 (US$108), high season CFP10,600 (US$123).

Budget

Gite Weouth, Tribu de Ouampoues, Hienghene, ph 42 8119. 4 rooms, camping. Restaurant, sea tours, pétanque, volleyball, 4x4 excursions. Price room CFP1,500 (US$17), tent CFP750 (US$9).
Monitel, RT3 Tiéti, BP 154 Poindimie, ph 42 7273, fax 42 7273. 5 rooms, 4 bungalows. Restaurant, bar, TV, A/C, pool, horse riding, beach. Price CFP6,500 (US$75) twin share, CFP7,500 (US$87) bungalow x 4.
Hotel de la Plage, BP 97 Poindimie, ph 42 7128. 1 A/C bungalow, 16 A/C rooms. Restaurant, bar, beach, TV room, bike rental, windsurf, horse riding, excursions, tennis, bougna on request. Price CFP6,500 (US$75) bungalow twin share CFP5,000 + A/C CFP800 (US$58 + US$9).
Gite Napoemien/Sci Aden, Tribu de Napoémien, Poindimie, ph 42 7477. 2 bungalows. Restaurant, camping, bougna on request. Price CFP1,500 (US$17) twin share, CFP1,000 (US$12) tent.
Hotel/Motel, le Tapoundari, 15 rooms without bath, 5 with bath. Restaurant, camping. Price CFP3,100 (US$36) single, CFP4,500 (US$52) twin share.
Gite Ouroue, Thio, ph 44 5163. 4 bungalows. Restaurant, camping. Price CFP3,000 (US$35) bungalow, CFP1,000 (US$12) tent, subject to change.

The South

Hotel Casy, BP 717 Mont Dore, ph 26 4777. At Casy Island, Prony Bay. 20 rooms. restaurant, pool, nautical activities, fishing excursions, Transit Noumea-Hotel CFP 3,500 (US$41). Price CFP6,500-7,500 (US$75-87) sea view, CFP6,000-7,000 (US$70-81) forest view twin.
Turtle Club, Ile Ouen, BP 121 Noumea, ph 28 5362. 20 rooms. Restaurant, bar, VTT (video TV transmission), canoe, kayak, windsurfing, pétanque. Price CFP6,500 (US$75).
Gite Wokoue E. Théin, Ile Ouen, BP 598 Mont Dore, ph 28 5767. 3

bungalows, campers. Restaurant, excursions, sports, camping. Price CFP5,000 (US$56) bungalow x 4. Camp. CFP1,000 (US$12).

Nukuhiva, Lot 2 Lotiss, Peyton, RT2 Plum, ph 43 4141. 7 bungalows with kitchen. Restaurant, pool. CFP6,000 (US$70) bungalow.

Le Vallon Dore, BP 113 Mont Dore, ph 43 3208, fax 43 6666. 7 bungalows with kitchen, 4 without kitchen. Restaurant, pool, picnic on islet. Price bungalow CFP6,000 (US$70).

Gite St Gabriel, A. Atti, Yate, ph 46 4277. 5 bungalows. Restaurant, excursions, sports camping. Price CFP4,000 (US$46) bungalow. New bungalow CFP5,000 (US$56).

Gite Iya, Yate, ph 46 4232/46 4223. 3 bungalows. Restaurant, camping, excursions on request. Price CFP5,000 (US$56) bungalow.

Gite Wadiana, Goro, ph 46 4190. 5 bungalows. Restaurant, excursions, camping. Price CFP3,500 (US$40), campers CFP800 (US$9).

Isle of Pines

Gite Kuberka, Baie de Kuto, ph 46 1118, fax 46 1158. 2 bungalows, 8 rooms, camping. Restaurant, TV, transfers, excursions, pool, car/bike rental. Price CFP4,800 (US$55) per bungalow. Camping CFP800 (US$9).

Relais Kodjeue, Baie de Ouaméo, ph/fax 46 1142. 9 bungalows, traditional; 6 bungalows, new; 6 rooms. Restaurant, transfers, excursions, tennis, car/bike/scooter rental, pool, diving centre, conference facilities, mini-store. Price CFP5,800 (US$67) traditional, CFP6,500 US$75) new, CFP4,100 (US$48) per person twin room.

Gite Manamaky, Baie de St Joseph, ph 46 1113, fax 46 1229. 3 rooms, traditional; 4 rooms, new. Restaurant, excursions, car rental. Price per bungalow: traditional CFP4,800 (US$56), new CFP4,800 (US$56).

Gite Nataiwatch, Baie de Kanuméra, ph 46 1113, fax 46 1229. 4 bungalows with kitchen, 8 bungalows with fans, camping. Restaurant, transfers, curios, excursions, car/bike rental. Price CFP4,900 (US$57) bungalow, camp CFP900 (US$10).

Gite Oure, Baie de Kanuméra, ph 46 1120. 4 bungalows, 4 rooms, camping. Restaurant, transfers, excursions en pirogue, island tour, glass bottom boat. Price CFP3,000 (US$35) bungalow, CFP1,500 (US$17) rooms, CFP1,000 (US$17) camp.

Hotel Koubugny, Baie de Kuto, ph/fax 46 1223. 12 bedrooms with A/C. Restaurant, transfers, TV, excursions, pool. Price on request.

NOTES

Loyalty Islands

Lifou

Lifou Plaisance, BP 63, Wé, Lifou, ph 45 1444/45 1355, fax 45 1333. 12 rooms with fans. Restaurant, transfers, excursions, island tour, bike/car rental, gym, pool, tennis, volleyball, snorkelling equipment, mini golf, sauna. Price CFP5,500 (US$64) twin share.
Motel 'Chez Rachel', Baie Chateaubriand, Luecilla, BP 95, Wé, ph 45 1243. 8 bungalows with kitchen, 3 rooms with kitchen, camping. Restaurant, TV, transfers, island tour, camping. Price CFP6,500 (US$75) bungalow, CFP6,000 (US$69) rooms, camping CFP500 (US$6) per person.

Budget
Gite Hinaxulu, BP 21, Wé, ph 45 1642. Huts. Restaurant, transfers, tour of Lifou. Price CFP1,500 (US$17) per person.
Gite Neibash, Baie de Luengani, BP 308, Wé, ph 45 1568. 3 bungalows, 1 hut, camping. Restaurant, TV, transfers, island tour, car/minibus, bike rental. Price CFP6,000 (US$69) bungalow, CFP2,500 (US$29) hut per person, camping CFP1,000 (US$12).
Gite Servigny, BP 401, Wé, ph 45 1244. 1 hut. Restaurant, visit to tribe, car rental possible. Price CFP1,500 (US$17) per person.
Relais des Cocotiers, Baie de Chateaubriand, BP 75, Wé, ph 45 1136. 6 bungalows. Restaurant, transfers, island tour. Price CFP 4,000 (US$46) per bungalow.
Fare Falaise, Tribu de Joking, Lifou. 1 hut - traditional Melanesian lodging. Meals with locals. Price CFP1,500 (US$17) per person.

Mare

Budget
Gite Si-hmed, Plage de Yedjele (Wabao), BP 150 Tadine, Mare, ph 45 4151. 7 bungalows, camping. Restaurant, transfers, beach, island tour, car/bike rental, canoe, kayak. Price CFP4,000 (US$46), camping CFP1,000 (US$12) per tent.
Hnala Village, BP 40 Tadine, ph 45 4396, fax 45 4387. 5 studios. Restaurant, TV, car rental possible. Price CFP4,500 (US$52).

Ouvea

Budget
Gite Beaupre, Baie de Fayaoué, ph 45 7132. 3 bungalows 3 single rooms. Restaurant, transfers, car rental, excursions. Price CFP3,500 (US$41) twin share, extra bed CFP500 (US$6).

Local Transport

Buses

Blue buses travel the most common routes in Noumea, and all start and finish at Baie de la Moselle. The cost is CFP100 (US$0.46), given to the driver.
The service operates 6am-6.45pm with buses every 15-30 minutes in Noumea.

Airport transfers

There is a coach service to the city and the fare is CFP1800-2,000 (US$21-23). Taxis charge CFP7,000 (US$81). The blue bus fare is CFP400 (US$5) but they do not run at night.
Package tours usually include transfers, so getting from the airport is not a problem for most people.

Taxis

The flag fall is CFP100 (US$1.16) and all taxis are metered. To call a cab phone 28 3512.

Bicycle Hire

Curios, Baie des Citrons, ph 26 2378. Charges are: CFP500 for 1 hour; CFP 1300 (US$15) for half a day; CFP1600 (US$19) for a full day; CFP 4,500 (US$52) for a week; CFP1,000 (US$12) for a month.
Deposit is CFP20,000 (US$232) for 1 week.
Bikes can also be rented on Lifou, Isle of Pines, Plage Loisirs, Anse Vata and Baie de Citrons.

Motor Bikes 600cc cost CFP5,000 (US$58) per day + 29CFP per km.

Car Hire

You can rent a car from the airport but it is advisable to organise it beforehand.
A current licence is accepted but the driver must be over 25 years.

Driving is on the RIGHT side of the road but if in the country, the locals may drive in the middle of the road. Roads in the country are sealed but narrow so take care. Seat belts are compulsory.

Rates vary from company to company. Leading firms are: Avis, Budget, Hertz, Pacific Car, Noumea Car. Most cars are French. Rates start per day plus mileage, petrol and insurance.

Air

The domestic airline is Air Caledonie and there are flights daily from

Magena Airport, 5 minutes from Noumea town centre, to the Isle of Pines, Mare, Lifou and Ouvea and Tiga as well as to the East and West coasts.

Charter flights are also available from Air Caledonie, ph 252 177.

Eating Out

Noumea

New Caledonia is a gourmet's paradise. There are so many restaurants it is impossible to list them all, and a complete list is available from the Tourist Office. Available are traditional French cuisine, seafood specialties, pancake, vegetarian, West Indian, Spanish, Italian, Chinese, Vietnamese, Thai, Japanese. Then there are snackbars, cafés, brasseries and bars selling food.

Some are far from cheap but most have a menu with prices listed outside. You will find that a particular restaurant has a special on one night but not the next. Read the menu before you venture inside.

For lunch or any snack meal, visit the supermarket and buy some French bread, ham, cheese and a bottle of wine etc. This is the cheapest way to eat.

French wines are world famous and so are their liqueurs. They are reasonably priced in New Caledonia. After all you are in a part of France so why not try the French cuisine?

French Traditional

L'Auberge du Mont Koghis - French Alpine cooking and pancakes (altitude is 500m), ph 41 2929.

Le Bilboquet Plage, Palm Beach Shopping Galleries, ph 26 4660.

Le Bilboquet Village, Noumea City. ph 28 4330.

Cannelle, Route de l'Anse Vata, ph 28 5118 - open for lunch and dinner.

Le Grand Chene, Kuendu Beach, ph 27 8989.

Seafood

La Bastide, 3 Rue René Coty, Mont Venus, ph 27 6370.

La Coupole, 57 Pr. R. Laroque, Rocher a la Voile, ph 26 4411.

La Bistrot, 22 3 Rue de Prony, Magenta Beach, ph 25 355.

Pancakes

Créperie de L'Anse Vata, ph 25 4595.

Créperie Bretonne, ph 27 3714.

Vegetarian

Vegetaria Snack, ph 28 1065.

West Indian
La Paillotte, ph 26 2090.

Spanish
La Concha, ph 26 4467
Le Don Quichotte, ph 26 4244

Italian
La Dolce Vita, 147 route de l'Anse Vata, ph 26 2441.
Pizzeria Magenta, ph 25 3636.

Chinese
La Grande Muraille, Ouen Toro Hill, Promenade P. Vernier, ph 26 1328.
Le Mandarin, 45 RT 14, Maghenta Beach, ph 25 4725.

Japanese
Le Mikado, 85 route de l'Anse Vata, ph 26 2030.
Le Samourai, Surf Novotel, Anse Vata, ph 26 4141.

Floating Restaurant
Le Mary D Princess, ph 26 3131.

Snacks and café
Bambino, ph 261177.
Café de la Paix, ph 28 1155.
Lapérouse, ph 28 2811.

Brasseries-bars
Bar Surf Novotel, ph 28 6688.
Fun Beach, in front of the Novotel, ph 26 3132.

There are not many restaurants outside the capital, so the choice is between eating at your hotel or cooking your own dinner if you have the facilities.

If staying in a Gite, a small family establishment with restaurant and bar, you will sample the best local cuisine. Many of the villagers are also willing to cook meals, so ask around.

NOTES

Entertainment

Night Clubs/Dancing

In Town

La Locomotive, 45 rue de Sébastopol, ph 28 2829.
Joker 2000, rue Frederic Surleau, ph 27 1777.
L. Eden, 44 rue Anatole France, ph 27 2142.

Anse Vata/Baie de Citrons

Starstruck, ph 26 1754.
Blackjack, ph 26 4286.
Metro Club, Club Med, ph 26 1696.
Macumba, ph 26 4722.
Le Privilege, ph 26 4433.
Piano Bar, Le Surf, ph 28 6088.
Club 501, ph 28 1838.
No Comment, ph 26 4904.
It is best to book. If there is a mix up with the booking, tell them Henri took the reservation. There is sure to be someone on the staff called Henri!

Casino (Casino Royal)

Located in Anse Vata in the grounds of Le Surf Novotel. Gamblers must be 21 years old, and smart casual dress is essential. There are two gambling rooms:
a) Games Room - Black Jack, Mini Baccarat, Roulette.
Admission CFP400 (US$5) and passport to be presented.

Open Mon-Thurs	8pm-2am,
Fri-Sat and Feast Day Eve	8pm-3am.
Sunday and Public Holidays	2pm-2am.

b) Slot Machines. Free admission.

Open Mon-Thurs	2pm-1am.
Fri-Sat and Feast Day Eve	2pm-2.30am.
Sunday and Public Holidays	2pm-1am.

Shopping

There are many duty free shops in Noumea, where the prices are about 20-30% off the retail price. Luxury articles are by far the best buy.

Genuine French bikinis, shoes, leather goods, perfume and fashions are much sought after, as are local handicrafts, carved woods, shells, lapidary, jade, Melanesian clubs and huts. Also cameras, jewellery, crystal ware, lingerie, sports equipment are all good buys. Rue de Sébastopol in Noumea has most of the shops but you can find good buys almost anywhere.

Sightseeing

Noumea

The only city and capital of New Caledonia is home to 40% of the population. It is a bustling cosmopolitan place.

Founded in 1850 Noumea is said to mean 'sunrise' in a Melanesian dialect. It covers 42 sq km of the southern peninsula.

Initially it was set up as a trading post, then it was used as a French military fortress. In 1943 it became the headquarters for the US military forces. The discovery of nickel and gold have had a strong influence on this unique city.

Most tourists arrive at Tontouta International Airport 45 minutes from the city. The domestic Magenta Airport is just a few minutes drive from the city. The large marina complex has a number of tour operators, yacht charter companies and dive operators.

There are many tour operators who have half and full day tours. All the hotels have literature on these and can make the bookings.

The colonial layout of the city centre is well worth taking time to appreciate. The *Place des Cocotiers* is a garden square in the centre of town. It is surrounded by magnificent flame trees. There are many excellent beaches and bays, Anse Vata, Baie des Citrons and Magenta being the most famous.

The **Museum**, which opened in 1971, displays the way of life of the Melanesian people from Vanuatu, Loyalty Islands and New Caledonia. It is located in Avenue du Marechal Foche near the Post Office, and is open daily except Tuesday and Public Holidays 9am-11.30am, 12.15pm-4.30pm. Admission free.

The **Cathedrale St Joseph**, in Rue Mg Douarre, celebrates Mass only on Sunday at 9am-10am.

The **Market** is open daily 5am-10am, and is for early birds and photographers. On offer are fish, vegetables, tropical fruits and local produce. Location Baie de la Moselle.

The **Aquarium** is located along the Anse Vata, and it is world famous for the large number of tropical fish. You will also see a stunning array of live fluorescent coral and nautilus, ancient creatures of the deep which have been successfully acclimatised by the Aquarium.

Parc Forestier - Botanical Gardens and Zoo. This nature reserve is full of zoological and botanical treats. Don't miss the cagou, New Caledonia's flightless bird and national symbol. The gardens are 4km from the city centre south of Montravel. Open May-Sept Tues-Fri 1pm-5pm, Sat-Sun and public holidays 1.30pm-5pm; October-April Tues-Fri 1pm-6pm, Sat-Sun and public holidays 1.30pm-6pm.

Admission is CFP300 (US$3.50) children 3-12 CFP100 (US1.16) A taxi from downtown costs approximately CFP700 (US$8).

Amédée Lighthouse offers a most enjoyable full day trip by boat, and make sure you take your swimming togs. The climb to the top of the lighthouse is hard for the not so fit, but you can snorkel from the pontoon or simply wait for the picnic lunch and entertainment.

Further Afield

South

Mont Dore, 30km south of Noumea, is at its best in late afternoon when the setting sun brings out the colours. See *Conception Church, Saint Louis Mission* and further on *The Forest,* a reserve with lush tropical vegetation and mountain views.

Yaté is known as the 'Botanical Paradise' and is 80km south of Noumea. It has hundreds of plants not seen anywhere else in the world. The Yaté Dam is 60m high and 230m wide. The village is reached through the gorge and has spectacular views of Goro village and waterfall.

Prony is a small uninhabited village 61km from Noumea, and access is by 4WD or by boat. Once an important convict settlement, some of the old buildings still stand. Access to the village is by 4WD or boat. Prony Bay is the departure point for Casy island.

North and West Coast

Dumbéa, 15km north of Noumea, is the site of a dam and Mt Koghi. Attractions include bush walks, horse riding and an 18-hole golf course. The town is famous for its yearly 'Giant Omelette' event.

Paita, a small town 26km from Noumea, has a panoramic viewpoint. A guided climb of Mt Mou (1220m) is a 4 hour excursion.

Boulouparis, 73km north of Noumea at the foot of Mt Ouitchambo has a race course and an 18-hole golf course.

La Foa, 110km north, is the start of cattle country. Explore *Dogny Plateau, Koindé village,* and the ruins of *Fort Teremba Prison,* which has an annual sound and light show. Nearby is an old military watchtower.

Farino, 300m above sea level, provides views of the area, and has walking treks and waterfalls. The local market is open every second Sunday of the month.

Bourail, 162km north of Noumea, is an important stopover. Highlights include the museum, the *NZ Pacific War Cemetery,* Arab cemetery, Nemeara Cattle Station, caves, forests, plus *La Roche Percée* (pierced rock) and *Poe beach.*

Poya, 209km from Noumea, is renowned for oysters, mangoes, cattle and mining. The Grande d'Adio stalagmite and stalactite caves are 5km from the town.

Koné, capital of the northern province, is on the west coast, 267km from Noumea, at the foot of Koniambo mountain range. Mt Koné peak (237m) can be reached by a well-defined track. Koné has an airport, and attracts lots of visitors to its annual rodeo.

Koumac, 368km from Noumea, forms the crossroads of the north-west coast. It is well-known for its church which has exquisite wooden sculptures. The town has an airport, and in the area are caves, a beach and river that is popular with swimmers.

Poum on Banara Bay, 56km from Koumac on the extreme tip of the island. It is a Melanesian village with the most beautiful beaches in New Caledonia.

East Coast

Ouégoa, on the northern most point, was one of the first centres to be colonised during the gold rush, and the old mine is still visible. The scenery between Koumac on the west coast and Ouégoa is spectacular. The *Col de Creve-Coeur* (200m) marks the climatic difference between the eastern and western slopes of the mountain range.

Balade is the site of Captain Cook's first landing in 1774 and also of the first mission. It was also here that Admiral Despointes took possession of New Caledonia on behalf of Napoleon lll in 1853.

Hienghene is located at the rocky mouth of the river of the same name. It has a interesting cultural centre, plus lagoons, valleys, waterfalls, coconut groves, coffee plantations, Melanesian villages and the highest peak in New Caledonia, Mt Panie (1639m). There are two limestone rocks towering 60 metres above the bay. One looks like a brooding hen (or Notre Dame, depending on the realms of your imagination), the other resembles the Sphinx.

The coastal road from Hienghene leads to **Touho**, in what is the most tropical region. The seaside village is surrounded by coffee plantations and palm trees, and is famous for its troca fishermen. Domestic flights operate into Touho Airport.

Poindimié, a relatively new town, is 308km from Noumea and has a great beach. A river flows through the centre and the wharf is on one side, the village and town centre on the other. The scenery is remarkable with coffee plantations, coconut trees and Melanesian villages in traditional style. The locals sell handicrafts and coconuts from roadside stalls. There are beautiful waterfalls inland at Nessapoué and Napoemien.

Ponérihouen is located in a mountain setting, and excursions can be taken to Tchamba Valley and village. The *Centre de Culture du Café, Ometteux* village and *St Paul's Church* in Pambou are worth seeing.

Houailou is the cross-over point to Bourail on the west coast. The *Nindiah Caves and Mission* are 7km away, and the Ba River and waterfalls are within walking distance. There is a *Nickel Mine* that can be visited, with permission.

La Crouen has alkaline waters with a temperature of 42C that are recommended for asthmatics and rheumatic sufferers.

Canala village nestles amongst the coconut trees and is the second oldest centre in New Caledonia. The spectacular *Ciu Waterfall* is 5km from the village, in the midst of a forest.

Thio is a mining centre in a beautiful valley 126km from Noumea. It is divided into two distinct areas: the village and *Thio Mission*. Nickel was discovered here in 1876, and permission can be obtained to visit Plateau Mines.

Isle of Pines

'Jewel of the Pacific', the Isle of Pines is called by visitors; Kunie by its Melanesian inhabitants. Discovered and named by Captain Cook in 1774, the island is 18km x 14km of unspoilt beauty.

It has prolific pine trees, perfect white sand beaches, aquamarine lagoons, and several small islets within the protective reef. As would be expected, water sports are the main activity for visitors.

Daily flights with Air Calédonie leave Noumea for the 70km trip.

A penal colony from 1872-1912, the ruins and cemetery can be visited. Lapita pottery and huge bird bones are testimony to life 200 years ago.

The island boasts some fabulous flora and fauna. Apart from the Norfolk pines, there are sandalwood and rosewood trees, wild orchids, ferns and palms.

The main village, **Vao**, has Melanesian architecture and an 1860 church. The traditional aspects of life on the island will ensure your stay is memorable.

Sightseeing attractions include the **Hortense Caves** which legend tells was the hiding place of Queen Hortense during tribal wars at the beginning of the century.

A rental car or motor bike is ideal for exploring, but there are tours available for those who prefer to be driven.

Bareboat or skippered yacht charters are available from Kanumera Bay or you may wish to cruise across the lagoon on a *pirogue*, a traditional Melanesian sailing outrigger.

The Loyalty Islands

Situated 100km from the mainland's east coast are the stunning Loyalty Islands of Lifou, Mare, Ouvea and Tiga. They are covered with swaying palms and scented sandalwood trees, and have white sandy beaches and dramatic cliffs. The climate is pleasant with moderate rainfall and there are no mountains.

Air Calédonie fly daily from Noumea and the flight takes 30 minutes. Transfers are also available through a ferry service.

Lifou is the largest (1150 sq km) and most accessible of these islands, and has a population of 8000. The administration centre of Lifou is *Wé* in Chateaubriand Bay.

Lifou is a paradise for snorkellers and shell collectors. There are several villages worth visiting and some caves. The culture and dialect is slightly different from the mainland. This is a great place to escape to if you want to unwind and relax.

Mare is the southernmost and highest of the Loyalty islands. It has an area of 650 sq km and a population of 5000. *Tadine* on the west coast is the most important centre and also the port.

Mare is a place of untamed beauty with deeply etched cliffs, basaltic rocks, dark tropical forests and tiny coves. The central plain was once a lagoon and is riddled with natural caves and water holes full of fish and turtles.

Other attractions worth seeing are *Warriors Leap*, the church at *La Roche* and the natural aquarium at *Tadine*.

Ouvea is the smallest of the islands, and has an area of 130 sq km with a population of 3540. It is long and narrow with white sandy beaches bordered by coconut palms, and a lagoon with plenty of marine life.

Fayaoué, surrounded by Melanesian villages, is the administrative centre. The scenery on the road from Fayaoué to St Joseph is stunning.

What to do? Enjoy the water, beaches, food and relaxation. There are flights by Air Calédonie from Noumea to Oulpoup Airport.

Tiga is a tiny island 6km x 2km. It has a Melanesian village in the north with a population of 351. Its main resource is copra. Flights from Noumea arrive at Tiga Airport.

Tour Operators

There are plenty of tourist organisations and your hotel or the Tourist Bureau will be able to advise you. Here are a few names:

Coach Companies

Are En Ciel, BP 1244, Noumea, ph 27 1980, fax 27 6277.
S.C.E.A., 3 rue La Republique, ph 28 6100, fax 27 5272.

Sunrise Tours PO Box 624, Noumea, ph/fax 27 6900.
Pacific Tourist Transport, PO Box 9 Noumea, ph 27 5323, fax 27 6900.
T.T.C., BP 4853, Noumea, ph 28 2774/26 1040, fax 26 4786.

Tour Companies

Alpha International, 143 rue de l'Anse Vata, ph 26 1313.
Center Tours, 27 bis avenue du Marechal Foch, ph 25 4040.
Discovery Tours, Galerie Palm Beach, Promenade Roger Laroque, ph 26 3131.
South Pacific Tours, Shop Centre Vata, ph 26 2320.
Blue Lagoon, c/o Kuendu Beach, ph 27 8989.

Cruises and Charter

Amac Voyages, PO Box A3, Noumea Cedex, ph 26 3838, fax 261662.
Noumea Yacht Club BP 1068, Noumea, ph 28 6666, fax 287 482 - cruises, charter with or without skipper.
Octopussy Charters 12R Higginson, Noumea, ph 27 8187 - with skipper.
Pacific Sun Sail BP 14311, Pontoon G, Pt Moselle, ph 25 4813/9287 - without skipper.
Amédée Lighthouse, PO Box 233, Noumea, ph 26 3131, fax 26 3979.
Coral Garden Underwater Observatory, c/o Lagon Loisirs, PO Box 62, Noumea, ph 26 2440, fax 26 2340.

Diving

Amédée Diving Club, PO Box 2675, Noumea, ph 26 4029, fax 28 5755.
Noumea Diving, PO Box 9574, Noumea, ph 25 1688.
Naticlub, Kuto Bay, Isle of Pines, ph 46 1122.

Sport & Recreation

Tennis

There are public courts at Ouen Toro behind Club Med and at 1 rue Kollen, Motor Pool. For reservations ph 26 4532. Price per hour CFP600 (US$7) + CFP400 (US$5) for evening tennis.

Squash

There are public courts at 21 rue J Garnier, Baie des Pecheurs. Bookings, ph 26 2218. Price per hour CFP1,800 (US$12).

Archery

Enquiries - ph 25 4893.

Golf

Dumbéa, 10 minutes from Noumea - 18 holes, ph 41 8000 24hrs beforehand. Equipment for hire.
Magenta - practice and tuition, ph 26 3226.
Paillottes de la Ouenghi (1 hour from Noumea) - 18 holes. Charming resort with golf, riding and tennis. Equipment for hire, ph 35 1735.

Ten-pin Bowling

Le Commodore, Anse Vata, ph 26 2602.

Roller Skating

There is a rink behind Anse Vata Hippodrome.

Swimming Pool

Ouen Toro, ph 26 1843.

Soccer

This is the favourite team sport with the locals. Ask your hotel to direct you to a match.

Le Cricket

This is almost as popular as soccer. It was introduced by the British missionaries in the Loyalty Islands and is played especially by women.

This is a real New Caledonian experience. A day of playing, singing, joking and dancing. Not to be missed. Ask your hotel or check the local paper for times and places of matches.

NOTES

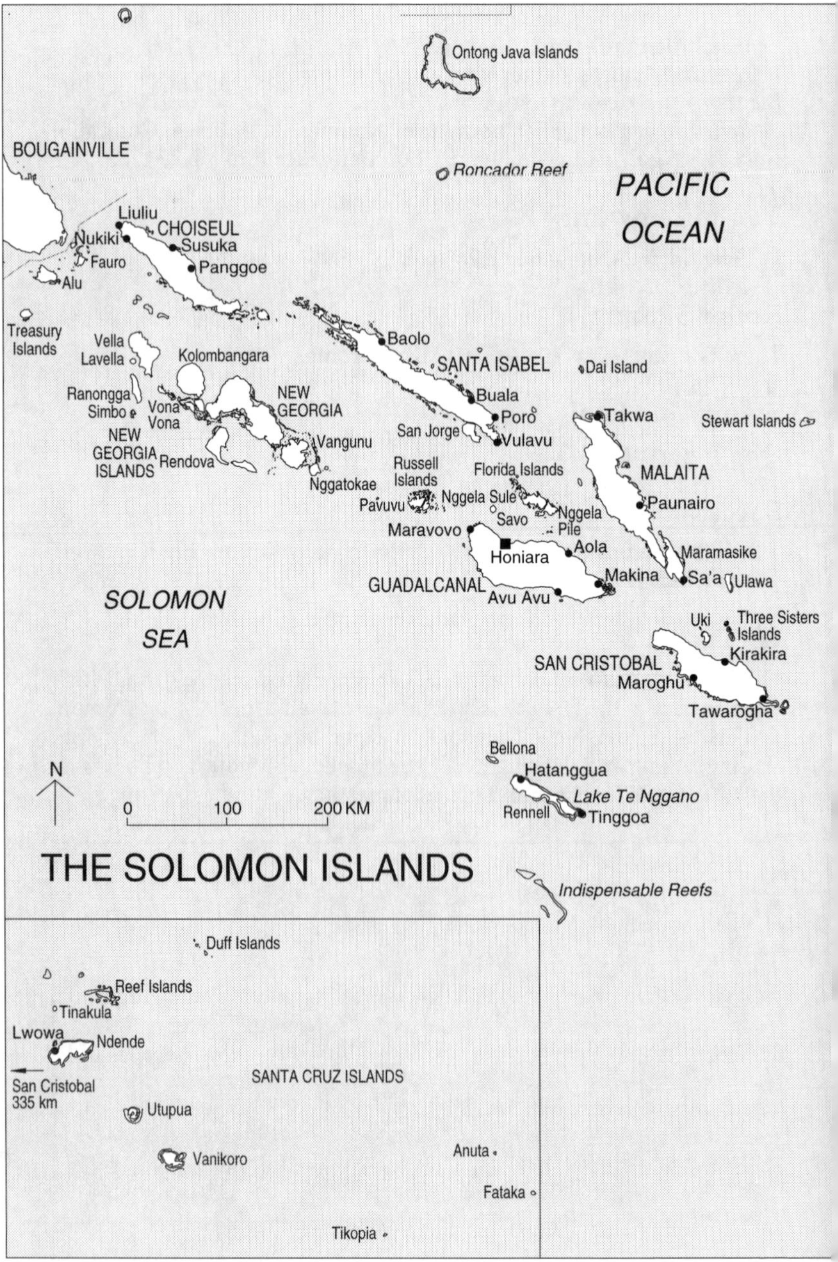
THE SOLOMON ISLANDS
Ontong Java Islands
BOUGAINVILLE
Roncador Reef
PACIFIC OCEAN
Liuliu
CHOISEUL
Nukiki
Susuka
Fauro
Panggoe
Alu
Treasury Islands
Vella Lavella
Kolombangara
Baolo
SANTA ISABEL
Dai Island
Ranongga
Simbo
Vona Vona
NEW GEORGIA
Buala
Poro
Takwa
Stewart Islands
NEW GEORGIA ISLANDS
Rendova
Vangunu
San Jorge
Vulavu
Nggatokae
Russell Islands
Florida Islands
MALAITA
Pavuvu
Nggela Sule
Savo
Nggela Pile
Paunairo
Maravovo
Honiara
Aola
Maramasike
GUADALCANAL
Avu Avu
Makina
Sa'a
Ulawa
SOLOMON SEA
Uki
Three Sisters Islands
Kirakira
SAN CRISTOBAL
Maroghu
Tawarogha
Bellona
Hatanggua
Lake Te Nggano
Rennell
Tinggoa
N
0
100
200 KM
Indispensable Reefs
Duff Islands
Reef Islands
Tinakula
Lwowa
Ndende
San Cristobal 335 km
SANTA CRUZ ISLANDS
Utupua
Vanikoro
Anuta
Fataka
Tikopia

REPUBLIC OF THE SOLOMON ISLANDS

The Solomon Islands, sometimes referred to as 'The Happy Isles', are a chain of hundreds of islands in the south-west Pacific Ocean. The largest islands are Choiseul, Guadalcanal, Malaita, New Georgia, San Cristobal (Christobal) and Santa Isabel (Yisabel). The many other islands in the chain include Bellona, Rennell and Santa Cruz Islands.

The larger islands are part of the Solomon Islands chain but not all the islands in the chain belong to the Solomon Islands. Bougainville, Buka and a few smaller islands in the northern part of the chain belong to Papua New Guinea.

The Solomon Islands lie 1600km north-east of Australia, and have a land area of 27,556 sq km, spread over 600,000 sq km of ocean.

The country's main islands were formed by volcanoes. They are rugged, mountainous and covered with tropical plants, and range from 40km to 190 km long, and 30km to 50km wide. Each island has a central spine of mountains some of which are more than 1200m high. The land drops sharply to the sea on one side of the island and gently to a narrow coastal strip on the other. Some of the outlying islands are atolls.

The Solomons are for a special breed of traveller. One who values genuine, simple hospitality and natural beauty. Ask yourself if you can live for two weeks without a luxury resort, TV and McDonalds. You need to be slightly adventurous. Enough to flyover the islands in a tiny plane, ride across the water in a very small boat and drive in a vehicle which would never pass registration at home. The Solomons are still unspoilt, and there are few roads.

The main exports are fish, timber, palm oil, cocoa and copra. The capital is Honiara on Guadalcanal.

History

Scholars believe that the first settlers on the Solomon Islands came from New Guinea. Ancestor worship was and, to a small extent, still is a common feature of all Solomon Islands societies. From tribe to tribe, island to island the belief in what form the ancestors took after death varied. One thing, common to all, was that the spirits of their ancestors had to be respected. Skulls and sometimes bodies were enshrined in specially constructed 'tambu' sites and added to by each succeeding generation. In some areas of the islands, a system of hereditary chiefs evolved, although a clan or tribe was more commonly governed by a 'Big Man'. He was someone with a forceful personality, who was brave in battle, had the ability to settle disputes, or had accumulated much wealth.

In 1568, the Spanish explorer, Alvaro de Mendana was the first European to reach the islands. He discovered alluvial gold on Guadalcanal and it is possible that he thought he had discovered King Solomon's great wealth, or maybe he simply wanted to encourage colonisation by Spain. Whichever was the truth, he named the islands 'Isles of Solomon'. During the next 200 years, few Europeans visited the islands.

From 1870-1911, about 30,000 islanders were recruited to work on plantations in Fiji and Queensland. Most were taken by force and treated badly. This practice was called 'blackbirding'. In 1890 the islands became a British Protectorate and 'blackbirding' ceased.

The islands remained almost untouched until World War II. The Japanese occupied the islands then the Americans arrived. Fierce fighting took place in 1942 between the warring nations, and thousands of lives were lost on both sides in land, sea and air battles. In 1943 the Japanese withdrew.

In 1976 the islands acquired internal self-government with Peter Kenilorea, leader of the Solomon Islands United Party (SIUPA), as chief minister. He became prime minister when they achieved full independence within the Commonwealth in 1978. Kenilorea was unable to devolve power to the regions while preserving the unity of the state and was replaced by Solomon Mamaloni of the People's Progressive Party in 1981. Mamaloni created five ministerial posts specifically for provincial affairs. Relations with the USA became strained by the government's refusal to allow nuclear-powered warships within the island's territorial waters.

In the 1984 elections SIUPA won 13 seats and the opposition, now The People's Alliance Party (PAP) 12. Sir Peter Kenilorea, as he now was, returned as head of a coalition government and immediately abolished the five provincial ministers. Kenilorea narrowly survived a series of no-confidence motions and resigned in December 1986 after he was accused of accepting US$47,000 of French aid to repair cyclone damage to his own village in Malaita. Kenilorea remained in the cabinet of his successor, Ezekiel Alebua, a fellow SIUPA member and became deputy prime minister in February 1988.

In the general election of 1989 SIUPA only won 6 seats and the PAP, led by Mamaloni, emerged as the dominant party with 14 seats. Mamaloni formed a coalition government which included members of the opposition. The coalition promised to reform the constitution, to establish a republic and reduce the number of 'foreign aid' personnel. In October 1990, Mamaloni resigned from the PAP after receiving a vote of no confidence but he continued as head of government. As a result the PAP and the opposition splintered into personality based factions.

The islands are now divided into eight administrative areas - seven provinces and the city of Honiara. The provinces are governed by elected assemblies, and Honiara is governed by a town council.

Climate

Temperatures range from 28C-34C with high humidity. Rainfall varies from 150-500 centimetres annually.

Population

The population is about 300,000, mainly Melanesian, and 90% live in villages. The majority of residents (95%) are Christians.

Language

The official language is English. Melanesian pidgin is spoken by locals.

Public Holidays

January 1 ....New Year's Day
March/April...........Good Friday-Easter Monday
June ....Queen's Birthday
July 7 ....Independence Day
August.....................Whitsunday/Monday
December 25 ....Christmas Day
December 26 ....Boxing Day.

Entry Regulations

US, Commonwealth and most West European citizens are not required to secure a visa. Others may be issued visas through British Consulates. Seven-day transit visas are available on arrival. All visitors must have a valid passport and onward ticket.

Customs

The duly free allowance is 200 cigarettes or 250gm of tobacco, 2 litres of spirit or equivalent. Electrical goods not to exceed SI$40,000 (US$14,00) dutiable goods.

Warning: Turtle shell and Turtle shell products are prohibited imports into Australia and many other countries.

Departure Tax

There is a departure tax of SI$30,000 (US$11), payable in local currency.

Embassies

Australia: High Commission, Honiara.
Canada: No representative. Apply to Canadian High Commission, Canberra.

New Zealand: High Commission, Honiara.
United Kingdom: High Commission, Honiara.
USA: No representative. Apply to US Embassy, Port Moresby, Papua New Guinea.

Money

The local currency is the Solomon Islands dollar (SI$). Notes are in denominations of $2, $5, $10, $20 and $50, and coins are 1c, 2c, 5c, 10c, 20c and 50c and $1.

Approximate rates of exchange, which should be used as a guide only are:

A$1	=	SI$2.59
Can $1	=	SI$2.49
NZ$1	=	SI$2.31
S$	=	SI$2.42
UK£	=	SI$5.18
US$	=	SI$3.38

Foreign currencies must be changed in Honiara before travelling to the outer islands. ANZ, Westpac and National Bank of the Solomons are all located in the town centre, and are open Mon-Fri 8.30am-3pm.

Communications

The main Post Office is centrally located in the main street of Honiara, and it is open Mon-Fri 8am-4.30pm. Telekom Ltd Solomon Islands provides comprehensive fax, telex and a world wide phone service. Facilities are available in most hotels.

The Solomon Islands Broadcasting Corporation broadcasts daily in pidgin and English. There is no television.

There are three local papers *The Solomon Star, The Solomon Voice* and *The Nius*. Your home newspaper might become available but it will be very out of date by the time you get it.

Miscellaneous

Time Zone

Local time is GMT + 11.

Business Hours

Offices and shops: 8am-noon, 1pm-4pm.
Shops and some commercial businesses are open Saturday 8am-noon.

Electricity

Supply is 240 volts where available. Major hotels in Honiara have 110 volt shaver outlets.

Dress

Bikinis are not to be worn in the streets. Brief attire must be kept to hotel and club pools and on dive and snorkelling trips.

Casual, light cotton clothes are the most practical. A cardigan or jacket should be included in case the evenings are cool.

Rest Rooms

Visitors must rely on restaurants and hotels. The Mendana Hotel and Point Cruz Yacht Club have public rest rooms.

Tipping

There is no tipping in the Solomon Islands. It is against Melanesian culture.

Village Life.

Health

A course of Malaria tablets should be commenced before leaving home. The Central Hospital in Honiara will see patients for a fee. There are hospitals and medical services in most of the provinces. There are a number of pharmacies in Honiara and also dental facilities.

Water

Boil all water before drinking. Bottled water is available in Honiara.

Insurance

Take out full insurance before you leave home.

Relics from World War II

Travel Information

How to get there

By Air

Solomon Airlines International, Air Nauru, Air New Guinea, Air Pacific and Qantas all fly to Honiara.

Domestic: Solomon Airlines serves 23 airports.

Henderson Field International Airport is 8km from Honiara. Hotels and tour operators meet visitors and there is a bus service.

By Sea

Cruise ships visit Honiara occasionally.

Tourist Information

Solomon Islands Tourist Authority, PO Box 321, Honiara town centre, ph (677) 22 442, fax (677) 23 986.

Western Province Tourism Association, PO Box 71, Gizo, ph (677) 60 171 or 60171.

Accommodation

Honiara

First Class

Solomon Kitano Mendana Hotel, PO Box 384, Honiara, ph (677) 20 071, fax (677) 23 942. On ocean front in town centre. 96 rooms, A/C, ensuite, tea/coffee making, fridge, phone, in house video, satellite TV. Restaurant, bar, function room. Swimming pool, activity desk (Associated Club for squash, tennis, golf), Island Dive, scenic tours. Telex, secretarial service, photocopying, free parking, laundry, boutique, hairdresser, shop, rent-a-car desk, travel desk, safe deposit. Price standard single SI$140 (US$51), twin SI$160 (US$58); deluxe single SI$200 (US$73), double/twin SI$220 (US$80); deluxe single sea view SI$250 (US$91), double/twin SI$270 (US$99); family garden view SI$310 (US$113); executive suite SI$450 (US$164) all + 10% tax.

Honiara Hotel PO Box 4, Honiara. Situated on Kukum Highway, Honiara, ph (677) 21 737/23 412, fax (677) 20 376. Close to town centre. New wing has Hilltop High modern rooms with balconies overlooking Honiara and the sea. Lift. A/C, ensuite, in house video, satellite TV, tea/coffee making, balcony. Original wing has same facilities. Budget

Rooms fully screened, fans, wash basin, share bathroom. Shops and services. Squash, tennis, pool. Tours. Live stage show Wednesday and Friday nights around the pool. Price New Wing with ocean views single SI$190 (US$66), double SI$220 (US$80); premier SI$230 (US$84); suite $260 (US$95). Original wing single SI$130 (US$48), double SI$150 (US$55), family (2 rooms) SI$230 (US$84), suite SI$220 (US$80); budget single SI$65 (US$24). double SI$80 (US$29) all + 10% tax.

Budget

Hibiscus Hotel, PO Box 268, Honiara ph (677) 21 205, fax (677) 21 771. In town centre. 15 rooms. Ensuite, A/C or fan, satellite TV. Restaurant, bar, entertainment. Hire car. Price single SI$85 (US$31), double SI$110 (US$40) + 10% tax.

Airport Motel, PO Box 251, Honiara, ph (677) 30 446, fax (677) 30 411. Two minutes from Henderson Airport. 17 rooms. A/C, ensuite, phone, tea/coffee making, cooking facilities, free continental breakfast. Private beach access, airport transfers, day/night tennis, restaurant, bar, function room. Price single SI$100 (US$36), double SI$130 (US$47) + 10% tax.

Testimony Guest House, PO Box 236, Honiara, ph 21 530. On Lengakiki Ridge, 10 minutes by taxi from town centre. 9 Rooms. Single, double and suite accommodation. Share facilities except in suites. Share cooking and common room, Free transport. Price on request.

United Church Rest House, PO Box 18, Honiara, ph 20 028. 5 minutes from town centre. 10 rooms. Share facilities, kitchen, etc. Basic accommodation. Cash payments only.

Church of Melanesia Transit House, PO Box 19, Honiara, ph 21 892. 3 minutes walk from town centre. 7 rooms. Share all facilities, cooking area. Basic accommodation. Cash payments only.

Pakoe Accommodation, PO Box 679, Honiara, ph 21 336/20 308. At top of Kola Ridge. 15 minutes by taxi from town, 15 minutes walk downhill to main road. 16 rooms. Budget backpackers accommodation with shared facilities.

West Guadalcanal

Tambea Village Resort, PO Box 506, Honiara, ph 23 639. 20 minute coastal drive from Honiara on western tip of Guadalcanal. 22 rooms. Melanesian style thatched bungalows on beachfront. Fans, fridge, ensuite, mosquito nets, electricity. Pool, bar, dining room, conference room. Snorkelling, horse riding, canoeing, kayaking, windsurfing, volley ball. Small charge for motorised activities and catamaran. Diving available. Tours to Savo volcano, bushwalking, coral islands, boat trips to Lambi Bay, Vilu War Museum, Clam Farm, Prawn Farm can be arranged on arrival. Battlefields tours arranged through Honiara Tour companies. Price single SI$140 (US$51), twin/double SI$160 (US$58), triple SI$180 (US$37), quad SI$200 (US$73) all + 10% tax. Children under 2 free. Transfers Airport/Tambea adult SI$30 (US$11), child 2-12 SI$10 (US$4) one way.

East Guadalcanal

Vulelua Island Resort, PO Box 96, Honiara, ph 23 684. On 5 acre coral isle 1 hour drive east of Honiara. 9 rooms. Self contained island-style thatched units. Bunk rooms available. Reef walking, fishing, tennis, excursions to nearby villages. No credit cards accepted. Travellers cheques or cash only.

Tavanipupu Island Resort, PO Box 236, Honiara, ph 22 672/22 991. At Marau Sound on eastern tip of Guadalcanal. 30 minutes by air from Honiara or 30 minutes by powered canoe. 6 rooms. Island-style thatched bungalows with private facilities. Dining room, bar. Diving, swimming, canoeing, fishing and trips to nearby islands. Price on request.

Central Islands Province

Tulagi Province Resthouse, PO Tulagi, Central Islands Province, ph 32 100 ext 4, caretaker-clerk to Assembly. In pre-war capital of Tulagi 3 hours by boat from Honiara. 6 rooms with two beds each. Share facilities. Basic backpackers accommodation.

Vanita Accommodation, PO Box 376, Honiara, ph 22 246/32 186. 3 hours by boat from Honiara. Close to main Tulagi wharf. 2 serviced rooms. Hot & cold meals, bar, caters for group functions on request. Daily or weekly rates on request.

Suani Resthouse, Bellona Island, Central Islands Province, ph 23 846. Bellona Island is 1 hour by air from Honiara. 1 building for up to 5. The island is a raised coral atoll inhabited by Polynesians. Basic accommodation.

Tahamatangi Guesthouse, Rennell Postal Agency. Approximately 1 hour by air from Honiara. On shore of Lake Tengano on eastern tip of Rennell Island (national wildlife park). 1 building for 5 people. Bushwalks, nature tours, visits to nearby islands. Basic accommodation. Cash payments only accepted.

Western Province

Gizo Hotel, PO Box 30, Gizo, Western Province, ph 60 199, fax 60 137. On the waterfront of Gizo town. 1½ hours by air from Honiara. 15 rooms. Self-contained. Has the only licensed restaurant in the town, bar. Regular entertainment by islanders. Local canoe trips, fishing, dives arranged. Swimming, snorkelling, small boat hire, cycling, canoeing, tours of Gizo environs. Only American Express and Mastercard accepted. Price standard single SI$110 (US$40), double SI$130 (US$47); Gnuzu Wing single SI$140 (US$51), double SI$160 (US$58). All + 10% tax. Airport transfers by outboard canoe extra.

Paradise Lodge, PO Box 60, Gizo, ph 60 021, fax 60 024. On hilltop overlooking lagoons. 12 rooms, all with views. Dining facilities, self catering, diving, land tours, bushwalking, fishing, handicraft sales.

Koburutavia Lodge, PO Box 50, Gizo, ph 60 257, fax 60 297. On hill top overlooking town. 1½ hours by air from Honiara. 7 rooms, 3 rooms accommodating 10 people. Trips to nearby islands, diving by arrangement, tours of Gizo.

Phoebe's Resthouse, PO Gizo, ph 60 161/60 244, fax 61133. On top of hill. 3 rooms accommodating 6 people. Share facilities, kitchen, living area. Basic accommodation. Cash only.

Agnes Lodge, PO Box 9, Munda, ph 61 133 fax 61 225. On Roviana lagoon on south-west point of Solomons, New Georgia Island. 1 hour by air from Honiara. 11 rooms to suit all travellers. Restaurant, bar. Diving, swimming, canoeing, picnic trips. Daily air service, weekly shipping. Price Naru wing standard twin private facilities SI$120 (US$44); Zazala wing, suite double triple & family SI$200 (US$73); Orchid Wing budget SI$72 (US$26); triple rooms share facilities SI$30 (US$11); Hope Honeymoon Cottage SI$200 (US$73) plus transfers SI$30 (US$11) per trip. All accommodation + 10% tax. Accommodation and meal package (divers deal) Zazala Wing SI$150 (US$55); Naru Wing SI$110 (US$40); Single supplement SI$50 (US$18).

Noro Lodge, ph 61 238, fax 61 225, a subsidiary of Agnes Lodge at the fishing village of Noro on Kulu Gulf. Accommodation from budget to business man. Licensed restaurant. Fans in all rooms, phone, laundry, meeting & function room. Transfers between Noro and Munda. Scuba diving, snorkelling, sport fishing, island picnics, swimming, lagoon tours, canoe hire, rainforest walks, World War II sites and wrecks, crocodile spotting, special family and children's pursuits. Price studio rooms private facilities SI$150 (US$55); standard private facilities SI$100 (US$37); Budget dorm-style SI$30 (US$11) per person + 10% tax.

Maqarea Resort, PO Box 65, Munda, ph 61 164, fax 61 165. On Hombupeka Island just off shore from Munda on Roviana lagoon, 1 hour by air from Honiara, 5 minutes in powered canoe from Munda. 4 thatched island-style bungalows for 4 people. Self-contained with private facilities. Snorkelling tours to nearby islands.

Lubaria Island Resort, PO Box 27, Munda. On Lubaria Island in the Rendova group. 1 hour by air from Honiara plus 45 minutes by powered canoe. 6 rooms. Traditional style thatched cottages, one western. Bushwalking, day trips to nearby islands and villages, swimming and canoeing.

Zipolo Habu Resort, PO Box 66, Munda, ph 61 164. On Lola Island in Vona Vona lagoon. 1 hour by air from Honiara then ½ hour by powered boat. 2 island style thatched bungalows with shared shower. Meals available as extra. Swimming, snorkelling, fishing, day trips. No credit cards, cash only.

Uepi Island Resort, Seghe Postal Agency, Seghe. In Marova lagoon 1 hour by air from Honiara and 1 hour by powered boat. 9 cabins and guest house accommodation with views of Marova lagoon, the longest saltwater lagoon in the world. Private facilities. Diving trips SI$80 (US$29) (a dive includes tank, weight belt, weights, boat, driver & dive guide). Bush walks, fishing, trips to nearby islands and villages, picnics. Price single SI$126 (US$46), twin SI$94 (US$34), child 3-10 SI$20 (US$7) + 10% tax. There is a compulsory meal supplement: Adult SI$90 (US$33) a day, child 7-12 SI$40 (US$15), 3-6 SI$20 (US$7) + 10% tax.

Matikuri Island Lodge, via Seghe Postal Agency, Marova Lagoon. 1 hour by air from Honiara, ½ hour boat ride. 4 rooms, featuring 3 island-style thatched bungalows with outside shower & toilet. 1 main complex with dining and cooking facilities.

Liapari Guesthouse, Liapari Estate, Vella Lavella, ph 60 216. On Liapari estate, a trading centre on the island of Vella Lavella 1½ hours by air from Honiara. 3 rooms. Diving, snorkelling trips, fishing, bush walks, trips to nearby villages by arrangement.

Shortland Islands Guesthouse, via Nila Postal Agency, Shortland Islands, near Korovou Police station, Faisi Island. 2 hours by air from Honiara, ½ hour boat ride from Balalae airstrip. 2 western style buildings with two beds in each. Dining room, kitchen, fridge, share shower & toilet.

Temotu Province

Ngarando Resthouse, Pigeon Island Mailbag, Reef Islands. Almost off the map on Pigeon island in Reef Island group. 4 hours by air to Santa Cruz, & 3 hours by powered canoe. 5 western-style guesthouses. Swimming, snorkelling, reef & beach walks, fishing trips. No credit cards accepted. Cash only.

Santa Ysabel (Isabel)

Mothers Union Resthouse, Buala, Santa Ysabel. The provincial centre of island of Ysabel, Buala is 45 minutes by air from Honiara. 6 rooms. Operated by the Mothers Union of the Church of Melanesia. Clean, comfortable basic accommodation.

Malaita

Auki Lodge, PO Box 9, Auki, Malaita Province. In centre of Auki town on Malaita Island, 30 minutes by air from Honiara. 6 self-contained rooms. Cultural tours, bushwalks, swimming, canoe trips. No credit cards. Cash only.
Malu'u Lodge, via Malu'u Postal Agency, Malaita. Caretaker. Malu'u headquarters. 3 hours by truck from Auki township on northernmost tip of Malaita Island. Backpacker accommodation for 6 in one main building. Snorkelling, canoeing, surfing, walks to nearby villages to see custom dancing & panpipes.

Ulawa Province

Kira Kira Resthouse, via Kira Kira Postal Agency, Makira, ph 50 111/2. Caretaker Clerk to Assembly. On Kira Kira station 1 hour by air from Honiara, on island of San Cristobal. 9 rooms with total of 20 beds. Cooking & dining facilities. Guests provide own food. Backpacker style.

Local Transport

There is plenty of public transport which allows you to visit most places around Honiara. Buses operate from 6am-7pm each day and the fare is 60c each way.

Hire cars are available and cost about SI$90-140 (US$33-51) a day. Avis and Budget have desks at the airport.

Taxis cost from SI$20-30 (US$7-11) an hour.

Eating Out

Honiara has many international restaurants so you will not be able to visit them all. The Tourist Authority can supply a complete list, but following is a selection:
Capitana Restaurant & Satellite Bar, Hotel Mendana, ph 20 071.
La Perouse Restaurant, near Guadalcanal Club, ph23 720-French cuisine.
Guadalcanal Club, ph 22 212 - snacks and main courses.
Hibiscus Hotel, ph 21 205 - selection of cuisines.
Family Favourites, ph 23 435 - snacks & light lunches.
Hong Kong Palace, ph 23 338 - Chinese.
Sea King Restaurant, ph 23 621 - Chinese.

Children from a village near Gizo, Solomon Islands (opposite)

South Seas Restaurant, ph 22 368 - Chinese.
The Kai Bar, ph 21 737 - selection of cuisines.
Honiara Hotel, ph 21 737 - selection of cuisines.
Kumho Court Restaurant, ph 21 687 - Chinese.
Super Club Restaurant, ph 22 163 - Chinese.
Mandarin Restaurant, ph 22 832 - Chinese.
Tambea Village Restaurant 28 miles along west coast, ph 23 639 - selection of cuisine.

Shopping

In Honiara there is an ample cross section of goods. Arts and crafts can be bought throughout the islands from local artisans.

King Solomon Arts & Crafts Centre, Honiara, and *Melanesian Handicrafts* in the BJS Agencies Building and NPF Plaza Arcade are open Mon-Fri 8am-12noon, 1.30pm-5pm; Sat 9am-noon. Wood carvings are particularly good.

ABC Arulingo Book Centre, Kingsley Arcade, Ashley Street, have books on the Solomon Islands, the Pacific and World War II, as well as postcards, greeting cards, maps, jewellery made from turtle-shell, gold-leaf, black coral, etc.

D.J.Graphics Ltd, next door to Sea King Restaurant, town centre have screen printed T-shirts, handicrafts and souvenirs.

Honiara Markets, in the town centre, is the best place to buy fruit and vegetables. Most hotels, even those on the outer islands, have boutiques.

Sightseeing

Honiara

Honiara is very small and you can do most of the sightseeing on foot. If you find the humidity is tiring you, hop on a local bus. Start at the Tourist Authority in the centre of town.

The **National Museum** is across the road. Here you will find a range of early Solomon Islands arts and crafts and tools. You can see a *Nguzunguzu*, a canoe prow head. There must be many of these around the world but Australia did return the one they had to its rightful owners. Admission is free.

Right next door, is the **Cultural Centre**. This is a true reproduction of the traditions and culture of the islands. Behind, in the next street, the National Archives are kept. You are in the centre of town and the shopping plaza is right beside the rest of the offices. If you walk following the water front, you will come to the **Main Markets**. Here,

Burial site on Skull Island near Munda (opposite)

apart from fruit and vegetables you can buy wood carvings and baskets.

You would have to retrace your steps to visit the **Botanical Gardens** which are a short distance from town on the western side. Palms and ferns which can be found throughout the islands flourish. Hibiscus, bougainvillea, frangipani, poinciana, poinsettia and oleander are plants which were introduced long ago. They have mixed in well with the orchids, flowering ginger and other plants that are native to the Solomons.

If you are driving, or going by taxi, you could include a visit to the Botanical Gardens on the way to **Tambea Resort**.

Drive up on to the mountainous ridge where many Europeans have their homes, to have a wonderful view of the surrounding countryside.

The drive along the western coastal road goes through coconut groves and rural villages. Here you will see many native parrots. The **Japanese War Memorial** is at Poha River. This was the site of an extremely fierce battle during World War II. In Vilu Village, there is a War Museum where the reminders of that terrible period in history, are displayed in the jungle.

The **Battlefields** are the main attraction of Honiara. Henderson Field, now the international airport, was the only landing strip during World War II. Here and around the airport, you will see Sherman tanks, wrecks and other war relics. Nearby is **Iron Bottom Sound**, so named because there are so many wrecks on its sea bed. There are at least 41 ships at the bottom of the ocean. Many of the wrecks can only be visited if you dive to them.

The locals have wanted the reminders of the war removed and the islands cleaned up but this is an impossible task. The best that can be hoped for is to rid the land of live ammunition.

Outside Honiara it is better to take a tour so that nothing is missed. **Gold Ridge**, 30km south-east of Honiara, can only be reached by 4WD. The drive takes about an hour, then there is another hour's walk to where the locals pan for gold.

An alternative is to visit one or all of the resorts, which are not far out of Honiara. Take the road east to **Vulelua** the resort where the locals go to get away from it all. It is so popular with the local population that visits are not allowed during peak holiday periods. You have to signal to the resort and then they will send a boat across. It boasts the finest seafood in the world. Further down the road at the very tip of Guadalcanal is the island resort of **Tavanipupu**. On the west end of Guadalcanal is **Tambea Village**, a pleasant place to have lunch, swim or just gaze across at Savo Island where the volcano is active but dormant at the time of writing.

From the shoreline of Honiara you can see the closest group of islands, the **Florida Islands**, where the pre-war capital Tulagi sits. In the 1966s Tulagi was used as a basis for Ernest Borgnine's TV series *McHale's Navy*.

For the best of the Solomons you have to fly out to the islands of Gizo, Munda and Shortlands.

Gizo

Gizo was almost missed by the war. It's main claim to fame is that it was the nearest civilisation to where US President J.F. Kennedy was rescued during his naval service. He was marooned on a tiny atoll called Plum Pudding Island, now known as Kennedy Island. He and his crew were eventually taken to Gizo and then to Honiara after a Japanese cruiser sliced the bow off his PT boat.

Gizo has not changed much since the war. It still has thatched huts and small buildings. It claims to have better dives than Honiara, because, the locals say, they have better wrecks and clearer water. However, in spite of the other claims, it does have incredibly large fish which are plentiful.

The endless number of lagoons, coral cays, white sandy beaches and unsurpassed beauty make it an ideal paradise. You can hire a boat which will take you to an uninhabited island where you can spend the day swimming, fishing or exploring. The boat will return to collect you later in the day.

Uepi (pronounced Wepi)

An hour flight from Honiara leads to Seghe, and a further ½ hour canoe ride takes visitors to the island resort of Uepi, located in the Marovo Lagoon, the longest salt water lagoon in the world. The island's marine life includes masses of fish just off the jetties.

On the down side is the fanged cone shell life which, if not handled carefully, can give anything from a faint bee sting to death within an hour.

For divers there are more wrecks. A Japanese Zero, a US P38 and at least two American landing barges sunk in 1942.

The hinterland has a multitude of bird life from sea eagles to honey eaters. A place to relax and forget the rest of the world.

Munda

Munda is at the edge of Roviana Lagoon on the island of New Georgia. Travellers to Gizo call in to Munda on the way.

This is also a World War II island and is supposed to have the best memorabilia.

Trips can be taken into the hinterland to visit World War II sites, cultural villages and crocodile viewing sites.

The Shortlands

Found at the northern tip of the Solomon Islands chain are the Shortlands where you find the Solomons as they once were.

There are no tourist facilities, but the beauty and isolation make it a memorable trip. Most people go for the day.

Malaita

This is for the adventurous. Not many tourists visit but backpackers who are prepared to rough it, travel in outboard canoes and market trucks, will see a very beautiful island.

It has rugged mountain peaks covered in rainforest and often shrouded in mist. There are cold, clear fast rivers and streams running through fertile valleys down to the sea.

The unique feature of Malaita are the artificial islands, constructed many generations ago. These islands were the home of the saltwater people. Over the centuries they built up their coral rock islands on shallow reef flats to escape head-hunting raids by other tribes. **Langalanga** and **Lau Lagoons** are liberally spread with these man-made islands. Langalanga is also the traditional home of the manufacture of shell money, a vital aspect of Malaita economy past and present. Pieces of bivalve shell *Spondylus* are ground into small disks, drilled and strung together usually in lengths of about 2m. Ten of these strings joined side by side are termed *tafuliae* and form the basic unit of shell money currency. The value of one tafuliae in Western terms is about SI$300 (US$110).

Those who do manage to reach Malaita will inspire curiosity from the locals. Children peer from behind their mother's dress. Walk down to the waterfront market and chat to one of the truck drivers. They will take you to any of the villages for a small fee. If you would like to spend a night in a village, ask for the 'bigman' who will arrange accommodation for you. Local customs are strong on Malaita so ask if there are any tambus you should observe.

Tours

The tourist agencies will arrange tours to suit the individual. Tours to outer islands can be booked in Honiara. Sightseeing on outer islands is organised by your hotel or guesthouse.

Honiara-Savo Island Day Trip

Savo Island lies 31km off northern Guadalcanal. It is an attractive volcanic island with a pair of craters, one enclosing the other. Although these volcanic cones are dormant at present, they are believed to be potentially dangerous. The island's several peaks are a mixture of eroded ridges and lava flows.

Alvaro de Mendana saw the volcano erupting in 1568 and called it Sasarga. In 1840 it erupted with considerable loss of life. The population of Savo, about 2500, is wholly Melanesian, and they live in 14 main villages around the island.

The highlight of the tour is to visit the nesting and hatcheries of the **megapode bird**. They use the heat of the volcanic soil to hatch their young from their large eggs. The bird is 28-38cm in size and digs a hole in the hot soil for nesting. The incubation period is 8-9 weeks, and when the young hatch they are fully feathered and able to run immediately and fly within 24 hours.

Ground temperatures rise to 85C (185F) and mud boils in several places. The best hot springs are at Fisher Voghala on the edge of the main crater.

The tour leaves at 8am and transport is a powered outboard motor crossing the open sea. The tour lasts about 7 hours.

Western Countryside

Drive along the coastal road through coconut groves and rural villages, and see the native parrots. Stop at the Japanese War Memorial at Poha River, where a fierce battle took place in World War II. Visit Vilu Village War Museum where reminders of the war are displayed in jungle surroundings. Continue along the coast road with views of Savo Island and the sea. At Tambea Village Resort there is a stop for lunch, after which there is time for a swim and to explore the resort. Tour takes 6 hours.

Eastern Battlefields

Tour the major Word War II battle sites, Mount Austen, Red Beach, Bloody Ridge and Henderson Field. The tour also includes a visit to Skyline American War Memorial and the Japanese War Memorial at Mount Austen. A stop is made at Betikama High School, famed for its wood carving and handicrafts. Time is made available to purchase handicrafts, and view World War II artefacts and live crocodiles. Tour takes 4 hours.

Laulasi Man-Made Island - Langa Langa Lagoon Malaita

Step back 600 years to visit the artificial islands of Laulasi, one of the world's unique living environments. The day starts with a 35 minute flight over Iron Bottom Sound, across the waters of the Battle of Savo and Tulagi, the old capital, to Auki. From Auki the Laulasi guides will take you by outboard canoe to Langa Langa Lagoon for a cultural program, which gives a glimpse of the Laulasi lifestyle, and a visit to a special custom site. Men will be taken to view the skull house while women will be led to other sites by the village women. The tour returns to Auki Lodge for lunch, then back to Auki for the return flight to Honiara. Full day tour.

Tenaru Falls Trek

A 30 minute drive leads to the start of the trek. A 40 minute hike leads to a village where you will be able to see typical traditional Solomon Islands lifestyle. There is another 1 hour trek to falls which are described as one of the finest in the Pacific. The flora and fauna are at their best on this trek. Takes 6 hours.

Cruise

Liveaboard luxury vessel MV *Spirit of Solomons*, which is air-conditioned and takes 26 passengers. Activities include fishing, snorkelling, wind-surfing, nature walks, river cruising, village tours, custom dancing and visits to 'Taboo' sites and Diving.

3 nights/4 days

Day 1 - Sail to the Florida Islands.

Day 2 - Anchor at Tulagi. Day trip to Gavutu Island and Tokyo Bay. See crocodiles. At night sail to Russell Islands.

Day 3 - At anchor. Spend the day on beaches, snorkelling, swim, fish or scuba dive. Traditional feast or BBQ.

Day 4 - Sail to another anchorage. Spot wrecks, birds. Enjoy watersports, take nature walks, look for orchids, almond trees, ginger and other exotic plants. Afternoon transfer to Yandina airport for your flight to Honiara.

4 day and 6 day cruises are also available visiting more islands. Contact Bilikiki Cruises Ltd, PO Box 414, Honiara, ph (677) 22 103, telex HQ66315, fax (677) 23 897 for more information and bookings.

Other cruise ships are the *Bilikiki* and the *Kirio*.

Tourist Organisations

Tour Solomons Ltd, PO Box 337, Honiara, ph (677) 21 630, fax (677) 21 637. They have all the tours plus special interest trips.

Guadalcanal Travel Service, PO Box 114, Honiara, ph (677) 22 587, fax (677) 23 887. All tours, transfers and diving.

Air Transport Ltd, PO Box 766, Honiara, ph 30 033, fax 30 713. They have helicopter, dive and fish tours. Scenic trips and special arrangements for photographers.

Zancos Express, PO Box 515, Honiara, ph 21 291, telex HQ66312. Excursions, airport shuttle service.

Sport & Recreation

Golf, tennis, horse riding, bushwalking, canoeing, wind surfing, fishing, kayaking, snorkelling and squash are available. Most hotels have the facilities.

Soccer is the main team sport and you can watch a match.

Hash House Harriers have runs on Mondays. Enquire at your hotel or guesthouse or look in the local paper.

However it is water sports which are the main recreation of the Solomon Islands. **Diving** to view the incredible number of wrecks from World War ll can take place anywhere on the islands. Apart from the relics of World War II there are fish of every size and colour, caves to explore and coral gardens. And, the water is clear and warm. All the instructors are specialists and will give lessons to the uninitiated.

Dive Solomons, PO Box 186, Honiara, ph 677 20 520, fax (677) 23 110. Your local travel agent can also make bookings.

Island Dive Services, PO Box 414, Honiara, ph (677) 22 103, are at the Kitano Mendana Hotel. They have two runs a day at 9am and 2pm. A mini submarine will transport 2 people to see wrecks at close quarters and marine life. The dive lasts about 1 hour with 40 minutes on the bottom.

Clubs

Point Cruz Yacht Club, *Guadalcanal Club* and *Honiara Golf Club* are open to cruise ship visitors.

Honiara Squash Club and *Guadalcanal Club* tennis courts are open to visitors.

The *Super Club* and *Club 88* are located in old Chinatown and are Honiara's alternative to Las Vegas.

NOTES

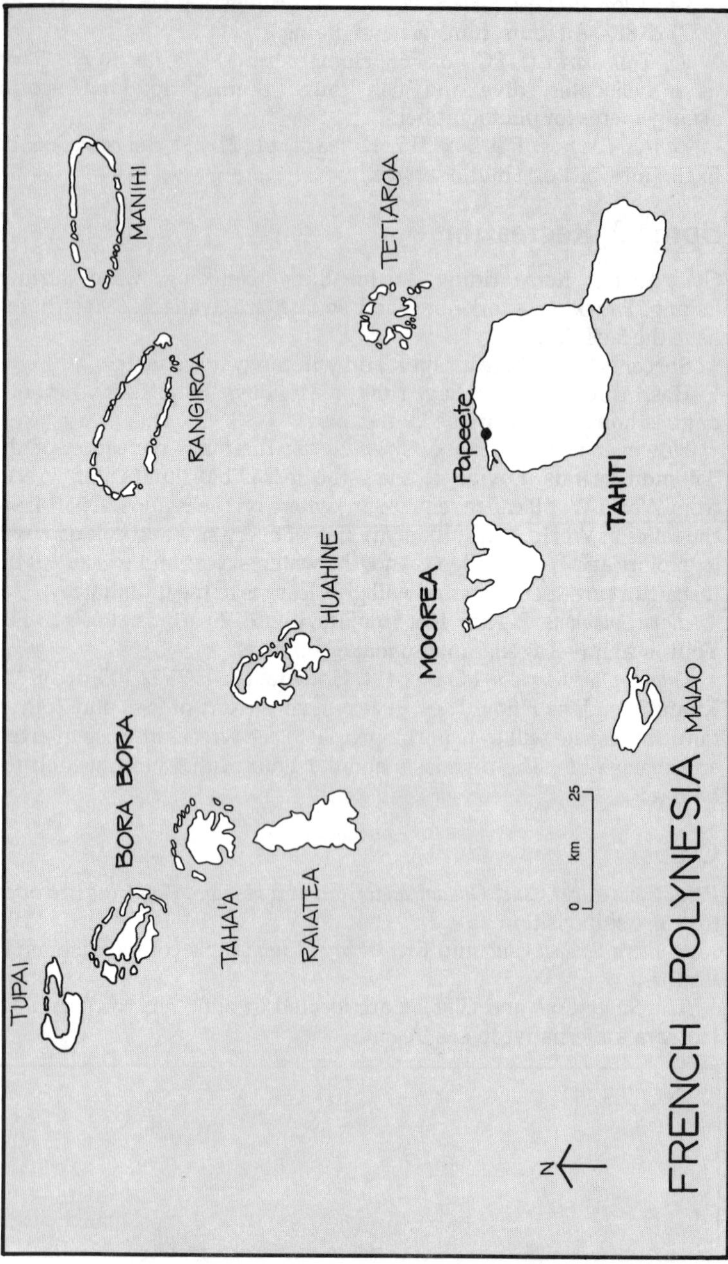
FRENCH POLYNESIA
TUPAI
BORA BORA
TAHA'A
RAIATEA
HUAHINE
MOOREA
MAIAO
TAHITI
Papeete
TETIAROA
RANGIROA
MANIHI
0 km 25
N

FRENCH POLYNESIA

Tahiti is the largest and best known of the 115 islands of French Polynesia which include the Marquesas, Tuatoma archipelago, Gambiers and Australs.

The total area of the islands and atolls is 4000 sq km and Tahiti occupies one quarter of that. The total population is over 188,600 and 71% live in Tahiti. Tahiti lies half way between Australia and California in the South Pacific.

Tourism is very important to the economy, and the main exports are: copra, sugar cane, vanilla and coffee.

The beautiful island of Tahiti has mountain peaks reaching over 2235m and is often called 'the island of love'. There are deep, green valleys covered with rainforests and ferns, and waterfalls cascading into rivers and streams. The flat coastal land is covered with fields of taro and flowers. It is ringed by a coral reef. The capital is Papeete.

History

The most generally accepted theory attributes an Asian origin to the Polynesians. It is thought that people from south-east Asia migrated to the area now known as French Polynesia between 1000 and 2000AD. According to ancient tradition, it was from these islands and in particular Raiatea, that they set out for New Zealand and the Hawaiian islands.

Because French Polynesia covers such a large area, it took many years and several explorers to discover and chart the islands. The Spanish and Dutch were making voyages through the archipelagos during the 16th and 17th centuries.

The first European to discover Tahiti was Englishman Captain Samuel Wallis in HMS *Dolphin* in 1767. The next year it was rediscovered by Frenchman Louis de Bougainville, followed by Captain James Cook in 1769 who was in the southern hemisphere to observe the transit of the planet Venus across the solar disc.

In 1788 Captain William Bligh arrived in HMS *Bounty* to collect breadfruit trees. The famous mutiny broke out and Fletcher Christian seized the ship and put Bligh to sea in a small, open boat. Bligh, with seventeen men, sailed that boat 4830km across the Pacific to Indonesia. He lived to see most of the mutineers caught and brought to justice. Fletcher Christian escaped the noose but met a violent death at the hands of the Tahitians in a dispute over women and land on tiny Pitcairn Island.

At first the Europeans thought they had discovered a lost Eden. The islands were extraordinarily beautiful, there were plenty of plants for food, and the lagoons were full of fish and shellfish. Beyond the reef, the ocean had schools of tuna. The climate was delightful and few clothes were needed. The houses were simple with no walls so the cooling breezes could flow through.

In reality, the natives lived in a rigidly structured society where most were no better than slaves. Thieving was rife. The climate was ideal for mosquitoes which carried filariasis, a parasite that once in the blood stream multiplies with horrifying results to the body. The people were also prone to large disfiguring ulcers. In later years these were diagnosed as yaws, a bacterial skin disease. Cures for these diseases were not discovered for another 200 years.

There were constant wars between different tribes, with the victors making slaves of the conquered and taking their land. They brought back, as trophies, the heads of men, women and children.

The Tahitians would probably have preferred to continue their way of life rather than change to the one the Europeans foisted upon them. Apart from introducing 'civilisation', they infected the Tahitians with venereal disease and measles, and introduced alcohol. The natives had no immunity to the diseases, and the alcohol turned Papeete into a centre of boozing and brawling until the French took possession in 1842.

The London Missionary Society christianised the natives by helping the Pomare family gain power. They remained the ruling dynasty until 1880 when Tahiti became a French colony. In 1857 it was made a French overseas territory and has been internally autonomous since 1984. It is headed by a High Commissioner representing the French Republic. The legislative body is the Territorial Assembly, consisting of 41 members elected by popular vote. This body elects the President of the Government and Head of the Territory who chooses his 10 ministers. French Polynesia also elects one representative to the French Senate and two representatives to the French Parliament.

The islands have not lost their Eden reputation and many famous people have lived there, written romantic tales or painted the magnificent scenery. They include Robert Louis Stevenson, Herman Melville, Charles Darwin, Pierre Loti (Julian Viaud), Jack London, Somerset Maugham, Rupert Brooke, James Mitchener, Marlon Brando and the one most talked about, Paul Gauguin in 1891-3.

Climate

Cooled by the gentle breezes of the Pacific, the climate of these islands is sunny and pleasant. Roughly speaking there are two seasons. From December-February it is warm and moist (22-32C). From March-November the climate is cool and dry (17-22C). Most of the rain falls during the warm season.

Population

The population is over 188,000 with 71% living on Tahiti, and 16% of the total population living in Papeete. The Polynesians of the Maori race make up 70%, Asians 4.3%, Europeans 11.5% and mixed races 14.2%.

Religion

Many religions are represented throughout French Polynesia. These include Protestant, Roman Catholic, Mormon, Seventh Day Adventists, the Reorganised Church of Jesus Christ of the Latter Day Saints, Jehovahs Witnesses, Judaism and Buddhism.

Language

The official languages are French and Tahitian. English is spoken in hotels, restaurants and tourist establishments.

Public Holidays and Festivals

January 1 - New Year's Day - a public holiday in all islands.
February-March - Chinese New Year.
March 5 - Commemoration of the arrival of the Gospel-Tahiti.
April-May - Good Friday - Easter Monday.
During this time many beauty queens are chosen to represent sports clubs, philanthropic associations, the Chinese community and other groups.
May - Taupiti O Papeete.
Miss Papeete is elected and a carnival atmosphere reigns, with rides, games and contests with the important activities taking place on the weekends.
May 1 - Labour Day: Ascension Day: Whitsunday and Monday.
May - Pacific Festival of Underwater Images.
Open to the public to contribute underwater colour slides and photos of marine life in the waters of the islands and other marine locals. Exhibited at OTAC, the Territorial Culture Centre.
June - Annual Moorea International Triathlon. An endurance test. Participants must swim 2km, cycle 60km and run 15km.
June-July - Marquesas Festival of Arts "Te Mata Vaa O Te Henua Enana" takes place in Taiohae, Nuku Hiva Traditional Marquesan songs, chants and dances, preparation of popoi and other culinary exhibits, tapa making, carving sculptures and tattooing.
July 14 - Bastille Day. Parties and a big parade and all night ball.
July - Annual Tahiti International Pro-Am Open. Generally played at the Olivier Breaud International Golf Course at Atimaono. The Tahiti Open is played toward the end of July.
July - Heiva I Tahiti, "Tiurai". This is the most important festival of the year. People come from all over the world to film the colourful events

and join in the fun. Highlights include songs, dance competitions, outrigger canoe races, contests of copra preparation, stone lifting, basket and hat weaving. There are permanent exhibits in the Arts and Craft Village, traditional costume making, fire walking ceremonies, historic re-enactments at *Marae Arahurahu* and other religious and cultural exhibits and events. It is a time to renew the warrior's might, the dancer's grace and the status of the tattoo. A time when heritage excels.

August - International marathon of Tahiti-Moorea. A 40km race with cash prizes, begins at Vaiare on Moorea, and a semi-marathon race of 20km with lesser cash prizes starts in Haapiti.

September 8 - Anniversary of the Statute of Internal Autonomy of French Polynesia.

September 27 - World Tourism Day.

October 6 - Day of the Tree. This is a week long event with environmental and folkloric activities.

October - Stone Fishing ceremony in Tahaa "Heiva No Te Pahu Nui O Tahaa". This two-day event includes boat races, fire walking and a fun-filled day on a *motu* islet in the Tahaa Lagoon.

November 1 - All Saints Day. Flower stands are set up all around Tahiti with families decorating graves in all the cemeteries in Papeete, Faaa, Arue and Punaauia November 11 Armistice Day. December 2 Tiare Tahiti Day. Tahiti's national flower "Gardenia Taitensis" is honoured with a Tiare Tahiti being presented to everyone on the streets of Papeete, in hotels and the airport.

December 24-25 Christmas. It is summertime in the islands and all the flowers are in bloom. Santa Claus or Père Noel, makes his appearance several times. Hotels and restaurants have special menus and entertainment.

December 31 - New Year's Eve. Hotels and restaurants throughout the islands make sure the ritual of St Sylvester is properly enjoyed.

Some events do not have specific dates and are subject to change. For further information contact OPAC, The Territorial Culture Centre, PO Box 1709, Papeete, Tahiti, ph (689) 42 8850.

Entry Regulations

A valid passport and an outbound ticket are required. Visas are necessary for all visitors except those from the EEC. There are special exemptions for citizens of USA, Canada and Japan. Cook Islanders using NZ passports may be issued a 3 month visa.

Failure to have an outgoing ticket means visitors must deposit the price of the return air fare to their place of origin.

Vaccinations are not required unless coming from a yellow fever or cholera area.

Customs

The duty free allowance is: 200 cigarettes or 100 cigarillos or 50 cigars or 250gm smoking tobacco, 50gm of perfume, 0.25litre of lotion, 55gm coffee, 40gm tea, 2 litres of spirits. Visitors under 17 years are not allowed to import alcohol or tobacco. Prohibited: narcotics, copyright infringements, weapons and ammunition. To import plants, flowers, fruits or vegetables, special permission is necessary from Service of Rural Economy, PO Box 100, Papeete, Tahiti, ph 42 9780. It is the same organisation and address for permission to import animals.

There is no departure tax.

Embassies

Australia and Canada: No resident representative. Refer to High Commission in Wellington, NZ, ph 64 (4) 637 411.
New Zealand: c/o Air NZ. Papeete ph 430 170.
USA: No resident representative. Refer to US Embassy, Wellington, NZ, ph 64 (4) 722 068.
United Kingdom: No resident representative. Refer to High Commission, Wellington NZ, ph 64 (4) 726 049.

Money

The currency used in French Polynesia is the French Pacific Franc (CFP). Notes are in denominations of 500, 1000 and 5000 francs. Coins are 1, 2, 5, 10, 25, 50, 100 francs.
Approximate rates of exchange, which should be used as a guide only are:

A$1	=	CFP69.48
Can$	=	CFP66.81
NZ$1	=	CFP62.02
S$	=	CFP65.05
UK£	=	CFP139.07
US$1	=	CFP90.76

There is an exchange counter at Faaa International Airport.

Banking Hours

Monday-Friday 8am-3.30pm.
Some banks open Saturday 7.45am- 11.30am.

Communications

Telephones, telegrams and telex services are available from the Post Office, Papeete. The Post Office is the centre of international communications. Stamps may be purchased and cables sent through Telefrance during postal hours. International and local inter-island calls can be made from hotels. IDD is available and the country code is 689.

The English language newspaper is the *Tahiti Sun Press*. TV is also available

Miscellaneous

Time

Local time is GMT - 10.

Business Hours

Offices:	Mon-Fri	7.30am-5pm.
Shops:	Mon-Fri	7.30am-5pm,
	Sat	7.30am-11am. Tourist shops stay open later.

Note. There is a very long lunch hour, usually 11am-2pm.

Electricity

Local current is 100 or 220 volts AC 60 cycle. Check at your hotel before using appliances, as you may need a converter. Take an adaptor in case the plugs are different.

Health

Tahiti has an excellent medical and dental service, pharmacies, government hospital, private clinics, an anti- stress centre and a cosmetic centre.
The local tap water is safe to drink.

Insurance

Always take out full insurance, especially medical cover.

Tipping

There is absolutely no tipping in French Polynesia.

Credit cards

Most major cards are accepted.

NOTES

Travel Information

How to get there

By Air

The airport of Tahiti - Faaa, 6km from town - is regularly serviced by connections from West Coast USA and Canada, Hawaii, France, Europe, New Zealand, Australia, Japan, South-East Asia, New Caledonia, Fiji, Cook Islands and Santiago, Chile via Easter Island.

Airlines providing these connections are the Air France Group, Hawaiian Airlines, Air New Zealand, Qantas, Lan Chile, Air Caledonie, Polynesian Airlines, Air Outre Mer (AOM). Charter flights are available aboard Corsair.

By Sea

Many cruise ships call at Tahiti.

Tourist Information

Tahiti Tourist Promotion Board Information Centres are in Faaa Airport where hostesses meet every international flight. Fare Manihini, PO Box 65, Papeete, ph 429 626, is open Mon-Fri 7.30am-5pm, Saturday and holidays 8am-4pm.

Tourism Committees outside: Moorea, ph 562 178; Raiatea, ph 662 334; Bora-Bora, ph 677 469; Huahine, ph 682 260.

Accommodation

Tahiti

First Class

Hyatt Regency, 8km from town, 20 minutes from the airport. 200 rooms and suites with A/C, fridge. mini bar, phone, radio, TV/V, bathrobe (suites only), terrace. Restaurant, bars, black sand beach, fantasy pool, children's pool, spa, tennis, jogging course, shop, room service, baby sitting. Beach hut/club. Price twin share A$196 (US$137); single A$309 (US$216); child 2-11 A$46 (US$32). Meal plan: full breakfast and dinner adult A$77 (US$54), child 2-11 A$39 (US$27) per day.

Tahiti Beachcomber Parkroyal, 7km from town, 5 minutes airport. 30 acres (13.5ha) on beachfront. 196 rooms and bungalows with A/C, fridge, tea/coffee making, mini bar, phone, TV/V, hairdryer, balcony. 2 restaurants, 3 bars, pools, shops, water sports. Laundry service, room service, babysitting. Price twin share A$222 (US$155); single A$340

(US$238). Meal plan: full breakfast and dinner adult A$92 (US$64), child 2-11 A$46 (US$32) per day.

Moderate

Sofitel Naeva Beach, 5 minutes from airport on white sandy beach. 224 rooms with A/C, mini bar, TV/V, balcony, phone. Restaurants, bars, pool, beach, water sports, tennis, shops, room service. Price twin share A$206 (US$144); single A$329 (US$230); child A$42 (US$29). Meal plan: full breakfast and dinner adult A$68 (US$48), child 2-11 A$34 (US$24) per day.

Standard

Le Royal Tahitian, 7 minutes from airport. 40 rooms with A/C, fridge, tea/coffee making, phone, TV on request. Restaurant, bar/lounge, laundry service, black sand beach, water sports, babysitting. Price twin share A$155 (US$109); single A$227 (US$159); child A$42 (US$29). Meal plan: full breakfast and dinner A$66 (US$46) per person per day, no reduction for children.

Le Mandarin Downtown, 10 minutes from airport, close to market. 37 rooms with A/C, fridge, mini bar, tea/coffee making, TV/V radio, phone. Restaurants, coffee shops, bars, room service. Price twin share A$156 (US$109); single A$289 (US$202); child A$42 (US$29). Meal plan: full breakfast and dinner A$51 (US$36) per person per day no reduction for children.

Budget

Te Anuanua, on border of lagoon, BP 1553, Papeete, ph 57 1254. 3 double bungalows with bathroom, hot water. Restaurant, bar, pool, linen, ping pong, games. Buffet Tahitian lunch Sundays. Price from CFP8,000-9,000 (US$93-105) per person.

Tahiti Budget Lodge, rue du frère Alain, town centre, BP 237, Papeete, ph 42 6682. 11 rooms/6 studios, 3 with private bath, A/C, hot water. TV lounge, kitchen equipment, sheets, own towels, transfers. Price per person 3 share CFP1,700 (US$20), with bath CFP4,700 (US$55).

Chez Sorensen 200m from airport. Commune de Faaa, Cité de l'air, route Mea Ma, ph 42 6330. 3 rooms, private bath, hot water, kitchen, linen, transfers. Price from CFP3,500-6,000 (US$41-70) per person.

Shogun Rue Cdt Destremeau, Centre Papeete, ph 43 1393, BP 2880, Papeete. 7 rooms with A/C, private bath, hot water, linen. Price CFP6,000-6,500 (US$70-75).

Note: The proprietors of budget accommodation outlets may not be able to speak English.

Marquesas, French Polynesia

Local crafts, French Polynesia

Moorea, French Polynesia

Moorea

Formerly named 'Eimeo', the island of Moorea is the sister island to Tahiti, and is located 17km north-west of Papeete. It still retains its natural beauty and peace while maintaining a proximity to the city. The tranquil waters of Cook's Bay and Opunohu Bay contrast with the volcanic peaks which rise from the island's basaltic base.

With its mountain slopes covered in pineapple plantations and white sandy beaches bordering crystalline lagoons, Moorea is spellbinding in its beauty. Ideal for the day visitor or longer stay.

Air Moorea operates an air-taxi service with 7 minute hops between islands and 19 scheduled departures from Tahiti.

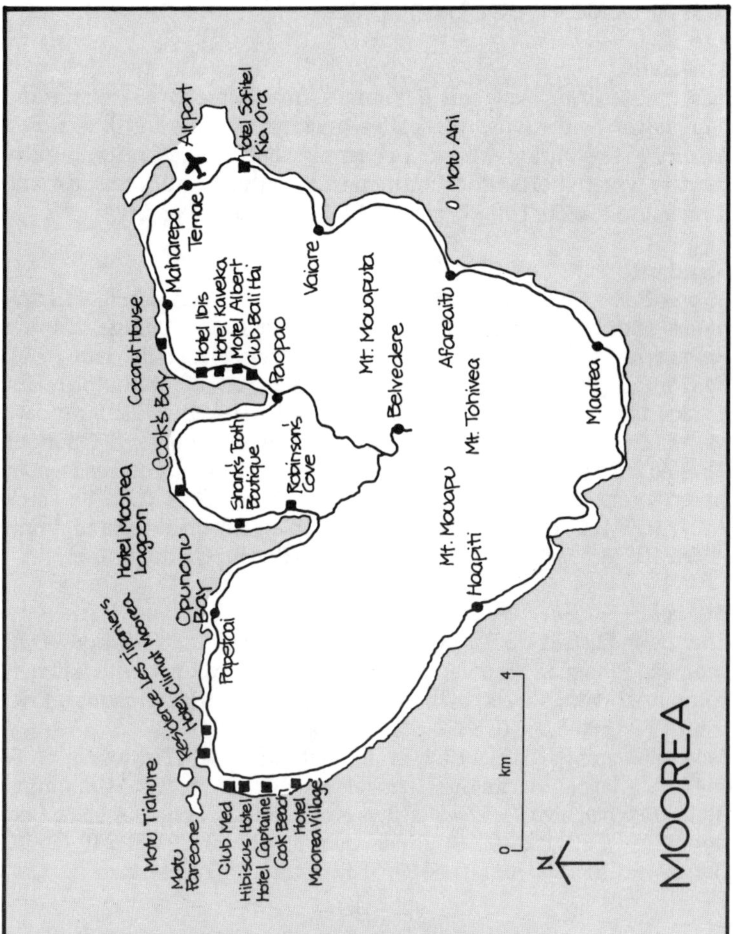

First Class

Moorea Beachcomber Parkroyal. On beachfront 28km from airport. 147 rooms and fan cooled bungalows with fridge, mini bar, tea/coffee making, TV/V, phone, hairdryer, radio. Restaurants, poolside cafe, bar, tennis, shops, room service, laundry service, water sports, babysitting. Price twin share A$198 (US$139); single A$352 (US$246); child A$22 (US$15). Meal plan; full breakfast and dinner adult A$92 (US$64), child A$46 (US$32) per day.

Sofitel la Ora on lagoon, 5 minutes from airport on white sandy beach of Temae. 80 bungalows, suites and villas with fan, mini-bar, phone, balcony. Restaurant, bar, laundry service, water sports, tennis, shops, babysitting. Price twin share A$188 (US$131); single A$331 (US$231); child A$22 (US$15). Meal plan: full breakfast and dinner adult A$68 (US$48), child 2-11 A$34 (US$24) per day.

Moderate

Bali Hai Moorea, 3km and 5 minutes from airport. 63 rooms and bungalows with fans, tea/coffee making, fridge in bungalows, hairdryer. Restaurant, 2 bars, pool, tennis, shop, room service, laundry service, water sports. Price on request. Meal plan: full breakfast and dinner adult A$50 (US$35), child 2-10 A$25 (US$18) per day.

Standard

Moorea Beach Club, 25km from the airport, on Haapiti beach. 40 Lanai rooms with A/C or fan, 43 bungalows with kitchen, fridge, balcony. Restaurants, bar, pool, water sports, shops, tennis. Price twin share A$108 (US$76); single A$171 (US$120); child A$22 (US$15). Meal plan: full breakfast and dinner adult A$57 (US$40), child 2-11 A$29 (US$20) per day.

Moorea Lagoon Hotel, 15km from airport between Cook and Opunohu Bays. 40 fan cooled bungalows with balcony. Restaurant, bar, beach, pool, water sports, laundry service. Price twin share A$111 (US$78); single A$177 (US$124); child A$22 (US$15). Meal plan: full breakfast and dinner AS$52 (US$36) per person per day, no reduction for children.

Budget

Chez Dina, District de Pao Pao, 13km from Airport, c/o Boutique Dina Moorea, Pihaena, Moorea, ph 56 1039. 3 bungalows with kitchen, communal bath, sheets, own towels. Bicycles, outrigger canoes. Price from CFP4,500-5,000 (US$52- 58) 3 persons.

Moorea Camping, District de Haapiti, Tiahura HAAPITI-Moorea ph 56 1447. 2 large dormitory bungalows. Toilet block. Communal dining/kitchen area. Cold water. Sheets own towels. Room for tents. Price dormitory CFP1,000 (US$12) per person; Camping CFP600 (US$7); Bungalow CFP4,000-5,000 (US$46-58). Reduction for longer stays.

Huahine

Huahine is 175km north-west of Tahiti in the Leeward Society Islands. It consists of two islands joined by an isthmus and enclosed by a coral reef. The lagoon is rich in sea life and has sandy beaches. It is a beautiful peaceful island, noted for its watermelon and cantaloupe industries.

Moderate

Sofitel Heiva, on a crystal clear lagoon 15 minutes from the airport by bus. PO Box 38, Fare, Huahine, ph 68 8525. 61 bungalows with fan, phone, mini-bar, hairdryer. Restaurant, bar, pool, water sports, TV/V room, library, laundry service, shops, tour desk, live entertainment. Price twin share low season A$170 (US$119); single A$313 (US$219); child A$26 (US$18). Meal plan: full breakfast and dinner adult A$68 (US$48), child 2-11 A$34 (US$24).

Standard

Bali Hai Huahine, on white sandy beach 5 minutes from the airport. 15 garden bungalows, 7 beach bungalows with fan and fridge. 2 restaurants, bars, water sports, tennis, shop, babysitting service, TV/V room. Price twin share A$75 (US$53) garden bungalows; single A$141 (US$39), child A$8 (US$6). Meal plan: full breakfast, lunch or dinner adult A$53 (US$37), child 2-10 A$26 (US$18) per day.

Budget

Chez Henriette in Baie de Haamene, BP 73, Fare Huahine, ph 68 8371. 4 bungalows with private bath, kitchen, sheets, outrigger canoe. Price from CFP3,000-5,500 (US$35-64).

Pension Meri, PK2 District de Fare, 1.5km from the airport, BP 12 Fare, Huahine, ph 68 8244, fax 68 8596. I bungalow with TV, private bathroom, hot water, sheets, own towels, kitchen. Price from CFP6,000 (US$70).

For more information contact Huahine Visitors Bureau in Fare ph (689) 68 8589 or 68 8156.

Raiatea

The second largest island in French Polynesia is 193km north-west of Tahiti. Uturoa, the principal village, is the Administration Centre of the Leeward Society Islands. It was known as Sacred Havai'i by the Polynesian Maohi, ancestors of today's Tahitians, and was the centre of royalty, religion, culture, history and heraldry. It has fertile valleys with farms and orchards. There are several passes through the lagoon which also encompasses the neighbouring island of Tahaa. Ideal for sailing and fishing.

Air Tahiti flies 3-4 times daily from Tahiti in 40 minute hops.

Moderate First Class

Bali Hi BP26 Temae, Moorea. 36 units with fan and shower. Restaurant, bar, dancing, entertainment, pool, water sports. 45 minutes from Papeete. Price US$93 (A$133).

Budget

Chez Marie-Fance, 2.5km from d'Uturoa, 5km from the airport, bordering the lagoon, BP 272 Uturoa, Raiatea ph 66 3710. 6 dormitory beds, 8 rooms, TV, private baths, communal baths with hot water, phone, pool, kitchen. restaurant, bar, linen, games, outrigger canoes, library. Price breakfast + lunch CFP3,000 (US$35); full board CFP4,500 (US$52); bungalow CFP6,000 (US$69); room CFP4,500 (US$52); dormitory CFP1,100 (US$13) each.

Hotel de Moana Iti, in the village of Opoa 35km from Uturoa, BP 724 Uturoa, ph 66 2182. 7 bungalows bordering white sandy beach. Lounge TV, hot water, private bath, linen, transfers, outrigger canoe, games. Restaurant specialising in seafood, bar. Price bungalow for 2 CFP14,000 (US$162); garden bungalow for 2 CFP12,000 (US$139); for 1 CFP8,500-10,500 (US$99-121).

Bora Bora

Bora Bora is 240km north-west of Tahiti in the Leeward Society islands, and is surrounded by a stunning multi-coloured lagoon. It is rich in natural and historical treasures. The principal village is Vaitape. A partially paved road circles the island passing colourful villages, archaeological sites and old army bunkers from World War II. Matira beach has white sand and the lagoon is world famous for its beauty. The two main peaks Mt Otemanu and Mt Pahia provide a dramatic backdrop to the white sandy beaches.

Air Tahiti has 4-5 45 minute flights daily from Tahiti. Charter flights are available on request.

First Class

Moana Beach Parkroyal, beachfront location 20 minutes from the airport by launch. 40 bungalows with fans, fridge, mini-bar, tea/coffee making, phone, radio, hairdryer, balcony. Restaurant, bars, lounge, water sports, TV/V room, shops, room service, laundry service, babysitting. Price twin share A$311 (US$218); single A$622 (US$435); child free. Meal plan: full breakfast and dinner adult A$97 (US$68), child 2-9 A$49 (US$34) per day.

Hotel Bora Bora, beachfront location 20 minutes from the airport by launch. 55 bungalows, junior suites and villas in garden, beach or over water locations with fans, fridge, tea/coffee making, mini-bar, hairdryer, bathrobes, balcony. Restaurant, beachside grill/snacks, 2

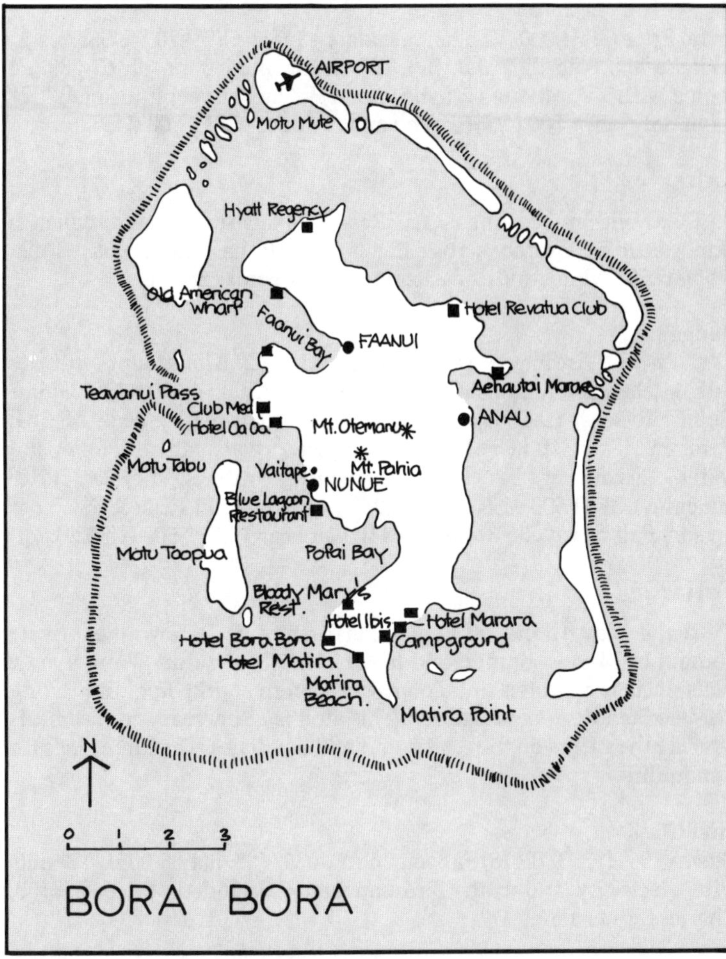

bars, water sports, tennis, table tennis, shops, TV/games room, volleyball, library, laundry service, babysitting. Price twin share A$304 (US$213); single A$607 (US$425); child 2-11 free. No meal plan.

Standard B

Beach Club Bora Bora, on beachfront 30 minutes from airport by launch and bus. 43 rooms with A/C or fan, fridge, balcony. Restaurant, bar, shops, water sports. Price twin share fan cooled A$146 (US$102); single A$264 (US$185); child A$14 (US$10). Meal plan: full breakfast and dinner adult A$57 (US$40), child 2-11 A$29 (US$20) per day.

Budget

Revatua Club, District de Anau, ph 67 7167 fax 67 7659, on mountain side. 16 rooms with A/C, private bath, hot water, kitchen, linen, activities

extra. Price CFP4,000 (US$46), breakfast + lunch CFP3,200 (US$37).
Chez Rosina, Baie de Pofai, BP 51, Vaitape, Bora Bora, ph 67 7091. 4 rooms with TV, private bath, hot water, kitchen, linen, transfers. Price room only CFP4,500 (US$52); bed and breakfast CFP6,500 (US$75).

Tahaa

Enclosed within the same reef as Raiatea is this small island, which is 3km north of Uturoa across the lagoon. It has numerous vanilla plantations, white sandy beaches and pretty coral gardens.

Budget

Chez Pascal, District de Tapuamu, ph 65 6042. 4 bedrooms, private bath, kitchen, linen, transfers. Price Room CFP2,000-4,000 (US$23-46).
Hotel Hibiscus, Haamene, 20 minutes from Uturoa by boat, BP 184, Haamene, Tahaa, ph 65 6106. 4 bungalows. private bath and toilet, hot water. Restaurant, bar, kitchen, linen, excursions, bicycles. Price bungalow CFP4,500-6,500 (US$52-75); dormitory CFP1,500 (US$17) per person. Full board CFP3,750 (US$44); half board CFP2,500 (US$29).

Tetiaroa

Once the playground of Polynesian royalty, it is now the private domain of Marlon Brando and is 42km north of Tahiti. Twelve *motu* islets enclose a protected lagoon with superb snorkelling and diving inside a 30m deep coral garden. This atoll is a sanctuary for sea birds who lay their eggs on the white sand of the beaches. The ideal place for tranquillity.

First Class

Tetiaroa Village, BP 2418, Papeete, ph 82 6302/82, fax 85 0051. 12 units with electricity and bath. Bird sanctuary. Secluded. Price US$150. Charter flights only.

Rangiroa

Rangiroa has a 68km long x 26km wide lagoon and is the largest atoll in the Tuamotu Archipelago. It is world famous for scuba diving, and has all water sports and boating facilities. Lagoon excursions include snorkelling through the pass along with hundreds of fish and sharks. Motor boat outings are available to visit Tiputa village, various *motu* islets, the bird sanctuary on *Motu Paio* and the Blue Lagoon of Taeo'o. Picnics are sometimes included in these trips, and all hotels and pensions can make the necessary arrangements.

Air Tahiti has 1-2 flights daily and it is a 1 hour 20 minutes hop.

First Class

Kia Ora Village Hotel, PO Box 4607, Papeete, ph 42 8675, fax 41 3040. 15 minutes by boat from Tiputa Village, 10 minutes by bus from the airport. 35 units, 2 bedroom bungalows, fans, bathroom, lounge. Restaurant, bar, dancing, entertainment water sports. Price US$290 (A$414).

Rangiroa Beach Club, BP 13019, Papeete, ph 96 0334, fax 95 0290, 2 minutes from the airport. 20 units. Restaurant, bar, entertainment, games room. Fishing, water sports. Rates on request.

Budget

Chez Henriette, Village d'Avatoru, 5km from the airport, ph 96 0468/96 0565. 4 bungalows, private bath, restaurant, linen, transfers from airport, shark feeding, games, picnics. Price CFP2,000-5,000 (US$23-58).

Pension Cecile, Village d'Avatoru, 2km from the airport, BP 98, Avatoru, Rangiroa. 3 bungalows, private bath, linen. Transfers from the airport, excursions, cultural activities, snorkelling, games. Price CFP4,000-6,000 (US$46-70).

Chez Lucien, Village de Tiputa, BP 69, Tiputa, Rangiroa, ph 96 0355. Sea side near disembarkation wharf. 2 bungalows, 2 rooms, private bath, hot water, linen. Restaurant, bar. Price CFP2,000-5,500 (US$23-64).

Tikehau

Tikehau is 300km north of Tahiti in the Tuamotus Archipelago. The atoll is almost a complete circle, with an interior lagoon 26km across and a pass for small boats through the coral reef. It is abundant in fish from parrot-fish to flying fish. Exotic birds, multicoloured fishes, painted shells and corals, and the black pearl farm in the middle of the lagoon, are some of the attractions of this paradise. With one village, only 312 inhabitants, and a temperature of 26-28C it is indeed the ideal place to stay.

Air Tahiti flies 3-4 times a week from Tahiti, a 55 minute hop.

Budget

Chez Isidore et Nini, Village de Tuterahera, Tikehau, ph 96 2238, 1km from the airport. 5 rooms, TV, private bath, kitchen, linen, transfers, fishing, shark feeding. Price CFP2,000-5,000 (US$23-58).

Chez Maxime, Village de Tuterahera, Tikehau Island, Tuamotu, ph 96 2238. In the village, 2km from the airport. 4 rooms, shared bathroom, TV, kitchen, linen, transfers from airport. Price CFP2,000- 4,500 (US$23-52) per person. Contact owner for a quote.

Manihi

Manihi is an atoll in the Tuanotu Archipelago, 520km north-east of

Tahiti. Its clear lagoon, 6km x 31km, has a deep navigable pass through the reef and shelters several black pearl farms. Activities are around the lagoon and your hosts will take you to fish parks, pearl farms, for picnics on *motu* isles, and spear fishing.

First Class

Kaina Village, BP 2540, Papeete, ph 96 4273. 16 units on a lagoon 10 minutes from the airport (90 minutes by air from Tahiti). Restaurant, bar, boutique. Scuba diving. Price US$177 (A$253).

Budget

Le Keshi, on a private isle, 20km by boat from the airport, ph/fax 96 4313. 7 bungalows, private bath, pool, linen, windsurfing, snorkelling, games. Price CFP6,000-8,000 (US$70-93).

The Austral Islands

The Austral Islands are located from 538km to 1074km south of Tahiti, and spread across 1280km of the South Pacific straddling the Tropic of Capricorn. The population of 6500 Polynesians live on the islands of Rurutu, Tubuai, Rimatara, Raivavae and Rapa.

The people grow crops and the women weave pandanus into hats, bags, baskets, fans, lampshades and mats. The Protestant religion is predominant and the churches form a social life for the villagers.

Archaeological diggings reveal human presence on Rurutu around 900AD. Giant sized stone tikis were found on Raivavae and resemble those on Easter Island. On Rapa there are the remains of a Maori fortress.

Air Tahiti flies to Rurutu and Tubuai three times a week. The cargo ship *Tuhaapae ll* sails once a month to Rurutu and Tubuai and every two months to Rapa.

Rapa

Chez Faraire, Village d'Area, Haurei-Rapa. 3 rooms, shared bath, hot water, kitchen, linen, transfers airport, walking excursions, deep-sea fishing. Price CFP3,500 (US$40).

Rurutu

Hotel Rurutu Village, BP 6, Rurutu, ph 940 392, or the agent Pacific Travel, ph 42 9385. 5km from villages of Moerai and Avera near airport and bordering the sea. 7 bungalows, double beds, private bath with hot water, kitchen. Restaurant, bar, pool. Transfers from airport. Car/scooter hire. Excellent meals. Contact hotel for activities. Price bungalow CFP3,500-9,500 (US$40-110) per person. Breakfast and lunch CFP3,500 (US$40).

Tubuai

Chez Taro Tanepau, Village de Mataura, 4km from the airport, ph 95 0382. 2 rooms, phone, private bath, hot water, kitchen, linen, towels, transfers. Price CFP3,000-5,000 (US$35-58).

Chez Karine et Tale, Village de Taahueia, 6km from the airport, ph 95 0452/76. 1 bungalow, TV, private bath, hot water, kitchen, linen, transfers. Price CFP5,000 (US$58), breakfast + lunch CFP2,000 (US$23).

The Marquesas Islands

This archipelago is situated about 1400km north-east of Tahiti. There are 6 small islands and 6 large ones of volcanic origin. There is no reef, which makes landing a boat difficult. The average temperature is 23C with high humidity.

Hiva-oa

Hiva-oa is the largest island in the group. It is where the painter Paul Gauguin and Belgium singer Jacques Brel are buried, and is the headquarters of the Roman Catholic Bishop of the Marquesas. Facilities include a post office, hospital, banks, restaurants, small pensions, and agencies for the rental of cars, boats and horses. The village of Puamau and the valley behind has the largest tikis.

Pension Maire, BP, 75 Hiva Oa, ph 927 455. In the village d'Atuana, 12km from the airport. 2 bungalows, private bathroom, hot water, TV, linen, kitchenette, bar, restaurant. Games. Price CFP5,500 (US$64). Contact proprietor for more information.

Pension Gauguin, Village d'Atuona, 15km from the airport, ph 92 7351, BP 34, Atuona, Hiva-Oa. 4 rooms, TV, shared bath, hot water, kitchen, linen. Price CFP5,000 (US$58).

Tahuata

Tahuata is separated from Hiva-Oa by the Bordelais Channel in the southern group. It is 15km long by 9km wide with the visible remains of a sunken volcano. Facilities include a post office, pharmacy, small pensions or rooms, boat and horse rentals. Recommended excursions to archaeological sites take 15 minutes by boat. Horseback rides to Hanatahau Valley to visit petroglyphs and sandy white beaches.

Chez Naani Barsinas Vaitahu, Tahuata, ph 929 226. 4 rooms, kitchen, shared bathroom, hot water, linen. Outrigger canoe. Price room CFP1,500-4,850 (US$17-56).

Fatu-Hiva

Fatu-Hiva is the most southerly of the group, and accommodation is available in small pensions or with private families. Rental of outrigger canoes, boats and horses is available. Local handicrafts, including tapa

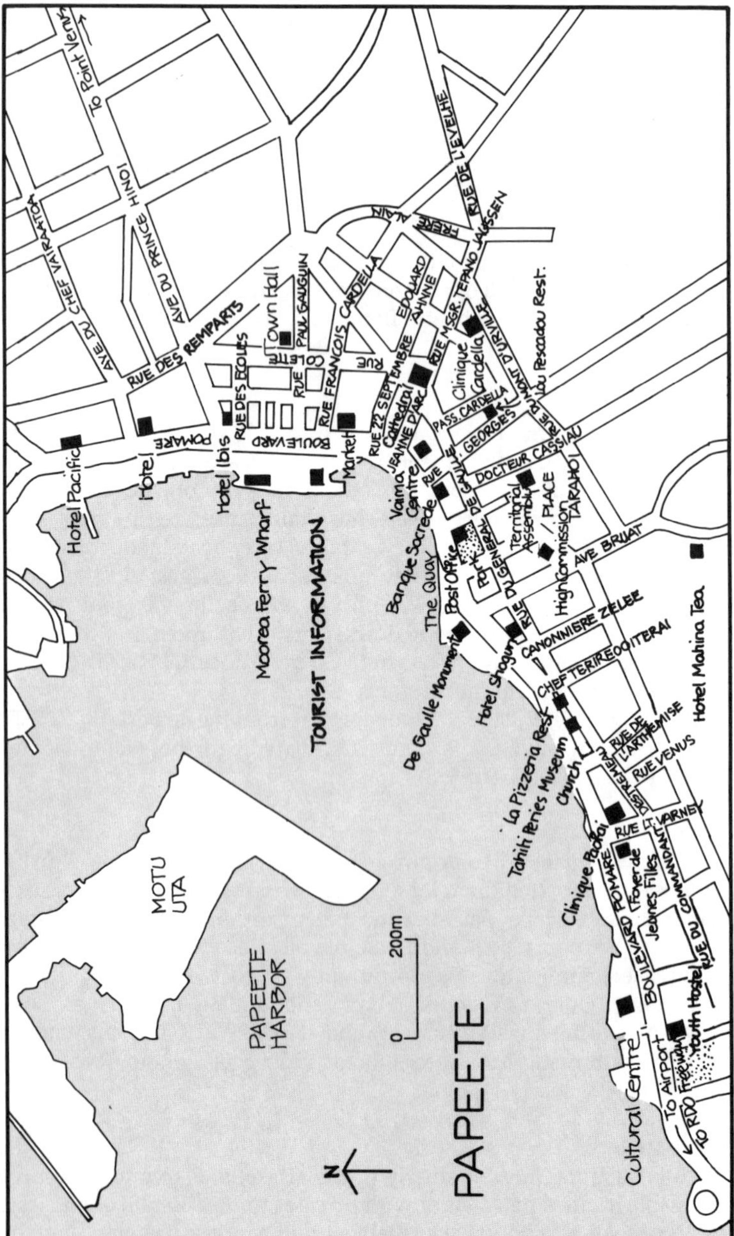
PAPEETE
PAPEETE HARBOR
MOTU UTA
0
200m
N
To Point Venus
AVE DU CHEF VAIRAATOA
AVE DU PRINCE HINOI
RUE DES REMPARTS
BOULEVARD POMARE
Hotel Pacific
Hotel
Hotel Ibis
Moorea Ferry Wharf
TOURIST INFORMATION
Market
Town Hall
RUE PAUL GAUGUIN
RUE COLETTE
RUE DES ECOLES
RUE FRANCOIS CARDELLA
RUE 22 SEPTEMBRE
RUE JEANNE D'ARC
Cathedral
Vaima Centre
Banque Socredo
The Quay
Post Office
Park
RUE DU GENERAL DE GAULLE
PASS. CARDELLA
RUE GEORGES
DOCTEUR CASSIAU
Territorial Assembly
PLACE TARAHOI
High Commission
AVE BRUAT
RUE EDOUARD AHNNE
RUE MSGR. TEPANO JAUSSEN
RUE DE L'EVELHE
Clinique Cardella
Lou Pescadou Rest.
RUE DUMONT D'URVILLE
De Gaulle Monument
Hotel Shogun
CANONNIERE ZELEE
CHEF TERIIEROOITERAI
La Pizzeria Rest.
Tahiti Perles Museum
Church
RUE DE L'ARTHEMISE
RUE VENUS
Hotel Mahina Tea
RUE LT. VARNEY
Clinique Paofai
Foyer de Jeunes Filles
RUE DU COMMANDANT
Youth Hostel
Cultural Centre
To Airport
To RDO Freeway

bark paintings, woven hats, mats, wood and stone carvings, are much sought after. Recommended excursion to Valley of Hanavave with unsurpassed tropical beauty and mountain back-drop.
Chez Cecile Gilmore, Village d'Omoa-Fatu, Hiva, ph 92 8054. 2 rooms, private bathroom, hot water, kitchen, linen. Price CFP2,500-4,000 (US$29-46).
Chez Norma Ropati, Village of d'Omoa, ph 92 8013. 4 rooms, shared bathroom, hot water, linen. Price CFP2,000-5,000 (US$23- 58).

Nuku-Hiva
Nuku-Hiva is the main island of the northern group. The town of Taiohae is the administration and economic centre of the whole Marquesas Group. Facilities include a post office, hospital, town hall, government offices, restaurants, small hotels and rooms for rent. There are rental agencies for the hire of horses, boats, cars and sail boats.

Recommended excursions to Hakaui Valley with 550m waterfall and look-out points and herds of horses, cattle, goats and wild pigs. Archaeological remains of 'Tohua' dance floors, and white sandy beaches at Anaho. Marquesan sculptors carve tikis and other artefacts of rare wood. Visit the Roman Catholic Cathedral where interior carvings represent the best of Marquesan sculptors.

Air Tahiti has 3 flights a week to Nuka-Hiva with connections to Hiva-Oa and Ua-Pou. There are no other air strips.

Inter-island passenger/cargo/copra ships sail from Tahiti on a regular basis. The *Aranui* with A/C cabins for 40 people has 16-17 day round trip cruises to all the inhabited islands of the Marquesas.
Hotel Moana Nui, BP 9, Nuku-Hiva, ph 920 002. Situated 300m from the quay at Taiohae. 7 bedrooms with private bath, hot water, linen. Transfers. Restaurant, bar. Price CFP5,500-8,500 (US$64-99), breakfast CFP3,000 (US$35) per person.

NOTES

Keikaha Nui Inn, BP 21, Nuku-Hiva, ph 920 382. Village de Taiohae, 2km from the quay. 6 bungalows with private bath, hot water, linen, kitchen. Restaurant, bar. View of bay close to beach. Price CFP14,200 bungalow per person, garden bungalow CFP8,500-11,700 (US$99-135).

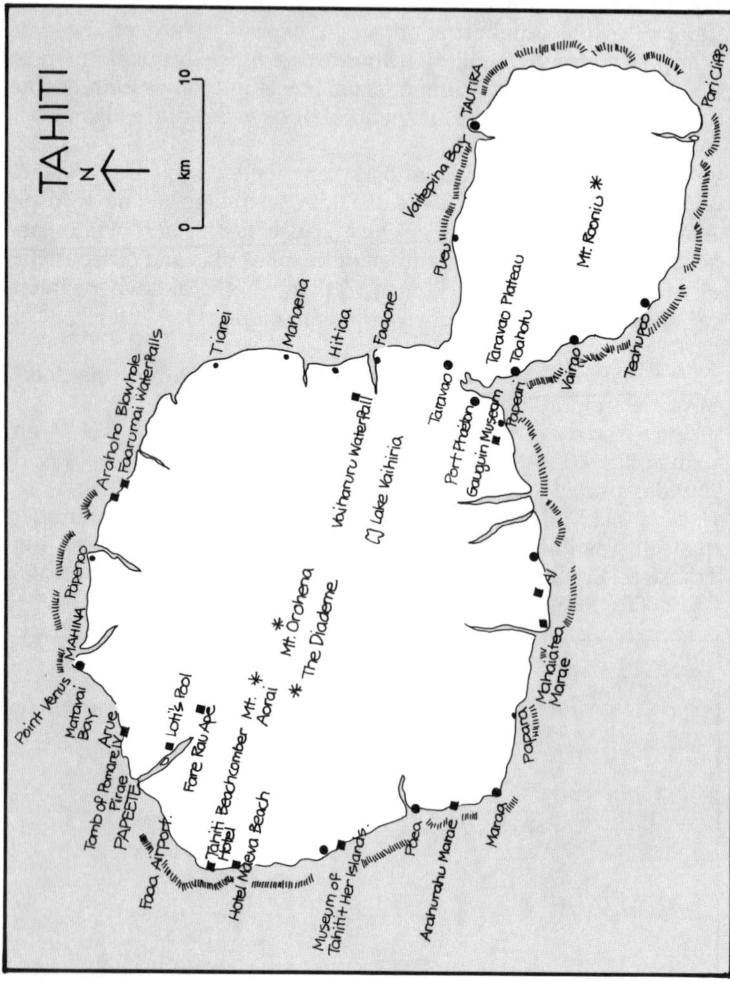

Tahiti

Tahiti has a 114km road which winds between the mountains and the sea. On the peninsula the road continues down each coast for 18km. An interior road leads past dairy farms and citrus groves to a panoramic view of the Plateau of Taravao.

Local Transport

Air

Air Tahiti makes regular flights to the other islands. The longest flight is to The Marquesas which takes 5 hours 5 minutes. The baggage allowance on inter-island flights is 12kg.

Bus

Le Truck is Tahiti's public bus service. The destination is posted on top of each Le Truck which always begins and ends its round-trip at the public market in the centre of Papeete. It operates during daylight hours with night transportation only to West Coast hotels as far as Maeva Beach.

Authorised stops along the route are marked by a blue sign with a drawing of Le Truck. Just wave the driver to stop. This form of transport is much more suitable for the young than the old.

Taxi

A Tiare Tahiti blossom insignia on the light on top of the cab indicates that the driver has some knowledge of English.

Taxi fares are controlled by the government and displayed in every cab. Taxi stations are at Station de Jasmin, ph 420 894; Station Vaima, ph 429 835; Station du Marche, ph 420 292; and Station Airport, ph 436 520.

Car hire

There are several rental firms including Avis, Budget, Eurocar and Hertz. Rates vary according to the type of car and whether the minimum daily mileage is included.

Drivers must be 21 years of age and have a driving licence valid for one year. Driving is on the **right** side of the road. Chauffeur-driven Silver Shadow Rolls Royces or Daimler Double-sixes are available for shopping tours, sightseeing, sunset cruise with champagne, airport transfers or visits to museums, or just hourly hiring. They are very expensive.

Moorea Boats

Moorea is linked to Tahiti by ferry service that operates several times a day, and a speed boat service. It takes 35-60 minutes and costs from CFP1,000 (US$12) one way.

Eating Out

All the major tourist hotels have up-market restaurants and bars. Papeete is renowned for its many restaurants in a variety of price ranges. As well as French cuisine, there are Italian, American, Chinese, Vietnamese and Polynesian dishes.

For the budget traveller, Les Roulottes, mobile diners which set up a shop each afternoon along the dock and serve hot food until the wee small hours are a practical alternative. These colourful wagons serve fast food at reasonable prices, as well as provide a bar stool to sit and watch the waterfront scene of Papeete by night.

All types of alcoholic drinks are available in Papeete, but they are very expensive, so we suggest you sample the local Hinano or Manuia beer.

Some of the deluxe hotels give patrons a complimentary drink. A favourite is made by dribbling five different coloured liqueurs into a tall glass, topping them with cream and ice cream. It is pretty to look at, certainly moorish, but deadly!

Entertainment

Papeete is a swinging town most of the time. The side-walk bars are usually very active seven nights a week.

Nightclubs close at midnight during the week but remain open until 2-3am on weekends.

Interesting places to drink and people-watch at the same time are:

Le Retro, a Parisian-style café in the Vaima Centre.

Le Tamure Hut in the Hotel Royal, Papeete. Open Wednesday-Saturday nights with dancing to old and new Tahitian tunes played by a live band.

Other nightclubs with a Tahitian atmosphere and music include:

La Cave, Hotel Royal, Papeete.

Le Pitate starts late.

Princess Helata in the suburb of Pirae is open till 4am weekends.

For European atmosphere and lots of disco music go to:

Le Bus, *Le Paradise*, *Le Galaxie*, *Le Surf* in Vaima Centre, *Le 106*, *Le Calypso*, *Le Lido* (mostly for young French draftees), *Le Piano Bar* (frequent transvestite shows), and *Le Zizou*.

Le New Orleans, behind the Cathedral features jazz.

Shopping

Shopping is a colourful experience in Papeete, and there are plenty of shops selling French goods. You'll find bright 'pareus' in hotel boutiques and small shops especially along the waterfront. Why not buy the fabric and make your own?

Black pearls are plentiful but expensive. The Tahiti Perles Centre in Pomare is worth a visit.

Wall hangings, tapestries, lampshades, candles, jewellery boxes, shell jewellery, paintings and engravings can be found in artisan shops. There is a good one on the waterfront in Papeete.

Handicrafts can be found everywhere. Works of art and basketry are popular. There are even locally made evening gowns but they are not cheap. Shirts and day dresses are more reasonable.

An inexpensive souvenir is Monoi Oil, made from coconut oil and the essence of flowers, usually Tiare Tahiti. It can be used as a moisturiser, perfume, sun tan oil, mosquito repellent, hair dressing or massage lotion. It can be bought in pharmacies, supermarkets, hotel boutiques and many other outlets.

Pottery can be purchased direct from the potters at their homes. Paintings by well known and local artists can be purchased from the many galleries.

Papeete Public Markets are open daily and the many stalls sell local produce, lovely floral arrangements and inexpensive souvenirs.

Duty Free shops can be found at Faaa International Airport, at Vaima Shopping Centre and on Boulevard Pomare.

Shops are open Mon-Fri 7.30am-5.30pm, and until noon on Saturdays. There is always a long lunch hour, 11am-2pm.

Sightseeing

Strolling around Papeete, driving around the island or taking a tour is enough to make the visitor want to stay. The scenery is spectacular with mountains, waterfalls and lush foliage. There is an abundance of parks and gardens, and they are all picturesque. It's no wonder artists like Paul Gauguin made this their home.

The **Museum of Tahiti and Her Islands** is at Pointe des Pecheurs in Punaruu, and is set in spacious gardens by the sea. The museum has exhibits depicting the pre-history and archaeology of the Polynesian settlement, and their social and religious life before and after the European missionaries. There are also displays of the natural environment of the islands.

The Museum is open daily 9.30am-5.30pm except Monday, ph 583 476. There is an admission fee of CFP500 (US$5.80).

The **Gauguin Museum** is at Pupeari. Here he owned land and a house. The museum is a memorial to his life and works, and is situated near the hill where he tried to commit suicide. Admission fee is CFP450 (US$5).

The **Harrison W Smith Botanical Gardens** are located adjacent to the Gauguin Museum in Papeari, 48km from Papeete. There are hundreds of varieties of trees, shrubs, plants and flowers from tropical regions throughout the world in the gardens' 138ha. Smith left his job as a university professor in Boston to devote his life to these gardens. The Tahitians called 'Grandfather of the Trees', and he died here in 1947. Open daily and there is an admission fee of CFP500 (US$5.80).

The Lagoonarium is built into the lagoon of Punaaia, 11km from Papeete. It is the largest natural environment observatory in the world, with four big fish parks containing several thousand sea creatures. The Auditorium has display cases containing the largest seashell collection in Polynesia, as well as exhibits of mother-of-pearl and black pearls.

Underwater projectors light up the fish parks at night for the diners at the Captain Bligh restaurant.

The Lagoonarium is open daily 9am-6pm, ph 436 290. There is an admission fee of CFP500 (US$5.80).

Art Galleries can be found in many locations. To name a few: *Galerie Winkler*, ph 428 177, on Rue Jeanne d'Arc; *Galerie Vaim'antic*, ph 436 896, in Vaima Centre; *Galerie Etienne Siquin*, ph 420 981, on Rue des Ecoles; *Galerie Oviri*, ph 426 382, in Punaauia on the mountain side, 4th house on left; *Galerie Reva Reva*, ph 433 267, 36 Rue Lagarde opposite the Chinese school; *Galerie du Dragon*, Rue Clappier above bar Taaina; *Galerie Noa Noa*, ph 427 347, on Boulevard Pomare; and *Fare Manihini*, upstairs at the Tahiti Tourist Bureau.

The best and easiest way to see Tahiti is on a tour. Any local travel agency or your hotel can make a booking. They run for half or a full day and include lunch, if you wish, on the full day.

Tours start from your hotel at 9.30am and return around 3.30pm-4pm. The average tour stops at One Tree Hill, historic Point Venus, the Blowhole of Arahoho and the Three Cascades of Faarumai. Passing Bougainville's market, by the bridge in Hitiaa, it continues to the Isthmus of Taravao. In Papeari a visit is made to the Gauguin Museum and Harrison Smith Botanical Gardens.

Usually, after lunch, it passes Olivier Breaud Golf Course at Atimaono with a short stop at Fern Grotto of Maraa Point. You will have a glimpse of wealthy beachfront properties amid old Polynesian style homes built of pandanus and woven bamboo. The tour can be modified to suit your taste.

There are day tours to Bora Bora, Moorea and Tetiaroa, 4WD tours to the inland mountains, and glass bottom boat tours.

The *Glass Bottom Boat Tour* starts from the Beachcomber Parkroyal

Hotel or Maeva Beach. You spend two hours viewing coral gardens and multi-coloured lagoon fish while Tahitian fishermen dive under the boat. Refreshments are provided.

Helicopter Tours

There are two standard tours available in sound-proof sightseeing helicopters. The 40 minute tour flies over the multi-hued lagoon and coral reef, Papeete and its suburbs, and the historic Matavai Bay.

The 50 minute tour flies around the island and to the peninsula of Tahiti and the Isthmus of Taravao. Special photographic flights are also available.

Tour Operators

Kia Ora Tours, ph 430 498; *Manureva Tours,* ph 427 258; *Pacific Travel,* ph 429 385; *Tahiti Tours,* ph 427 870; *Tahiti Voyages,* ph 425 763; *Aute Voyages,* ph 426 607; *Paradise Tours,* ph 424 936, *Compagnie Maritime Polynesienne,* ph 428 402; *Bernadette's Bora Bora Day Tours,* ph 677 115; *Pacific Helicopter Service,* ph 431 680; *Tahiti Helicoptere Service,* ph 433 426. Tourist hotels have brochures, can offer assistance, and can make bookings.

Yacht base, Papette

Sport

Golf

The *Olivier Breaud International Golf Course* is in the communes of Papara and Mataiea, 40km from Papeete along the west coast. It was designed by Bob Baldock, a well known golf architect from California.

The course is open daily 8am-5pm and Golf Tours and transfers are available Mon-Sat from Hui Popo Co. Pickups from major hotels begin at 8am. Departure from the course is at 3.30pm. For further information, ph 574 032 or 574 341.

Horseriding

Club Equestre de Tahiti, ph 427 041, is open daily except Monday. Riding is possible in the mountains or by the sea with breakfast included. Picnic outings by request.

L'Eperon de Pirae, ph 427 987, closed Mondays, offers riding in the mountains, a 1 hour seaside ride including breakfast and a picnic ride in the mountains for 4-10 people. Lessons are also available.

Equestrian Centre of Hotel Puunui PO Box 7016, Taravao, is located in the grounds of the hotel in the mountains of the Tahiti-Iti peninsula. Open daily with 4 outings per day.

Bowling

The only bowling alley is in Arue. Open Tues-Sat 5pm-1am, Sun 7pm-10pm, closed Mon. Rental of necessary equipment available. Restaurant and bar on premises, ph 429 326.

Squash

Hotel Matavai has 2 lighted courts, used on a first come first served basis, ph 425 768.

Tennis

Tennis courts are located at some hotels; Tahiti Beachcomber Parkroyal, Sofitel Maeva Beach, Hyatt Regency, Tahiti Country Club. There are also courts at the Tennis Club in Fautaua, ph 420 059. The Sports Clubs also have courts, and there are some that are privately owned.

Mountain Climbing

Tahiti Special Excursions can arrange unusual treks for those who wish to explore Tahiti's interior valleys, climb mountains, walk across the island or investigate old lava-tubes, burial caves and hidden grottos.

These excursions are classified according to difficulty and take 1-4 days. For further information, ph 437 201.

The Alpine Club also has information, ph 481 059.

Deep-Sea Fishing

On the Papeete waterfront there are numerous sport fishing boats for hire. Many of them are represented by the Mer et Loisirs floating office in front of the Papeete Post Office.

Bonito boats are also available for fishing expeditions using the traditional Tahitian techniques for fishing with bamboo poles. These outings can include a picnic visit to Tetiaroa atoll to join the *Auroch* which is permanently moored there as a nautical base offering sleeping accommodation for fishing and scuba diving parties, ph 439 799.

Scuba Diving

Tahiti Aquatic Maeva is located at Hotel Sofitel, Maeva Beach, PO Box 6008, Faaa, Tahiti, ph/fax 41 0854. Also has water skiing.

Tahiti Plongée is based at Hotel Te Puna bel Air with diving programs for anyone 4-78 years old, ph 41 0062/43, fax 42 2606, PO Box 1702, Papeete.

Yacht Club of Tahiti Diving Centre is managed by bi-lingual highly qualified diving instructors. There are diving outfits for 25 people and the centre organises 2 dives a day except Sunday, ph 42 2355/42 7895, fax 42 3707, PO Box 1456, Papeete.

Water Skiing

The Nautical Activity Centre at Hotel Te Puna Bel Air is the home of the Ski Naurique Club of Tahiti, a water skiing association open to non-members, ph 421 038 or 582 998.

Force 6 in the Watersports Pavilion adjacent to Hotel Beachcomber Parkroyal. Here you can go water-skiing, windsurfing, scuba diving, deep-sea fishing, charter a yacht, take a glass bottom boat ride or anything else to do with water sports, ph 425 110.

Tahiti Jet Ski Club organises sporting events and open house with demonstrations and equipment testing. In Mataiea opposite golf course, ph 574 285.

Surfing

Surf Clubs in Tahiti welcome visitors and will show them where to find the big waves. For information on custom-made surfboards, surfing conditions and accessories for surf, skate and boogy boards, ph 424 539.

Surfboard sales and repairs - ph 438 691.

Sailing

Sailing holidays can be combined with island hopping, visiting the Leeward Society Islands by yacht and flying back to Tahiti, or with scuba diving excursions to the best locations. Contact associations for further information. *Tahiti Aquatique,* ph 428 042; *Sea and Leisure,* ph 439 799; *Tahiti Cruising Club,* ph 426 889; *Tahiti Yachting Club,* ph 427 803.

Jackboat, located near Maeva Beach *motu,* rents small motor boats with no licence required. Half day rates to package plans for a weekend, ph 421 370.

Spectator Sport

Soccer, the favourite sport of Tahitians, can be seen on almost all the islands. In Tahiti, crowds gather at the Faytaua Stadium or the Stade Pater both in Pirae, near Papeete, on week nights and weekends.

As there are so many **athletic clubs** in Tahiti, it is best to call the local paper *La Depeche,* ph 424 343, to find out what sporting events are on and where.

Horse racing is held on special occasions at Pirae Hippodrome. The jockeys sometimes ride bareback, only wearing a brightly coloured pareu and a crown of flowers. On-course betting exists but the payouts are very small.

Outrigger canoe racing competitions are held frequently to determine the champions of each pirogue club, each community, each island and finally which team is the best in Polynesia. The winners then compete for international titles, paddling against teams from Hawaii, California and other Pacific Islands.

Moto-cross racing is a popular event, with competitions held at the moto-cross course in Taravao and in other parts of the island.

There are regular automobile rallies, bicycle, sail- boat races, Delta plane and hang gliding shows. Archery competitions, boxing matches, basketball and rugby games and track events.

Huahine

Local Transport

Air

Air Tahiti has 2-3 daily 30 minute direct flights to Huahine.

Bus

The hotels and pensions provide mini-buses, at a charge, from and to the airport.

Le Truck services operate between the centre of Fare and each village, coordinating their runs with the ferry schedules and school hours.

Hotels and pensions have mini buses to and from the airport. Cars, bicycles and boat hire can all be arranged through your hotel.

Ferry

Huahine is serviced by four ferries - *Raromatai Ferry, Temehani, Taporo V* and *Vaieanu.*

A high-speed monohull which seats 450 passengers operates three 3 hour voyages per week from Papeete.

There are a number of charter boats that offer cruises around the islands. Contact Huahine Visitors Bureau in Fare, ph (689) 68 8569 mornings (689) 68 8634.

Eating Out

Most hotels have restaurants on the premises which offer a variety of cuisines. These include French, Chinese and local food. There are also a number of food bars.

Shopping

The boutiques in the hotels and some of the shops in the town have original creations. Paintings on silk, scarfs, cushions and pareus are widely available.

There is a variety of local handicrafts, including pottery, dishes, lamps, vases, hand-painted clothing and jewellery from seashells and mother-of-pearl.

Roti Tarona Artisan Centre sells *tifaifai* quilts and wall hangings, woven hats, sculptured bowls, handpainted clothes, monoi oil and sea shells.

Sightseeing

Maeva Village Archaeological sites. This old fishing village, built beside Lake Fauna Nui, is an open-air museum with its stone *marae,* fish weirs and sacred Matairea Hill lending clues to a civilisation that existed here at least 1000 years ago. Kings and chiefs lived and worshipped side by side in this royal village, and their descendants still carry on some of the traditions.

A tour of the sites includes a visit to the **Fare Pote'e** replica of a Polynesian meeting house built on stilts over a lake.

Circle Island Tour: mini-bus tours around Huahine-Nui, Huahine-iti or both islands can be arranged through your hotel or pension.

Sport

Most hotels offer activities such as swimming, windsurfing, water skiing, deep sea fishing, bicycles, outrigger canoes, pedal boats and snorkelling. Diving can be arranged.

Camping trips and buggy rides are available, including a visit to Maeva Village and a vanilla farm.

There are social moonlight horse rides along Lake Fauna.

Raiatea

Raiatea is the second largest island in French Polynesia. A partially paved road winds its way around the island.

Local Transport

Air

Air Tahiti flies 3-4 times daily from Tahiti, and a direct flight takes 40 minutes.

Bus

Le Truck service is available daily during business hours.

Taxi

The taxi stand is located near the market in the centre of Uturoa.

Bicycles

Most hotels have bicycles for hire.

Car Rental

Cars are available from local hire companies.

Ferry

Raiatea is serviced by the Vaieanu, Raromatai ferry, *Temehani II* and *Taporo IV*. A high speed monohull that seats 450 passengers operates three 4 hour voyages per week from Papeete.

Cruises can be arranged through your hotel desk or contact the Raiatea Visitors Bureau on the ferry boat deck in Uturoa, ph (689) 66 2333/66 2318.

Eating Out

Local cuisine as well as French, Chinese and Italian are offered by a number of local restaurants and snack bars. Even small hotels have restaurants on the premises.

Sightseeing

Small hotels offer a variety of sightseeing tours as well as lagoon excursions or horseback riding. See your hotel or contact Raiatea Visitors Bureau.

Faaroa River Excursion is a very popular tour. The river is explored on board an outrigger speed canoe. A green haven bordered by wild hibiscus 'pareu' trees and modern homes, it was the historic departure point for hundreds of Maohi families on their migratory voyages to Hawaii and New Zealand.

The tour of the Faaroa River, the only navigable river in Tahiti and her islands, also includes a visit to a *motu* for a swim, to snorkel or just to lie on the beach.

The **Marae Tainuu Tour** heads off to the north-west coast. It includes a brief stop at a marina, then passes vanilla plantations and continues to the fishing village of Tevaitoa. Here the Tremehani Plateau rises in a formidable wall of basalt, hiding sacred caves behind threads of waterfalls.

Maeae Tainuu is the main attraction as it is the largest temple site on this side of Raiatea. A Polynesian sun stone was found there, plus 10 stones engraved with turtles, depicting a sort of treasure hunt that Maohi warriors had to perform to achieve valour and esteem.

Marae Taputapuatea is Raiatea's most famous landmark and was the most important *marae* in eastern Polynesia. There is an open-air temple where pre-Christianised Polynesians, the Maohi, worshipped a pantheon of gods. Raiatea was formally known as Havai'i, the spiritual home for the Maohi. This Sacred Island became the cradle of royalty and religion, the centre of culture, history and heraldry.

The sacred passage of Te-Ava-Moa at Opoa offered frequent scenes of grandeur as great double canoes sailed into the lagoon, streaming pennants from many islands, when delegations from as far away as Tonga, Rurutu and New Zealand came to give their respect and sacrifices to Oro, the bloodthirsty war god, who even demanded human offerings.

These pagan rites ended with the arrival of the missionaries.

Tours to Marae Taputapuatea are available on request, and include pies and juice or a Silver Service breakfast.

There is a 4WD excursion that travels through pineapple and vanilla plantations into the valleys and to the crest of the mountains. At the Queen's Bathing Pool you can dive from a 5m overhanging rock into the pool below. The tour ends at a colonial home beside the Faaroa River.

NOTES

Tahaa

Enclosed within the same lagoon as Raiatea, and separated by under 5km, is the island of Tahaa. Most day tours are by outrigger speed canoe, crossing the protected lagoon in 30 minutes and arriving at the village of Tiva.

Tahaa has not really been discovered by tourists - yet.

Sport and Recreation

Horseriding

The Kaoha Nui Equestrian Tourism Centre has a program of riding sessions four days a week including Sunday, ph 662 246.

Deep-Sea Fishing

Jeanne-Pierre Constant has half and full day sport fishing charters, ph 663 683 or 663 097.

Scuba Diving

Raiatea Plongée Centre has all the necessary equipment for 12 divers and there are two daily outings. A special outing on Sunday has 2 dives and a picnic lunch. Instructors speak English, French and Spanish, ph 663 710.

Walking Tours

Hikers who want an overall view of Raiatea and neighbouring islands can take a self-guided round trip trek to Mt Tapioi. The road is not extremely steep but good walking shoes, water and a camera are essential. The walk takes about 3 hours.

There is a guided tour to find the Tiare Apetahu flower. Polynesian legend claims that the flower represents five fingers of a beautiful Tahitian vahine who fell in love with the son of a royal chief. She died of a broken heart when she could not marry him because she was a commoner. For more information, ph 662 334.

Sailing

ATM Yachts South Pacific, whose main office is in Paris, have their marina at Faaroa Bay in Raiatea. Sailboats from 10m-14m plus 15m catamaran are available for bare boat or skippered charter with provisions if desired, ph 662 318.

The Moorings is a marina base with a fleet for 2-8 passengers. All yachts are equipped with radio and telephone. Bare boat or skippered charters are available. Windsurfing and scuba diving equipment can be rented, ph 663 593.

Moorea

Local Transport

Air

Air Moorea operates an air taxi service with 7 minute hops between islands and 19 scheduled departures from Tahiti.

Bus

Le Truck transports passengers between the ferry dock in Vaiare and their hotels for a nominal fee.

Taxi

A taxi service is available from Moorea Airport and by phone from hotels.

Ferry

The passenger and car ferries *Tamarii Moorea-8-H* and *Tamarii Moorea* provide a 1 hour crossing from Papeete to Vaiare Bay.

Two new catamarans are now available, a must for everyone:

Aremith, a 120 luxury A/C catamaran for 320 passengers, permits a relaxed and convivial trip to and from Moorea. A 30 minute excursion.

Tamahine Moorea has comfortable seating for 180 passengers, although it has no air conditioning. The trip takes 30 minutes, and facilities include a bar.

Eating Out

A broad and interesting variety of food, including French, Chinese and local style, is available in a number of restaurants. Tourist hotels have restaurants on the premises.

Entertainment

The *Tiki Village Theatre* presents the Polynesian of yesterday in an authenticated village. Visitors can see artisans at work, weaving leaves, making floral crowns and sculpting wooden tikis.

Shopping

Moorea has many talented artisans whose creations are sold in hotel boutiques and in shops around the island.

The public market in Pao Pao beside Cook's Bay has locally made shell jewellery, hats, tote bags, baskets and mats woven from palm fronds, pandanus and banana plants. Black pearls can be purchased from several boutiques.

Sightseeing

Exploring Moorea can be accomplished by taxi, guided bus tours, rental car, mobylette, vespa and bicycle. Rental agencies are located at the airport, the Vaiare boat dock and hotels.

Circle Island Tour takes 4 hours with visits to small villages and stops to photograph the views of Moorea's mountains, valleys, lagoons and bays. The frequent stops include at the Catholic Church in Pao Pao, where a nativity scene painted by the late Pierre Heyman portrays the Holy Family as Polynesian.

The **Moorea Highlights Tour** passes through Opunohu Valley with its farms, masses of spiky pineapple plants on the mountain slopes, and grazing cattle. The partially paved road is shaded by acacia trees. It includes stops to see Moorea's stone *marae* temples and archery platforms used by Polynesian royalty in pre-Christian days.

Le Belvédère look-out point offers an unqualified panorama of Moorea's two bays, Opunohu and Cook. These tours can be combined and booked through your hotel reception or a tour operator.

Opuhi Plantation is a small botanical garden in the Pao Pao valley along the road leading to the pineapple plantations, only 5 minutes from the circle island road.

Teva's Tropical Aquarium Centre offers 36 salt water aquariums filled with exotic lagoon fish, sea anemones, live coral, seashells and even moray eels. The centre also has sales and exhibits of seashells, jewellery, shark's teeth, coral and black pearls, which Teva fashions into creative designs. Open daily, ph 561 133.

Vai Miti Artisan Workshop in Maharepa, near Hotel Bali Hai, has demonstrations on how to paint pareus, using engraved blocks of mahogany wood, ph 561 612.

The **Moorea Distillery and Fruit Juice Factory** was built to process the sweet pineapples that grow in abundance on the slopes of the mountains. Sold in cartons with no preservatives or additives, the fresh juices contain pineapple, passion fruit, apples, grapefruit, oranges and limes. There is a counter where visitors can taste samples of liqueurs and spirits made from coconut, coffee, carambola, corosol, ginger, guava and mango, ph 561 133.

The **Tiki Theatre Village** is a cultural and folklore centre built beside the lagoon in Haapiti, past Moorea's hotels and boutiques. Visitors arrive from the sea in outrigger canoes. They are welcomed by a Polynesian chief, who comes to greet them in his royal canoe accompanied by the sound of conch shells.

Built of bamboo and thatch, the Tiki Theatre Village offers visitors the same Polynesian welcome and hospitality as was extended to the 18th century Europeans who first visited these islands.

A traditional dance show is performed and lunch is served at 1pm. The village is open daily from 10.30am-3.30pm except Wednesday afternoon. Each Tuesday and Saturday the Village presents a Tahitian *Tamaara's Show* with visitors arriving at sunset. For more information, ph 561 086.

Water Tours

There are plenty of cruises around Opunohu and Cooks Bay lasting about three hours, with lunch included. There are also sunset cruises.

Cruises can include the Tropical Aquarium Centre, snorkelling, swimming and diving. All charters have a limited number of passengers according to the size of the boat. The skippers are experienced in sailing these waters.

Helicopter Tours

The helicopter service has flightseeing tours of Moorea. Special photographic flights can be arranged, ph 431 680.

All tours can be arranged through hotels or the Moorea Visitors Bureau ph (0689) 56 929/56 2648.

Coral Atoll.

Sport and Recreation

Moorea offers sportsmen an abundance of opportunities to experience all it has to offer from horse riding and hiking, to scuba diving and deep sea fishing for prize catches such as swordfish, marlin, tuna and mahi-mahi.

Fully qualified guides accompany each tour.

Scuba Diving

All diving centres have qualified instructors. The number of dives per week varies and packages are available with accommodation.

Bathy's Club, PO Box 1019, Papetoai, Moorea, ph 56 3144/56 1919, fax 56 3810/56 1888.

M.U.S.T, PO Box 336, Moorea, ph 56 1732/56 1583, fax 56 2918.

Scubapiti, PO Box 1072, Papetoai, Moorea, ph 562 038.

Tennis

There are courts at the Hotel Sofitel Kia Ora, Hotel Bali Hài, Club Bali Hai, Moorea Lagoon, Tiare Moorea, Moorea Beach Club, Club Med and Moorea Village. They include lights for night matches.

Deep-Sea Fishing

All the sport fishing boats in Tahiti are available for deep-sea fishing around Moorea. Full and half day expeditions are obtainable, ph 42 6729.

Horse Riding

Rupe Rupe Ranch is located close to Club Med in Haapiti, ph 562 210.

Bora Bora

Local Transport

Air

Air Tahiti has four or five 45 minute flights daily from Tahiti. Connecting stops are in Moorea, Huahine, Raiatea and Rangiroa.

Charter flights are available on request.

Bus and Taxi

Le Truck and taxi services are the main modes of transport on Bora Bora. A 29km partially paved road circles the island.

Ferry

Bora Bora is serviced by *Raromatal Ferry, Vaieanu*, the *Temehani IV* and *Taporo IV* two to three times a week. Check timetables which may vary.

A high-speed monohull that seats 450 passengers operates three 5 hour voyages per week from Papeete.

Cars, bicycles, scooters and boats are available for hire.

Eating out

The hotels have restaurants and bars with a variety of food. Most have a Tahitian *Tamaara'a* feast with traditional foods cooked in an underground oven. They also have traditional dancing.

There are many smaller restaurants serving Chinese, Italian and Mexican cuisine. The local seafood is a must. Even hamburgers and sandwiches are available in the many snack bars.

The *Yacht Club* is noted for its Bloody Marys, homemade ice cream and sorbets. It also serves fresh seafood, steak and duck.

Chez Christian at the Revatua Club has French cuisine and a good wine list.

Enjoy a happy hour in one of the many bars where cocktails are the popular drink.

Entertainment

Most hotels present regular Tahitian entertainment including dances and folklore shows. Disco dancing is also offered.

Free snorkelling equipment and outrigger paddle canoes can be obtained from most hotels.

The larger establishments have regular demonstrations of pareus tying, making floral leis, how to prepare *poisson cru*, dance the 'tamure' or weave baskets and mats. There is still plenty to do should you strike a rainy day.

Shopping

The boutiques in the major hotels are well stocked with goods both mundane and exotic like black pearls. Small hotels also have boutiques with pareus, T Shirts, suntan lotion and film.

If you see a pareu blowing in the breeze, you will know there is a boutique there. Goods which can be bought include clothing, wall hangings, posters, paintings, postcards, books, photographic equipment, clothing, and always the black pearls. You can also buy a replica of an old sailing ship in a bottle.

The *Artisan Centre of Bora Bora* is on the quay in Vaitape.

Sightseeing

Circle Island Tours travel the 29km circuit of the island passing modest homes surrounded by flower gardens, snack stands and small boutiques. The *marae* temples where Polynesians worshipped in pre-Christian days are visited as well as the naval base and heavy artillery guns left behind by the Americans who were stationed on the island in World War II.

These tours are done by Le Truck with English speaking guides from Bora Bora Tours, ph 677 028, or Otemanu Tours which pick up from hotels at 2pm daily except Sunday, ph 677 049. The tour is a leisurely 2½ hours.

Bora Bora Jeep Safari have a comprehensive tour of the island which is very popular but not for the faint hearted, ph 677 034.

The Hotel Bora Bora and Hotel Moana Beach have relaxing **tours in outrigger sailing canoes**. These sail out to the coral gardens, past Point Matira and the basaltic rock called Otemanu (Mountain of Birds). Contact Hotel Bora Bora, PO Box 481, Papeete, ph 482 600, or Hotel Moana Beach, PO Box 256, Vaitape, ph 677 373.

There are many independent operators who offer canoe trips around the lagoon.

Feeding the Sharks has become a popular excursion and is available to all visitors wherever they may be staying.

There are many variations of this tour with some operators including a boat trip around the island, a picnic on a *motu*, reef walking and snorkelling.

The tour from the Hotel Sofitel Marara includes a 3 hour trip around the island, then donning masks and snorkels the tourists descend into the water and walk until they reach a rope. This is attached to two coral heads. The guide kneels on one side of the rope and the tourists on the other. Left-overs from last night's dinner are then offered to whatever fish swim by. Some fish don't realise the significance of the rope but the guide will assure you that they are only interested in the food. The sharks are the last to arrive and the audience is likely to become smaller. For those who are game to stay 40 to 50 blackfin or blacktip sharks may be seen at very close range.

Shark feeding tours are also presented by Hotel Moana Beach, Bora Bora Hotel, Bora Bora Beach Club, Revatua Club, Matira Excursions, Blue Lagoon, Hanalei Tours and Bora Bora Aquarium.

The Galacteus Light Show takes place on a *motu* islet inside the coral reef, facing the village of Anau each Tuesday night. Visitors are transported from their hotels by Le Truck to the jetty at Anau where they board a boat shaped like a white swan. They go ashore to a theatre under the stars and are entertained by the Galacteus, young French people who present original music, fashion designs, comedy and dances from Africa to Asia. A light show features a Polynesian sky and the lost continent of Mu, connecting the ancient Lemurians to the Polynesians of today. Books and cassette tapes are for sale after the show. For more information, ph 677 428.

Catamaran Cruises

The *Taaroa* is a Formula 40 ultra modern racing catamaran based at Bora Bora Beach Club. A 4 hour sailing excursion departs every morning at 9am in light breezes and shallow waters to the *motu* islands. Here the passengers are guided through the jungle to reach the Pacific side of the islet. They walk on the living coral reef and at a natural aquarium in the lagoon, snorkel among myriads of fish in just over a metre of clear water. Fresh water, plastic shoes and face masks are available on board.

Taaroa Sunset Cruise leaves the dock each evening at 5pm. When the sails are lowered, after the sun sets, rum punch drinks are served to the strains of classical music, ph 677 046.

Vehia Sailing Excursions from Hotel Bora Bora leave at 9.30am several times a week for a barbecue picnic cruise. The *Vehia* sunset cruise which leaves the dock at 5pm is legendary for honeymooners, lovers and other romantics, ph 677 079.

Moana Adventure Tours operate from the Hotel Bora Bora. They offer glass bottom boat rides, reef trips, snorkelling, shark feeding, boat trips around the island, airport express speedboat service, speed boat rental, off-shore fishing, scuba diving, *motu* picnics and a VIP cruise, ph 677 034 or Hotel Bora Bora Reservations, Papeete, ph 428 600.

Calypso Beach Club at Bora Bora has water-skiing, scuba diving, snorkelling, shark feeding shows and visits around the lagoon. It also has a 3 1/3 hour excursion designed for Senior Citizens. A covered double canoe takes them around the island with stops to visit *motus* and to play Cousteau in warm shallow crystalline waters, ph 67 7464/67 7785, fax 67 7034.

Sport and Recreation

Scuba Diving

Certified divers can explore the lagoon depths up to 15m or dive outside the coral reef up to 27m, and lessons are available from certified divers for those with no experience.

Calypso Club Hotel Beach Club, Bora Bora, ph (689) 67 7785/67 7464, fax (689) 67 7034; *Bora Diving Centre*, PO Box 182, Bora Bora, ph (689) 67 7184, fax (689) 67 7483.

Deep-sea Fishing

There are numerous places where you can arrange excursions for half or full days both on Bora Bora or in Tahiti.

All boats are fully equipped with the latest motors and experienced crews. Some carry beer and refreshments.

Toerau is a Fantacy 7m equipped with a 155hp turbo diesel Volvo Penta, with 25 knots cruising speed. Equipment includes 4 Penn international reels, 4 Fenglass 36kg rods, 2 flying gaffs and 2 professional gaffs. The skipper makes his own lures using ancient Polynesian techniques, ph 677 063.

Tennis

The *Hotel Bora Bora Tennis Club* has two courts with complimentary use of equipment for hotel guests. This complex also includes volleyball and a half basketball court.

The *Hotel Sofitel* has a court which is free for hotel guests, and they have priority. There is a minimal charge for non- residents.

For information about anything to do with Bora Bora, phone the Visitors Bureau on (689) 67 7636/67 7031.

Package Tours

There are package tours from most countries to French Polynesia. These usually range from 4-6 nights including air fares, accommodation and transfers. Many tours also have 'special' meal plans for those taking the package. As French Polynesia is far from cheap, a package deal is a good idea. At least you know how much you are up for apart from personal items. Package tours can range from A$1099-1299 (US$802-948). Consult your local travel agent as to the best buy at the time you are thinking of visiting.

NOTES

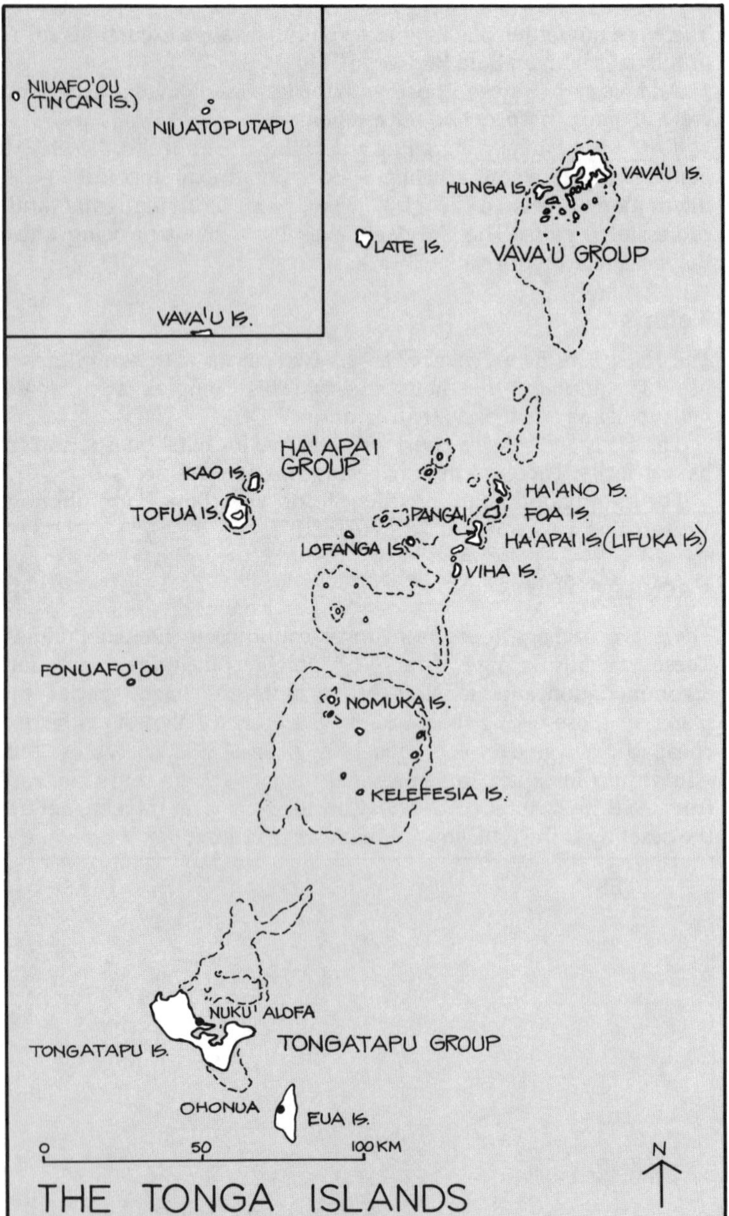

NIUAFO'OU
(TIN CAN IS.)
NIUATOPUTAPU
VAVA'U IS.
HUNGA IS.
VAVA'U IS.
LATE IS.
VAVA'U GROUP
HA'APAI
GROUP
KAO IS.
TOFUA IS.
HA'ANO IS.
PANGAI
FOA IS.
HA'APAI IS.(LIFUKA IS.)
LOFANGA IS.
VIHA IS.
FONUAFO'OU
NOMUKA IS.
KELEFESIA IS.
NUKU'ALOFA
TONGATAPU IS.
TONGATAPU GROUP
OHONUA
EUA IS.
0
50
100 KM
N
THE TONGA ISLANDS

KINGDOM OF TONGA

The Kingdom of Tonga, also known as the Friendly Isles, is the only modern day monarchy in the Pacific. It is an archipelago of 170 islands, 36 of which are inhabited. It covers 748 sq km and lies just below the Tropic of Capricorn. It is also just west of the international dateline, making it officially the first place in the world (to the inhabitants' delight) to see the sun rise at the dawn of each day.

The islands are divided into four groups - Eua, Haàpai, Vavau and Tongatapu, where the capital Nuku'alofa is located.

Tonga is a constitutional monarchy. The King appoints a Prime Minister and a cabinet of six assists him. The Legislative Assembly consists of seven nobles elected by the hereditary nobility and seven commoners elected by the people. Elections take place every three years and all Tongans who are at least 21 and can read and write are eligible to vote.

In the 1990 elections, the number was increased to nine elected representatives of the people in the Legislative Assembly. Three pro-democracy candidates were successful, and they have been gathering support for some dilution of the power of the king.

The economy depends mainly on agriculture, with three-quarters of all the workers being farmers. The government owns all the land but any male is entitled to a plot which he rents from the government. The administration has also helped establish small-scale manufacturing, mainly around Nuku'alofa. The chief exports are bananas and copra. Some oil has been found in recent years. Tourism is becoming increasingly important.

The capital of Tonga is Nuku'alofa.

History

Tonga's early history is based on myth. Recognised rulers go back to 900AD, but according to archaeologists Tonga was settled as early as 500BC. It is thought that the first settlers were Polynesians who came from Samoa. The Tui Tonga, the supreme ruler, was believed to be the son of the Creator God Tangaloa Eitumatupuà. His influence was at its height in the 13th century when his domain covered part of the Lau Group in Fiji, Rotuma, Futuna, Ulvea, Tokelau, Samoa and Nieu. The collapse of this empire dealt a severe blow to his authority. The growth of the population and its control became a burden. Political unrest followed, and a number of Tui Tongas were assassinated. Consequently, the 24th Tui Tonga created a new office of 'Hau', Temporal Ruler, in 1470. The Tui Tonga, because of his divine origin became Sacred Ruler.

The first 'hau', Moungamotuà, was a younger brother of the Tui Tonga. He founded the dynasty of Tui Haàtakalaua. In the 17th century, the sixth in his line created yet another dynasty, Tui'Kanokupolu. Administration for the dynasties was carried out throughout the islands by close relatives. The result was peace and quiet during the 16th and 17th centuries.

The first Europeans to set foot on Tonga were Dutch navigators Willem Cornelis Schouten and Jacques Lemaire in 1616, and Abel Tasman in 1643. Englishman Samuel Wallis and even Captain Bligh visited the islands.

Captain James Cook made several voyages in the area between 1770 and 1777. On his last visit, he noted that Tongatapu was the residence of the Tui Tonga and other high ranking chiefs. It became known as 'Land of Chiefs'. The other islands served as gardens and produce was dispatched to Tongatapu at certain times of the year. These subordinate islands became known as 'Land of Servants'.

Methodist missionaries from Britain started to move into the islands in the 1800s. From the 1790s to 1820s there had been civil war. While Christianity was endeavouring to get a stronghold, there was a struggle for power between Taufaàhau, the young chief of Haàpai, and the Tui Tonga. By 1826 the Wesleyan Mission was effectively established and Taufaàhau was baptised in 1831. He chose the name George after the English King. He fought the nobles of Vavau and destroyed the Tui Tonga of Tongatapu. In 1845 he was proclaimed King George Tupou l. He ensured the loyalty of the nobles by giving them land which they could rent out. Aided by Rev. Shirley Baker, a Methodist, whose statue stands in Pangai, Hapài, the king was able to ensure independence from British Rule and make Wesleyan the official religion.

Christianity changed the Tongan culture. New taboos were introduced, based on the ten Commandments and Wesleyan beliefs. The missionaries also introduced reading and writing so by 1839 it was possible to officially announce a written code of laws - the Code of Vavau - which was limited to the king's subjects in Vavau. It was not until 1850 when the king was acknowledged as Ruler of the Islands that a Code of Laws for the whole of Tonga was in force. This became the basis of the Tongan Constitution which was adopted in 1875. In the 1862 Emancipation Edict, King George abolished the system of semi-serfdom.

King George died in 1893 and was succeeded by his great-grandson Tupou II. There had been treaties with France and Germany but on May 18 1900, Tonga signed a Treaty of Friendship and Protection with Great Britain.

Queen Salote Tupou III succeeded Tupou II in 1918. She worked hard to improve education and health in Tonga. Under revised treaties with Great Britain in 1858 and 1967, Tonga regained control of its internal affairs.

Queen Salote died in 1965 and was succeeded by her son King Taufa'ahau Toupou IV. In 1970 Tonga gained independence within the Commonwealth.

Climate

The climate is pleasant being slightly cooler and less humid than most tropical areas. The temperatures range from 18-25C from May-September and 24-32C October- April. Trade winds blow a constant 13-18 knots year round.

Population

The estimated population is 100,000, almost all of whom are Polynesian. The predominant religion is Methodist. Under the Constitution, no work or recreation is allowed on Sunday and the people obey this law.

Most Tongans live in small villages, where they grow crops and fish. Many islands have no running water or electricity.

The law requires all children 6 years of age and over to attend school. The government operates 60% and the church 40% of the schools, all of which teach English.

Language

The official language is Tongan, but English is widely spoken. Although you probably will not need them, here are a few words and phrases which might be useful.

Hello ....Malo e lelei
Good morning........Malo e lelei ki he pongipongi ni
Good evening.........Malo e lelei ki he efiafi ni
Welcome..................Talitali fiefia
Good bye.................Alu a: nofo a (in reply)
How much? ....Oku fiha?
How many? ....Ko e meà fiha?
Cheap.......................Maàmaà
Expensive................Mamafa
Stop ....Tuu
Good ....Lelei
Bad ....Kovi
One...........................Taha
Two ....Ua
Three........................Tolu
Four..........................Fa
Five...........................Nima
Six............................Ono

Seven........................Fitu
Eight..........................Valu
Nine ....Hiva
Ten ....Hongofulu
Twenty ....Uofulu or Uaanoa
One Hundred ....Teau
Thousand ....Tahaafe
Where is the...? Hotel.............. Oku tuu i fe à e hotele
Hospital .... falemahake
Market........... maketi
Palace .... palasi
Restaurant .... falekai
Police .... Fale polisi?
Where can I buy? .... Teu fakatau mei fe ha...?
Where is the toilet? .... Ko feà e fale malolo?

Public Holidays

January 1 ....New Year's Day
March April ....Good Friday-Easter Monday
April 25....................Anzac Day
May 4 ....HRH Crown Prince Tupoutoà's birthday
June 4 ....Emancipation Day
July 4 ....HM King Taufaàhau Tupou IV's birthday
November 4 ....Constitution Day
December 4 ....King Tupou I Day
December 25 ....Christmas day
December 26 ....Boxing Day

Festivals

Red Cross Week: various activities to support the Red Cross, highlighted by the Red Cross grand ball. May.

The *Haàpai Festival* takes place during the first week in June.

The *King's Birthday* and *Coronation Day* (public holiday) and *Heilala Festival* July 4.

Vava'u Festival Week coincides with the Crown Prince's birthday on May 4.

The *Royal Agricultural and Industrial Shows* take place from the last week in September to the first week in October throughout the Kingdom.

Entry Regulations

All visitors must have a valid passport and onward ticket, proof of adequate funds and relevant health certificate. No visa required for visits of less than 30 days. If visitors wish to extend their stay, permission must be requested from the Principal Immigration officer.

Vaccinations for yellow fever and cholera are needed if coming from an infected area.

Customs

The duty free allowance is 200 cigarettes and 1 litre of spirits. Tonga is a duty free port.

Prohibited imports are: firearms, ammunition, drugs and pornographic material. Birds, animals, fruit and plants need certification from Quarantine.

Restricted Exports: valuable artefacts and certain flora and fauna.

Departure Tax

There is a departure tax of T$15 (about US$11) payable at the airport in local currency.

Embassies

Australia: Australian High Commission, Salote Road, Nuku'alofa, ph 212 244/5.
New Zealand: NZ High Commission, Tungi Arcade, Tautaàhau Road, Nuku'alofa, ph 21 122.
UK: British High Commission, Vuna Road, Nuku'alofa, ph 21 020/21.
USA: No resident representative. Refer to US Embassy in Fiji.
Canada: No resident representative. Refer to High Commission, Wellington, NZ.

Taiwan has an Embassy but France, Germany, Nauru, South Korea, Spain and Sweden are represented by Honorary Consuls.

Money

The basic unit is the Pa'anga (Tongan dollar) shown as T$ and equal to 100 seniti. Notes are in denominations of T$1, T$2. T$5, T$10, T$20, T$50. Coins are T$1, T$2, (pa'anga) and 1,2,5,10, 20 and 50 seniti.

Approximate rates of exchange, which should be used as a guide only are:

A$	=	T$0.94
Can$	=	T$0.90
NZ$	=	T$0.84
S$	=	T$0.88
UK£	=	T$1.88
US$	=	T$1.22

Duty Free shopping is available in Tonga and goods may be purchased in any currency. You must spend your Tongan money before you leave though, as it is not accepted anywhere else. In Tonga the exchange rate is controlled so you don't really know what your value for money is. Major credit cards are accepted in superior accommodation and by tour operators. Overseas currency can be exchanged at the Bank of Tonga.

Communications

The Post Office is located in Taufaànau Road, and is open Mon-Fri 8.20am-4pm. Visitors must collect their mail from the post office. Locals have their mail delivered to the nearest corner shop and they must go there to collect it.

IDD service is available and the country code is 676.

Telex, fax and cables can be booked through Cable and Wireless. Many hotels have telecommunication facilities.

There are two weekly papers, *Tonga Chronicle* and *Times of Tonga,* in Tongan and English, but there is no international news. The Embassies usually have current news.

Radio A32 broadcasts in Tongan and English. A small privately owned cable TV operation exists in Nuku'alofa.

Tax

A government tax of 5% applies to all goods and services and a room tax of 2.5% is also applicable. This means that there is a 7.5% tax on all accommodation.

Miscellaneous

Time

Local time is GMT + 13.

Business Hours

Main stores	Mon-Fri	8.00am-5.00pm,
	Sat	8.00am-12noon.
Banks -	Mon-Fri	9.30am-3.30pm,
	Sat	9.30am-11.00am.
Government Offices -		
	Mon-Fri	8.30am-4.30pm.
Post Office	Mon-Fri	8.30am-4.30pm.
Private Business -		
	Mon-Fri	9.00am-5.00pm.

Electricity

Local supply is 240 volts AC50. An adaptor may be necessary for power points.

Tipping

Tipping is not expected or encouraged in Tonga.

Dress

Casual attire is recommended for most occasions. Men are required to keep their torso covered, so T-shirts are okay, but no bare chests. The Police are very strict and you will be sent to get a shirt if you are not wearing one.

Women must not show their midriff. In the outer islands they are more sensitive about this.

Bathing suits, shorts and bikinis are fine for the beach or pool but not to be worn in other public places.

Sunday

On Sunday nothing happens. It is the Lord's Day. You are expected to eat, go to church and sleep. You cannot swim or play sport, and no shops are open.

The restaurants in the hotels are open, and the only service provided is transport organised by hotels to take visitors away from Tongatapu.

Emergency Number

Dial 911 for police, fire and hospital.

Medical

The Government provides comprehensive medical and dental care for residents and visitors. There are modern hospitals in Nuku'alofa, Ha'apai and Vava'u. There are also dispensaries, chemists and pharmacies. Private medical practitioners are also available for visitors.

Insurance

It is advisable to take out full insurance.

Water

All under water supplies are chlorinated.

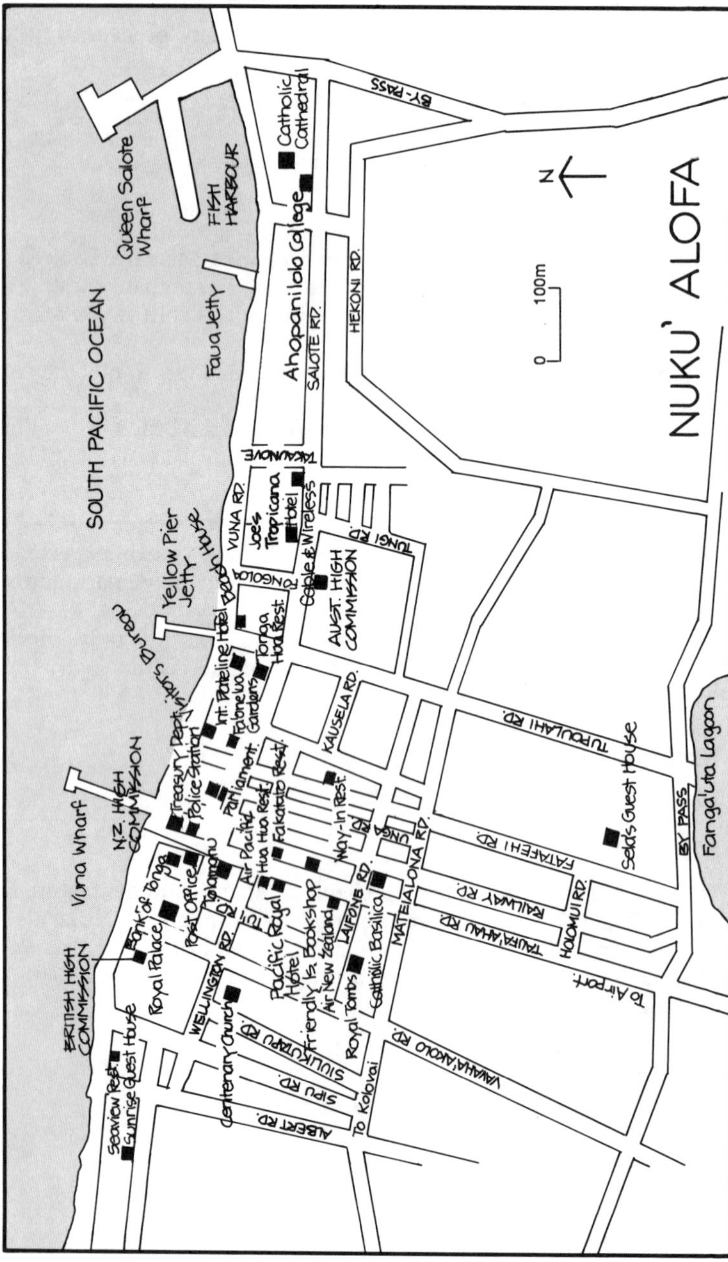
NUKU' ALOFA
SOUTH PACIFIC OCEAN
Queen Salote Wharf
FISH HARBOUR
Faua Jetty
Yellow Pier Jetty
Beach House
Visitor's Bureau
Vuna Wharf
N.Z. HIGH COMMISSION
BRITISH HIGH COMMISSION
Seaview Rest.
Sunrise Guest House
Royal Palace
Bank of Tonga
Post Office
Treasury Dept.
Police Station
Int. Dateline Hotel
Parliament
Air Pacific
Hua Hua Rest.
Fakalato Rest.
Tonga Hua Rest.
Way-In Rest.
Pacific Royal Hotel
Friendly Is. Bookshop
Air New Zealand
Royal Tombs
Catholic Basilica
Centenary Church
Joe's Tropicana Hotel
Cable & Wireless
AUST. HIGH COMMISSION
Catholic Cathedral
Ahopanilolo College
Sela's Guest House
Fanga'uta Lagoon
VUNA RD.
TAKAUNOVE
SALOTE RD.
HEKONI RD.
BY-PASS
BY PASS
TUNGI RD.
FONGOLOA
KAUSELA RD.
TUPOULAHI RD.
UNGA RD.
MATEIALONA RD.
FATAFEHI RD.
RAILWAY RD.
HOLOMUI RD.
TAUFA'AHAU RD.
LAIFONE RD.
WELLINGTON RD.
SIPU RD.
ALBERT RD.
To Airport
To Kolovai
N
0 100m

Travel Information

How to get there

By Air

Air Pacific, Royal Tongan Airlines, Air New Zealand and *Polynesian Airlines* provide regular services from Sydney, Auckland, Fiji, Western Samoa, Los Angeles and Hawaii.

Samoan Air links Vava'u and Tonga with Western Samoa via Pago Pago.

The main airport is 45 minutes from the centre of Nuku'alofa. Most hotels arrange for their guests to be met at the airport. There is also an international airport at Vava'u.

By Sea

Most cruise ships include Tonga in their South Pacific itineraries. They either dock at Queen Salote Wharf in Nuku'alofa or the Halaevalu Wharf on Vava'u.

There is an ever increasing number of blue-water cruising yachts, and the Tongan Visitors Bureau produces a *Yacht Arrival Information* pamphlet.

Tourist Information

Tonga Visitors Bureau, Vuna Road, PO Box 37, Nuku'alofa, ph 21 733.

Vava'u Office - PO Box 18, Neiafu, Vava'u.

Accommodation

Nuku'Alofa

First Class

International Dateline, Nuku'alofa, 10 minutes walk from town. 76 rooms with A/C, private facilities, tea and coffee making, phone, music, fridge, views of harbour. Pool, cocktail bar, restaurant, floor-shows, local cultural groups, shop, pool, lift, laundry/dry cleaning, tour desk. Happy Hour Fridays. 2 conference rooms for 70-100 people, baby sitting. Credit cards, American Express, Diners Club, Visa and Mastercard. Price A$73 (US$51) first night, A$55(US$39) extra nights + 7.5% tax.

Standard

Hotel Pacific Royal in heart of Nuku'alofa, 20 minute drive from airport. 60 rooms with A/C, shower, tea and coffee making, phone, fridge.

Restaurant, bar, pool, laundry, tour desk. Price twin share A$75 (US$53) 1st night A$57 (US$40) extra nights + 7.5% tax.

Budget
Hotel Nuku'alofa, in the heart of town close to Palace and markets, handicraft shops and waterfront. 10 rooms with A/C, shower, tea and coffee making, phone. Restaurant, bar, laundry, tour desk. Price A$52 (US$36) 1st night twin share, A$34 (US$24) extra nights + 7.5% tax.

Tongatapu

First Class
Royal Sunset Island Resort on Atata Island, 10km, or an hour by boat, from Nuku'alofa. 26 beach bungalows with separate bedrooms, lounge, 2 single beds, fans, tea and coffee making, private facilities, snack making, kitchenette, sink, fridge. Pool, library, entertainment, water sports, scuba diving, children's facilities, tennis. Price A$112 (US$78) 1st night A$85 (60) extra nights + 7.5% tax.
Fafa Island Resort, 7km, or 30 minutes by boat, from Nuku'alofa. 14 rooms with fan, shower. Restaurant, bar, library, entertainment, shop, tour desk, laundry, windsurfing, snorkelling. Free twice daily boat service. Price 1st night A$87 (US$61), extra nights A$41 (US$28) + 7.5% tax.

Standard
Ha'atafu Beach Resort, 21km from Nuku'alofa on west peninsula of Tongatapu. 6 rooms. Restaurant, bar, snorkelling equipment. Perfect for surfers. Price, breakfast and dinner included, 1st night A$94 (US$66), extra night A$60 (US$42) + 7.5% tax.

Budget
Angeles Guest House, ph 23 930 - 8 rooms. Tea/coffee making, fridge, cooking facilities, hot/cold water, shower. Price single T$20 (US$14), double T$30 (US$21), triple T$35 (US$25) triple + 7.5% tax.
Fasimoe Afi Guest House, ph 22 289. 5 rooms. Bed and breakfast, hot/cold water, restaurant. Price single T$15 (US$11), double T$30 (US$21) + 7.5% tax.
Good Samaritan Inn, ph 41 022. 15 rooms. Bed and breakfast, hot/cold water, shower, restaurant/bar, beach-front. Price single T$30-40 (US$21-28), double T$50-70 (US$35-49), dorm T$10 (US$7) + 7.5% tax.

Vava'u

Moderate
Tongan Beach Resort, on the Isle of Vava'u on a beautiful beach. 12 double rooms with ocean views, fan, shower, tea and coffee making,

fridge. Restaurant, bar, pool, entertainment, library, shop, laundry, tour desk, cultural tours, windsurfing, snorkelling, scuba diving. Mostly for lovers of water sports. Price 1st night A$83 (US$58), extra night A$55 (US$39) + 7.5% tax.

Standard
Paradise Intercontinental Hotel, 1.5km from main town of Neiafu overlooking part of Refuge Harbour. 45 rooms with A/C, bath, shower, tea and coffee making. Restaurant, bar, entertainment, pool, library, shop, laundry, tour desk, cultural talks, windsurfing, snorkelling, scuba diving. Price A$44 (US$31) per night + 7.5% tax.

Budget
Hamana Court House, ph 70 507. 6 rooms with Tea/coffee making, fridge, cooking facilities, shower. Price single T$15-25 (US$10.50-17.50), double T$22-35 (US$15-25).
Hill Top Guest House, ph 70 209. 13 rooms with tea/coffee making, fridge, cooking facilities, shower. Price single T$20 (US$14), double T$25 (US$17.50) + 7.5% tax.
Vava'u Guest House, ph 70 300. 8 rooms with cooking facilities, fan, shower. Restaurant. Price from single T$9 (US$6), double T$14 (US$10) + 7.5% tax.

Haàpai

A 35 minute flight from Tongatapu are a group of atolls. There are few places to stay or tourist facilities.

Moderate
Sandy Beach Resort, ph 60 200. 12 rooms with A/C, tea/coffee making, hot/cold water, shower, fan, cooking facilities. Restaurant, pool, snorkelling equipment. Price T$130 (US$91) per room per night + 7.5% tax.

Standard
Niu'akalo Beach Hotel, a few minutes from the village of Panh'ai on Ha'apai's main island of Lifuka. 16 simple beach-front rooms with private facilities. Restaurant, bar, entertainment, laundry, tour desk, cultural activities, snorkelling. Price A$24 (US$17) per night.

Budget
Captain Cook Resort, ph 60 014. 4 rooms with cooking facilities, shower. Beach-front, snorkelling equipment. Price single T$8 (US$6), double T$12 (US$8) + 7.5% tax.
Fonongava'inga Guest House, ph 60 038. 9 rooms. Fridge, cooking facilities, shower, hot/cold water. Price single T$8 (US$6), double T$15 (US$10.50) + 7.5% tax.

Èua

Haukinima Guest House, ph 50 088. 8 rooms, cooking facilities, shower. Price single T$15 (US$10.50), double T$20 (US$14) + 7.5% tax.

Niuatoputapu

Niuatoputapu Guest House. 5 rooms, cooking facilities, shower. Price single T$18 (US$12.60), double T$22 (US$15) + 7.5% tax.

Local Transport

Air

Royal Tongan Airlines has many daily flights connecting Tongatapu with the outer islands.

Sea

Small craft roam the Pacific calling at many islands, and arrangements can be made to join these cruises through the Visitors Bureau. It is best to make enquiries as soon as possible after arriving in Tonga.

Sailing Safari

Set sail and discover over 50 isles with palms, clear water and fish on *Melinda* a 50ft (164m) yacht with toilet, shower, hot and cold water. It has skipper and hostess, accommodation for 2 crew and a maximum of 6 guests. For more information, ph 21 733.

Land

On Tongatapu, Èua and Vava'u, land transport varies from air-conditioned buses and taxis, to motorcycles, bicycles and horses. There are also ferries to outer islands.

Car Hire

Avis and Budget have cars to rent on Tongatapu at competitive rates.

Driving is on the **left**, and the speed limit is 45kph in town and 65kph in the country.

Visitors must be over 18 years of age and hold a current driving licence which they must take to the Central Police Station together with their passport, and for T$10 (US$7) can have a temporary Tongan driving licence.

Eating Out

The hotels have dining rooms, and there is usually a special night every week when a Tongan feast is served followed by a floor show.

There are a few small restaurants specialising in French, German, Taiwanese, Japanese, Indian, Italian, Korean and local cuisine. The Tongan National Centre is recommended.

Shopping

There is a large duty free shop in the Dateline Hotel that stocks almost anything you desire. There is another in the main street that specialises in electronic equipment. When cruise ships dock the duty free store at Queen Salote Wharf opens. There is another duty free at Fuaàmotu Airport, and duty free centres in Neiafu on Vava'u.

Tonga has always been noted for its high quality handicrafts, and most visitors buy a basket or hat. There are handicraft shops in hotels and all over the islands. The markets have good buys. There are supermarkets, bakeries, butchers and fruit and vegetable shops for those with self catering facilities.

Sightseeing

Nuku'alofa

The main points of interest in the town can be seen on a walking tour.

Tuivakano Residence, Salote Road, is on the estate of the Honourable Tuivakano and includes the village of Nukunuku. He was Tonga's oldest serving nobleman and sat in parliament for many years.

The **Royal Palace and Chapel** is a Victorian white-framed building that is surrounded by massive Norfolk pines, and dominates the waterfront. The building was prefabricated in New Zealand and erected in 1867. Apart from the addition of a second storey verandah when the Chapel was built in 1882, it remains the same.

King George Tupou II (1893), Queen Salote Tupou (1918) and King Taufaàhau Tupou IV (1967) were all crowned in the Chapel. King George Tupou I was the last monarch of the Tui Kanokupolu line to be crowned under the Koka Tree in Hihifo. The coronation chair contains a piece of wood from that historic tree.

Visitors are not allowed in the Palace grounds. The small octagonal building named 'Palesi' in the corner of the gardens was for many years a rest house for chiefs who were guests of royalty.

Sia-Ko-Veiongo, Salote Road, is an area to the west of the Palace and is a royal estate. There is an old home, on Mt Zion (also known as Chapel Hill or Zion Hill), overlooking the Palace gardens. The hill was the site of the 18th century fortress of Aleamotuà when he was Tui Kanokupolu. In 1830 the first missionary chapel was built here, and a large Wesleyan church was built on the site in 1865 under the patronage of King George Tupou I. The former chapel was moved 6.5km west to the Siaàtoutai Theological College property.

On the crest of the hill is the neglected grave of Captain Croker of the British sloop HMS *Favourite* who was killed at sea, June 24 1840, when he and his men attacked the fortress.

Ahomeè's Residence, Taufaàhau Road is the home of Tongan noble Honourable Ahomeè, whose chiefly ancestor, Tevita Ahomeè, offered up the first prayer before a congregation of 5000 gathered to celebrate Emancipation Day, June 4 1862, following the promulgation of the Code of 1862. The Code formed the basis for the present constitution.

Nuikasa, Vuna Road, was the home of Setaleki Mumui, a son of the Tui Kanokupolu, Tupou Malohi. During the 1800s, the nobleman sailed to Britain on several occasions where he stayed with friends in Newcastle. After his final trip back to Tonga, Mumui built this house on royal land and named it 'Niukasa' which is a direct Tonganisation of his favourite city, Newcastle. It has been a private residence since the death of the last of Mumuis' heirs in 1960.

The **British High Commissioner's Residence**, Vuna Road, is situated on the left of the Palace, facing the sea. The house was originally owned by Motekial Halaholo and his wife Sisilia Tupou. It was given to the government in exchange for a waterfront lot at Kolomotuà about the turn of the century. In 1901 it was leased to the British Government for the use of its senior representative. Set in spacious grounds, overlooking the waterfront, its flag-pole is surrounded by four cannons from the ill fated *Port au Prince* wrecked off Haàpai in 1806.

Malaeàloa, the cemetery on Vuna Road, derived its name from *Malaè*, meaning field, and *loa*, meaning difficulty or tragedy. The area is fenced with toa (casuarina) trees, and the site was especially selected as a chiefly burial ground.

The wife of King George Tupou l, Queen Lupe Pauu, (Charlotte) and Queen Takipois,. second wife of King George II are buried here. The first person to be buried in this cemetery was Tui Kanokupolu Mumui.

Ovalau, Vuna Road, is a weatherboard residence that was built in Levuka, the old capital of Fiji, but shipped to Tonga and re-erected on the present site in the early 1950s. It was occupied by the manager of the old trading company, Morris Hedstrom, until the manager moved to new quarters in Sopu. The building was leased to the New Zealand Government as a residence for High Commission senior staff.

Faiàkoka, Vuna Road, was apparently first occupied by the Veéhala

A Polynesian lass

Accommodation at Bora Bora

Catholic Cathedral, Nuku'alofa, Tonga

One way to get around Viti Levu, Fiji

Royal Palace, Nukuàlofa

Wharf scene, Pangai, Haàpai group

family. Later it was home to a British Consular representative. More recently it became government quarters. The late Queen Salote lived in this house during the Royal Visit of HM Queen Elizabeth II so that the Queen and Prince Philip could stay in the Palace.

In 1976 it was leased to the New Zealand Government as a residence for its High Commissioner. It was in a very neglected state but has now been restored to its former glory.

The oldest part of **Cecil Cocker's Residence** in Wellington Road was built around 1880. The builder was the son of the first British Consul, Joshua Cocker, and the house was re-constructed by Joshua's son James, in 1925. His son, Cecil Cocker, a senior civil servant, now lives here with his family.

Opposite the Cocker house, slightly to the west is **Faletuuloto**, the residence of the Chief Tuitavake.

The **President's House, Free Wesleyan Church of Tonga**, in Wellington Road, is believed to have been built about 1871 for the Rev. Shirley Baker. It is an impressive mansion, and has been the home of successive Presidents of the Wesleyan Church in Tonga. It is best viewed from the grounds of the adjoining cemetery church.

The **Cemetery Church** in Wellington Road, took three years to complete and was opened by Queen Salote in 1952. It measures 56.8m by 21.3m and seats over 2000.

Otualea, Wellington Road, was originally part of the Palace grounds, and was known as *Kai Pongipongi* (breakfast) because this was where the people who worked and lived in the Palace had their meals.

The present name of the house comes from the beach of Otualea in Vava'u. It was originally a government house which was given to Siaosa Tukuàho, an uncle of Queen Salote, in an exchange of properties. The reason for the exchange, was that the expatriate officials living there complained about the many neighbouring church bells ringing in the early hours of the morning.

The house was extensively rebuilt in 1946 to accommodate Queen Salote's relatives coming to Nuku'alofa for the double wedding of her sons, Prince Tungi (now King) and Prince Fatafehi Tuipelehake (later Prime Minister).

The **Old Free Wesleyan Church** is a classic example of early Tongan church architecture. It was built in 1888 and held 800 worshippers. It was originally erected on the site of the present Cemetery Church but was moved in 1949.

Malaékula. This area was named after the Katoanga Kula Festival organised by HM King George Tupou I, and held in 1885. The Tongan National Anthem *E Otua Mafimafi* (God Almighty) was first performed here during the festival.

These large park-like grounds are sacred to all Tongans as the burial ground for royalty since 1893. At one time, the grounds around the royal tombs were used as a golf course. Cows grazing is now a more usual sight.

Queen Salote College, Mateialona Road. Between 1975-79 large sums of money were raised to celebrate the Golden Jubilee of the Wesleyan Church in Tonga (1876). These funds provided for the building of five new churches. King George Tupou I requested the fund to build a ladies' college to be known as Queen Charlotte's College, after his wife. The reason is not clear but it was not until 1923 that a separate Ladies' College was established from the nucleus of the girl's section of Tupou College and named Queen Salote College.

Queen Salote Memorial Hall, Mateialona Road. In 1966 as a mark of love and respect, the people of Tonga raised funds to build a memorial hall to Queen Salote on government ground, adjacent to Tonga High School. A design was selected and work commenced but someone in authority absconded with the funds so the hall could not be completed.

The **Anglican Church** was founded in 1900 by Shirley Baker after he had been dismissed from the Wesleyan Church and later the Free Church of Tonga. The Anglican church was established under licence from Bishop Willis of Dunedin, New Zealand. The present church was completed, 1929-30, as a memorial to Dr Alfred Willis DD who was assistant Bishop of Tonga 1902-20.

Takamahu Market, Salote Road, is built on the site of the Queen Victoria Hall, a social centre in Nuku'alofa for many years. Open every day except Sunday it has a number of handicraft and souvenir stalls as well as cheap fruit and vegetables.

Fatai, Vuna Road, is the sea-front residence of Prince Tuipelehake, who became Prime Minister of Tonga. The house is on land originally owned by his grandparents. During her last illness, the late Queen Salote lived in Fatai as she could no longer manage the stairs in the Palace.

Vuna Market, Vuna Road. Originally the customs house stood on this site opposite the Treasury. The market was constructed in 1955 for the sale of fruit, vegetables and meat, and is adjacent to the roadside fish market. A sign is erected outside the market to indicate the type of meat available each day.

Vuna Wharf was constructed 1906, enlarged in 1933, and further improved since then. It served as an arrival point for visitors over many years but there was a need for a modern wharf to be built. An earthquake in 1977 so damaged Vuna wharf that it is unsafe. The Queen Salote Wharf was built in 1965 at Maufanga.

St Mary's Cathedral, Vuna Road. Built in classic Tongan style with a high roof and comparatively short walls, this Catholic Cathedral is the most beautiful building in Nuku'alofa. Financed and built by the Catholics on the island, it is situated opposite Queen Salote Wharf and is well worth a visit.

Langa Fonua, Taufaàhau Road. William (Viliami) Cocker built this house for his five daughters who lived in New Zealand and visited Nuku'alofa in winter. It is now the headquarters of Langa Fonua, a woman's cooperative movement, founded in 1953 by Queen Salote. Its aims were to improve living conditions and to foster handicrafts. The late Queen was President until her death, and the current president is Queen Mataàho. The association was established and is still operated by women.

Basilica of St Anthony of Padua, Laifone Road, was the first Basilica in the South Pacific. This magnificent building was opened on January 8 1980 by King Taufaàhau Tupou IV. The two storey building is 36m in diameter and 29m high. It was built by local people, including the young, without the use of cranes. Beneath the Basilica is a well-equipped community centre and a Japanese tea-room open to the public.

Further Afield

The **Tongan National Centre** is on the main road to the airport, 3km from Nuku'alofa. The centre is set out like a Tongan village. It has an amphitheatre, education centre, exhibition centre and *fales* (native houses) where visitors can watch tapa and canoe making, wood carving, basket and mat making. The centre features kava ceremonies and umu feasts (earth oven), and has a restaurant with views of the lagoon, a traditional fishing ground. It also houses the museum and Tongan art exhibits.

Blow Holes. On the coast at Houma, 14.5km from Nuku'alofa, there are a series of holes in the coral reef, through which the sea water spurts up to 18m in the air. The area is locally known as *Mapu à Vaea* (the Chief's whistle) because of the sound made by the gushing water.

If sailing on that side of the island, there is a spectacular view of the spurting water. If walking near the blow holes, wear sturdy shoes as the coral cuts and can lead to infection. Be very careful as several tourists have been washed off the rocks and have drowned. It is impossible to climb back onto the rocks.

Flying Foxes. At Kolovai, 18km from Nuku'alofa, you will see trees literally filled with flying foxes, some of which have a wing span of 1m.

Haàmonga Trilithon. Nuku'alofa has been the seat of government and the royal family for over a century, but legend records that the first Tongan kings ruled from the eastern village of Niutoua, where the monumental Haàmonga (trilithon) stone stands. The trilithon consists of two large vertical stones with a third horizontal connecting stone morticed into the tops of the upright pillars.

The uprights are about 5m high, 4.23m wide and 1.4m thick. The lintel is 5.8m long, 1.4m wide and 0.61m thick. The visible portions of the uprights are estimated to weigh between 30-40 tonnes each.

The eleventh Tui Tonga, Tuitatui, built the trilithon about 1200AD.

Lapaha, the northern district of Muà, is 9km from Nuku'alofa on the shores of a lagoon. Because it was the centre of Tongan culture for at least six centuries it has the richest archaeological monuments in the Kingdom.

Ten kilometres from Ha'amonga, are the **Terraced Tombs** or *langi*. The first was built around 1200AD for an ancient dynasty and was formed by quadrilateral mounds faced by huge blocks of coral rock rising in terraces to heights of 4m.

Captain Cook's Landing Site. Near Mu'a stands the Ovava tree, under which Cook is alleged to have rested after anchoring the *Endeavour* just off-shore in the lagoon.

Caves. 20km from town, on the coast, are impressive underground stalactite and stalagmite caves of unknown length through which flows a deep underground river. A local guide and a strong torch are highly recommended.

Vava'u

The Visitors Bureau has a book crammed with information on places you should see and things to do in this interesting harbour town with a population of 5000. Here are some not to be missed.

Along Fatafehi Road, past the Vava'u Club and the European cemetery, is the **Fangatongo Royal Residence**. There is a beautiful view of the Port-Of-Refuge Harbour and part of the archipelago.

A steep path past St Peter Chanel Chapel (named after a French priest who visited Vava'u in 1837 and was martyred in the Wallis Islands) leads to the summit of **Mt Talau** from which there are glorious views of the town, harbour and other islands. There is a walking tour available to Mt Talau.

Sailoame Market has a cornucopia of tropical fruit and delicacies. Try *limu fuofua*, made from tasty seaweed, and *ifi*, roasted Tahitian chestnuts.

Tours

Keitahi and Ene'io Beach Tour

These are two beautiful beaches on the main island. Visitors are driven across the island from Neiafu through villages and plantations to swim and enjoy Tongan hospitality. Picnics or feasting can be arranged.

Panoramic Coastal Drive

A scenic drive around the west coast of Vava'u stopping at Feletoa, the scene of a battle in 1808. The tour then proceeds to Tefisi and Longomapu villages to enjoy the view of Refuge Harbour and numerous islands.

Tu'anuku Lake Tour

Tu'amiku is a freshwater lake about 14.5km from Neiafu. Visitors can watch villagers call and catch by hand *lapila*, or King fish, and can sample pan-fried fresh fish beside the lake.

Swallows Cave Tour

Boats wend their way down Refuge Harbour to the Swallows Cave on the island of Kapa. This multi-coloured chamber is a sanctuary for thousands of swallows in the autumn, and can be entered by boat.

Mariner's Cave Diving Tour

The drowned grotto on the island of Nuapaapu gave refuge to a young chief and his beloved in ancient times. Boats wait at the entrance of the cave while guides take divers through the heart shaped entrance into the mystical blue-lit cavern. Snorkels and flippers are required.

Nuku Island Tour

Spend the day on a perfect castaway island. Swim, snorkel and collect shells on this magnificent beach. A barbecue lunch or picnic is provided.

Haàpai

The island is flat like Tongatapu, but has a far fresher feel. The houses are better kept and the people friendlier.

Pangai is the main town and houses the local general and merchant store, police station, a variety of schools, the Tongan Church, Catholic Church and hospital.

The Pangai shoreline has two jetties and there are many small fishing vessels. It does not boast 'organised' fishing trips but if you wish to take one, ask at the local store or restaurant. There is a local bus that goes up and down the island from the transmission station at one end, to the causeway at the other. The causeway was built by the Kiwi army to link Foa with Haàpai.

The present King of Tonga was born in Pangai in the house known as the **King's Residence**. Each Christmas the royal family retire to Haàpai to celebrate the feast and enjoy their holidays. The house is typically European, constructed of wood with enclosed verandahs. The gardens extend to the shore. It is, without doubt, the best house on the island.

From Pangai at night, you can see on one of the nearby islands, the molten lava of a **live volcano**. Its ever changing red and purple colours are in stark contrast to the dark night.

Life on Haàpai is extremely tranquil. A few cars, children laughing in school, the snorting of pigs, the chatter in the local market, the ringing of church bells daily and the shouting of rugby players are the only sounds of Haàpai.

Villagers are poor but cheerful. On the way out of Pangai on the right hand side of the road, in a cemetery Tongan-style appears a 'Churchillesque' type statue. It is the tomb of Shirley Baker, the controversial protestant minister who changed his religion three times, but was instrumental in the fortunes of the present royal dynasty in the 19th century.

Felemea is a beautiful village on the island of Uiha. Visitors can participate in all aspects of village life from kava ceremonies, feasting and dancing to hunting *feke* (octopus) with village fishermen in outrigger canoes.

With advice from the people at your guest house, you can persuade one of the local fisherman to organise a **swimming and snorkelling** outing. Negotiate the deal with the guest house owner. You will have a great time and probably go to a nearby island about 40 minutes away. Here, protected by reefs, you can swim and snorkel in safety.

Foa Island

This is another tree-lined paradise. It has brilliant sandy beaches lapped by aqua coloured water. All the islands are surrounded by coral reefs. Foa is adjacent to another island which can be reached by good swimmers. There is no rip but you must wear shoes as the coral can easily cut your feet and cause infection.

Transport: get the bus to the causeway then settle down for an hour's tramp to the beach. It's worth it.

Èua Island

An ideal retreat for hikers, adventurers and naturalists. Ornithologists will appreciate the bird life.

On the southern end of the island is **Matalanga-'a-Maui**, a high, natural stone bridge through which sea-water churns. Less than a kilometre away are the 100m sheer cliffs of **Lakufa'anga**, at the base of which turtles can usually be seen playing in the sea. Natural forests, in which parrots chatter and scream, add to the enjoyment of the excursion.

Hafu Pool. The clear Heike stream rushes down from the hills into the beautiful natural **Hafu Pool** which is enhanced by an abundance of hibiscus and other tropical plants.

Transport on Èua is by horse or on foot but visitors can hire a Land Rover or lorry.

Package Deals

There are many package deals to Tonga. The most popular are those that include another island. Samoa is one suggestion and Fiji the other. It is possible to have a round trip Pacific Island package which will include New Caledonia, Vanuatu, Fiji and Tonga. Many packages at reasonable prices, include Samoa, Tonga and the Cook islands.

Package deals include air fares, accommodation and transfers. Check with your travel agent for the best bargain.

Activities, Sport and Recreation

Popular sports include rugby, soccer, boxing, cricket, volleyball and basketball. Indigenous games are still played especially *hiko* which involves expert juggling.

Diving and Reef Viewing

The coral reefs in Tonga are virtually untouched. The rare and much sought-after black coral is found in abundance, and caves and sunken ships await the adventurous diver.

There are five marine reserves and three island parks off Tongatapu that are government protected.

Dolphin Pacific Diving. Rates: 2 tank boat dive T$88C (US$62), certified scuba diving instructors for all level of courses. Equipment available for hire. Underwater video and photography services available. Average visibility 100 ft.(328m). Average depth 50ft.(164m). Type of diving: walls, hard and soft corals, caverns and wrecks. PO Box 104, Neiafu, Vava'u, ph (676) 70 380.

Beluga Diving. 9m inflatable boat brings you to the coral reefs. Rates: 2 dives close by T$88 (US$62), 2 dives further afield T$99 (US69), 4 Dives include full equipment and guide. Full courses available. PO Box 2660, Nuku'alofa, ph/fax (676) 23 576.

Deep Sea Fishing

Charter boats are available. MV *Zeus* twin engined live-aboard gameboat. She is aluminium, fully rigged for all types of sport and fully crewed and operated by experienced gameboat and fishing couple. Available for full and half day charters. Rates: Full day T$700 (US$490), half day T$350 (US$245) plus T$65 (US$46) a day per person on extended charters. All rates + 5% tax. Royal Sunset Island Resort, PO Box 960, Nuku'alofa, ph/fax (676) 21 254.

Summer Breeze is a sailing yacht fully equipped for ocean passages. 2 double berths, 2 single, full galley, freezer, toilet, hot shower, GPS navigation system. Available for charter daily to the islands or for extended cruising. Rates: T$660 (US$462) per day/night. Up to 5 guests. Includes all food, linen, captain and crew + 5% tax. Daily charter rates on application. Reservations as above, PO Box 960, Nuku'alofa, ph/fax (676) 21 254.

Swimming

There are many, many beaches to choose from on all the islands, and most are protected by the coral reef.

Horse Riding

Hotels and tour operators can make arrangements. Most horses do not have saddles and are not schooled. Previous riding experience is highly desirable.

Tour Operators

Orient Pacific, ph 132 747 - all destinations and local.
Teta Tours, PO Box 215, Main Road, Nuku'alofa, ph 23 690, fax 23 238.

Schoolboys, St. Joseph's College, Pangai, Haàpai Islands

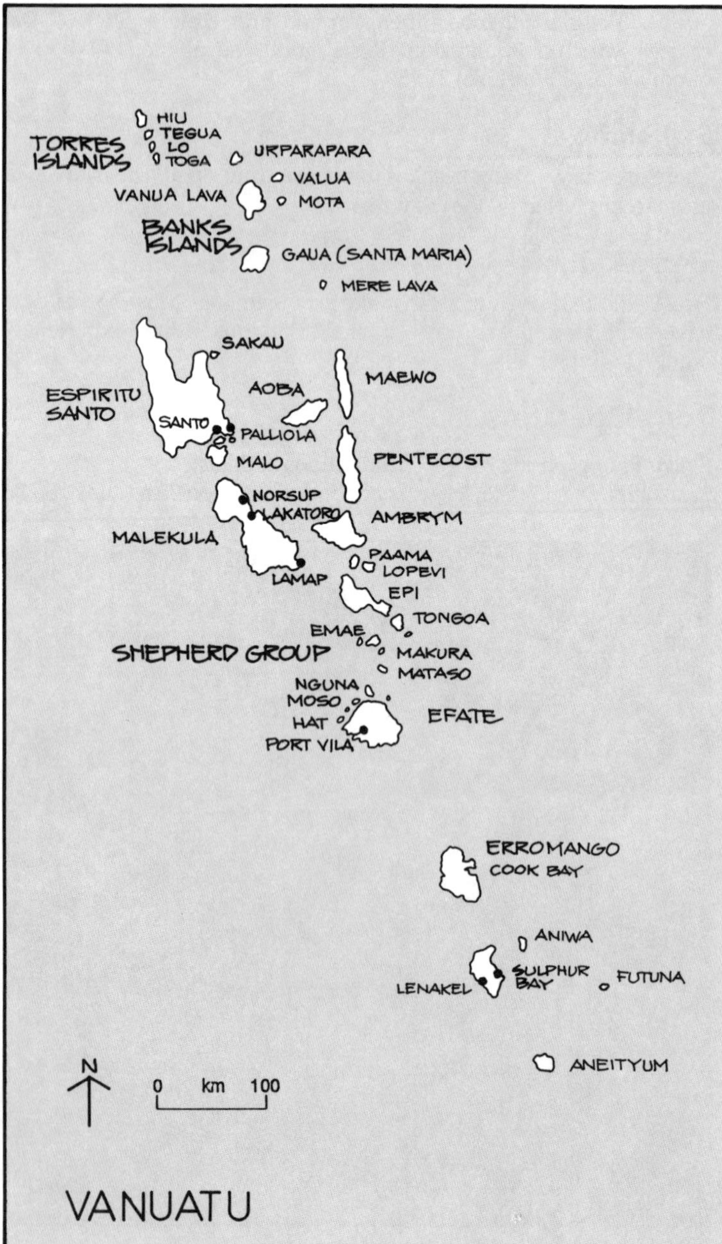
HIU
TEGUA
TORRES ISLANDS
LO
TOGA
URPARAPARA
VALUA
VANUA LAVA
MOTA
BANKS ISLANDS
GAUA (SANTA MARIA)
MERE LAVA
SAKAU
MAEWO
AOBA
ESPIRITU SANTO
SANTO
PALLIOLA
MALO
PENTECOST
NORSUP
LAKATORO
AMBRYM
MALEKULA
PAAMA
LOPEVI
LAMAP
EPI
TONGOA
EMAE
SHEPHERD GROUP
MAKURA
MATASO
NGUNA
MOSO
HAT
EFATE
PORT VILA
ERROMANGO
COOK BAY
ANIWA
SULPHUR BAY
LENAKEL
FUTUNA
ANEITYUM
N
0 km 100
VANUATU

REPUBLIC OF VANUATU

Vanuatu, which means 'Land Eternal', consists of a group of 80 islands north-east of New Caledonia. It covers an area of 14,760 sq km, and was formerly known as the New Hebrides. The main islands are: Espiritu Santo (the largest), Efate where the capital Port Vila is situated, Tanna, Malakula, Ambrym, Pentecost, Epi, Erromango, Anatom, Aoba, and the smallest Aniwa.

Most of the islands have narrow bands of cultivated land around the coast with dense rainforests and mountainous interiors. Some are raised coral islands with wide beaches and deep harbours. There are five active volcanos in the group.

Vanuatu's exports are cocoa, coffee and beef. The economy depends on tourism, fishing and manganese mining.

Once a 'condominium' administered by France and Britain, it is now governed by its own indigenous people.

History

It is thought that the islands have been inhabited for 5000 years. The Ni Vanuatu, predominantly Melanesian, have populated these islands for centuries. Open warfare rarely existed but sporadic killing, wife stealing and cannibalism were common. Today there are more than 105 distinctly different cultures and languages still existing in these islands.

In May 1606, Portuguese navigator Pedro Fernandez de Quiros landed at Big Bay on Espiritu Santo thinking it was Terra Australis Incognita (Australia). This aroused the interest of the Spanish who declared the country theirs but did nothing to colonise it. In 1786 Louis Antoine de Bougainville sailed through and six years later Captain James Cook discovered the full extent of the islands and named them the New Hebrides.

Australian sandalwood traders soon followed, introducing ravaging diseases, which rapidly decimated the local population. They were a lawless breed and would not hesitate to kill any native who stood in their way. When the price of sandalwood dropped, they turned their attention to sea cucumbers, pearls, turtle shell and whales.

The missionaries decided Vanuatu should be Christianised but the first two emissaries were killed. More were killed during the next 25 years so Vanuatu, along with Fiji, became known as the Cannibal Islands.

Christianity won through but not the way the missionaries

intended. In 1860 the Australian sugar industry based in Queensland needed cheap labour. They recruited workers from Vanuatu by indentured contracts or slavery. Many died on the ships taking them to their new home or while working on the cane fields. Some survived and a few remained in Queensland as free men. Those who returned to Vanuatu, introduced changes in their culture and a new language. Pidgin English was the only form of communication with their overseers. It became known as 'bislama', now the official language of Vanuatu.

By the late 1800s France had decided it wanted Vanuatu as a colony. Britain had little interest in the land but Australian traders did. The Protestant missionaries hated French Catholicism and lobbied the British Government to annex the islands.

In April 1904, a politically expedient but ridiculous compromise was reached: both governments were to administer the islands. It satisfied nobody, least of all the indigenous people.

During World War II, the Americans came. They made a lasting impression on the people, precipitating the development of cargo cults, like the one started by John Frumms of Tanna. After the war, villages formed co-operatives forcing the Europeans to raise cattle in order to make money. This necessitated the purchase of land from the owners, who thought they were only selling the rights of use. These events led the people to push for independence.

In 1978 they were given partial self-government. There were two political parties, the New Hebrides National Party supported by British interests, and the Union of New Hebrides Communities supported by France. Independence was delayed because the National Party changed its name to Vanua'aku Party (VP). The government of National Unity was formed in 1978 with Farther Gerard Leymang as chief minister and VP leader, and Father Walter Lini as deputy.

In 1980 a revolt by French settlers on the island of Espiritu Santo was put down by French, British and Papua New Guinean troops. Later that year independence was granted and the New Hebrides became the Republic of Vanuatu within the Commonwealth.

The first president was George Kalkoa who adopted the name Sokomanu. The first Prime Minister was Walter Lini. Lini pursued a left-of-centre, non-aligned foreign policy and supported the Kanak separatist movement in New Caledonia. This soured relations with France and provoked opposition within parliament. Despite VP retaining its majority in the 1987 general election, the opposition continued prompting Lini to expel from parliament his rival Barak Sope. Lini was then dismissed as PM and parliament was dissolved by President Sokomanu who appointed his nephew Sope as head of the interim government. However, the High Court ruled this inadmissible and security forces loyal to Lini arrested the president, Sope and the opposition leader Maxime Carlot and reinstated former health minister Fred Timakata. He was elected president in January 1989.

In 1991 the VP voted to replace Lini as its leader with Donald Kalpokas. In the December 1991 general election none of the parties won an overall majority. Finally it was agreed to form a coalition government under Maxime Carlot, on the understanding that Lini would not be a member of the government.

Since independence, Vanuatu has sought to promote greater cooperation among the states of the Pacific region. The aim is to preserve Melanesian cultural tradition and campaign for New Caledonia's independence.

Climate

Summer is from November-March with an average temperature of 28C; Winter is April-October and the average temperature is 23C.

Population

The total population is 159,000. The Melanesian inhabitants who were born in Vanuatu are called Ni Vanuatu. There are a number of Australians, New Zealanders, French, British and Chinese.

Religion

The majority of the people are Christians.

Iririki Island Resort, Vanuatu

Language

English and French are widely spoken, with Bislama being the official language. There are also 105 'mother tongues' in common use.

Here are a few words in bislama to show you how it sounds.

I or me .... Mi
My name .... Nem blong mi
Hullo.. Gudmoning or gudnaet
Goodbye.................................. Tata
How much is this? .... Wanem praes blong hem?
I don't understand.................. Mi no ave.

Public Holidays

January 1 .... New Years Day
March 5 .... National Chief's Day
March/April.............................. Good Friday/Easter Monday
May 1 .... Labour Day
July 30....................................... Independence Day
August 15................................. Assumption Day
October 5.................................. Constitution Day
November 29 .... Unity Day
December 25 .... Christmas Day
December 26 .... Boxing Day

Entry Regulations

A valid passport is necessary for all visitors. Nationals of Commonwealth countries, Belgium, Denmark, Eire, Fiji, France, Germany, Italy, Japan, Luxembourg, Netherlands, Norway, Philippines, South Korea, Switzerland and the USA do not require a visa.

Visas can only be obtained from The Immigration Department, Port Vila, Vanuatu.

Customs

The duty free allowance is 200 cigarettes or 250gm of tobacco or 50 cigars, 1.5 litres of spirits or 2 bottles of wine, quarter of a litre of toilet water, 10 centilitres of perfume plus 2,000 (about US$19) Vatu in unused goods.

Departure Tax

There is a tax of 1500 vatu (about US$14) per person except children under 2, payable in local currency.

Embassies

Australia: Aust High Commission, Melitco House, Port Vila, ph 22 777.
New Zealand: NZ High Commission, Prouds Building, Kumul Highway, Port Vila, ph 22 933.
US: No representative. Refer to US Embassy, Wellington, New Zealand, ph 64 (4) 722 068.
UK: British High Commission, Melitco House, Port Vila, ph 23 100.
Canada: Canadian High Commission in Australia ph (062) 73 3844, is accredited to Vanuatu.

Money

The local currency is the Vatu (VT), and 1 Vatu = 100 centimes.
Notes are in denominations of 5000, 1000, 500. 100. Coins are 1,2,5,10,20 and 50.

Major currencies are accepted in most places. The locals are so used to the many different exchange rates that they can accurately give change to any currency. As rates of exchange vary from day to day, check the up-to-date rate before changing money.

Approximate rates of exchange, which should be used as a guide only, are:

A$	=	VT84.73
Can$	=	VT81.48
NZ$	=	VT75.63
S$	=	VT97.32
UK£	=	VT169.60
US$	=	VT110.69

Major credit cards are widely accepted.

Communications

World-wide satellite communications are available from Vanuatu to anywhere in the world, 24 hours per day, seven days per week. The country code is 678.

There is a tri-lingual weekly newspaper called the *Vanuatu Weekly*. *What to do in Vanuatu*, a free tourist paper, is issued regularly and is widely available.

Miscellaneous

Time Zone

Local time is GMT + 11.

Business Hours

Small shops open early and close late.
Banks are open Mon-Fri 8.30am-3.00pm. Westpac at the airport is open for all flights.
Shops are open 7.30am-11.30am, 1.30pm-5.30pm. Some stay open until 7pm. All open Saturday morning, and some specialty and supermarkets open Sunday morning.

Electricity

Local supply is 220-240 volts AC. Take an adaptor as some plugs are French.

Tipping

Tipping and bargaining are against Melanesian custom.

Dress

Light and casual but not brief in public. Tropical clothes for evening wear, no ties.

Emergency Phone Numbers

Police........................22 222
Doctor........................22 826
Hospital....................22 100
Ambulance..............22 100
Dentist......................22 306
Fire............................22 333
Taxis..........................22 870.

Medical

Good hospitals exist in Port Vila and Luganville, Espiritu Santo. No vaccinations are required unless coming from an infected area. Anti-malarial tablets should be taken prior to departure if visiting the outer islands. There are no dangerous animals or insects.

Water

The urban water supply is safe to drink.

Insurance

It is recommended that all travellers have comprehensive insurance policies.

All the islands provide a haven for yachts. (opposite)

Travel Information

How to get there

By Air

International: *Air Vanuatu* from Australia and New Zealand; *Air Caledonie* from Noumea with connections from Australia, New Zealand, Fiji, Tahiti, Guam and Hong Kong; *Air Pacific* from Brisbane and Nadi with connections from New Zealand, Japan and USA; *Solomon Airlines* from Honiara, Port Moresby, Nadi, Auckland and Cairns.
Domestic: *Vanair* services all major islands in the country.
Airport: Bauerfield, only 10 minutes from Port Vila.

By Sea

Port Vila is a popular port of call for many cruise ships.

Tourist Information

The National Tourism Office, PO Box 209, Port Vila, ph (678) 22 685-22 515-22 813.

Accommodation

Efate

De Luxe

Royal Palms Resort and Casino, PO Box 215, Port Vila, ph 22 040, Fax 23 340. Situated at Tassiriki Park. 144 A/C rooms, most with private balcony, 24 hour room service, tea/coffee making, in house video, phone, telex, fax, photocopy, conference rooms, safety deposit boxes, currency exchange, tour desk, car rental, parking, shops, local doctor on call, laundry/ironing, baby sitting, children's club and daily activities. Restaurants, coffee shop, bars, pool, beach, ballroom, golf, tennis and non-motorised water sports. Casino: slot machines, roulette, baccarat, blackjack etc. Open 11.30am until late. Price single or double standard room A$160 (US$126); 2 bed suites A$350 (US$276) + 10% tax.
Le Lagon, PO Box 86, Port Vila, ph 23 817, telex 1032 NH. 108 rooms, bungalows, suites-island style. 24 hour reception, room service. Safety deposit boxes, A/C, tea/coffee making, phone, in-house video, TV. Restaurants, bars, shops, laundry/valet, foreign exchange, doctor, baby sitting, conference room, secretarial service, tour desk, parking, pool with spa, nightclub. Tennis courts, golf, beach, ballroom, water sports, aerobics, games room, cultural

Windsurfing off a local beach. (opposite)

demonstrations, children's programs. Price Lagoon rooms US$120; suites from US$240 plus 10% tax.

First Class

Windsor Hotel International, PO Box 810, Port Vila, ph 22 150, fax 22 678. 20 studio suites - kitchen, fan, tea/coffee making, balcony. One suit for handicapped. 10 x 1 bed apartment - kitchen, microwave. Automatic washing machine & iron. 2 x 2 bed apartments same as above but with spa. 53 orchid rooms A/C motel-style with balconies, fridge, TV, phone, tea/coffee making. 1 Executive suite A/C TV spa, 3 phones, bar, balcony. Laundry available. 5 minutes walk from town, pool, tennis courts, bar, restaurant, Club 21 gaming lounge. *Duke of Windsor's* pub/nightclub, old English style pub at other end of town, beer garden and bistro. Price studio suites VT7,300 (US$68); apartments VT11,000 (US$103); Orchid Rooms VT11,800 (US$157); Executive Suite VT25,000 (US$333) + 10% tax.

White Sands Golf and Country Club PO Box 906, Port Vila, ph 22 090, fax 22 090. 16km from Port Vila on south coast. 8 x 2 bed bungalows, 2 x 1 bed bungalows. Sitting room, bath, fans, fridge, bar. Restaurant, bar, 18 hole golf course, beach across road, pool, tennis courts, croquet, volleyball, walks, snorkelling, shell collecting. Free shuttle bus from town. Price single/twin share VT10,000 (US$93) + 10% tax.

Iririki Island Resort, PO Box 230, Port Vila, ph 23 388, fax 23 880. Situated on a private island, half a kilometre from the town. Free 24 hour ferry service taking 3 minutes. 72 self-contained bungalows on stilts. A/C, lounge. tea/coffee making, phone, fridge, in-house video and music, bath and shower, fan. Pool, beach, restaurant, water sports (non motorised) all other sports catered for at hourly rates. Price single/double A$148-270 (US$104-189) + 10% tax.

Iririki Centre Ville Hotel, PO Box 230, Port Vila, ph 23 388, fax 23 880. In the middle of Port Vila business district. All guests have full use of Iririki Island Resort facilities including ferry. 21 A/C rooms, studios and suites. Desk, phone, fridge, tea/coffee making. Restaurant. Studios and suites have kitchen. Price A$120-170 (US$84-119) + 10% tax.

Erakor Island Resort, PO Box 24, Port Vila, ph 22 983, fax 22 083. On a private island, 5 minute drive from town. Free 24 hour ferry service. 13 bungalows. Fridge, tea/coffee making, fan. Restaurant, bar, beach, snorkelling equipment. Windsurfers, canoes, catamarans for hire. Other sports easily arranged. Price single VT9,500 (US$89); twin/double VT10,500 (US$98); 2 storey sleeps 5 VT13,500 (US$126) including tax.

Standard

Kaiviti Village Motel, PO Box 152, Port Vila, ph 24 684, fax 24 685. 5 minute walk from town close to supermarket, restaurant. 9 2-bedroom self catering units, bath, lounge, kitchen, balcony. 28 studios. Fans, A/C in 14. Pool, bar phone, laundry, baby sitting, fax/typing, snack bar. Price double/twin VT7,500 (US$70); apartment for 4 VT10,000 (US$93); for 6 VT2,000 (US$27) including tax.

Budget

Coral Motel/Apartments, PO Box 1054, Port Vila, ph 23 569, fax 23 569. On airport road 5 minutes from town. Budget style. 10 studio units, kitchen, transport at door, 24 hour TV and in-house movies. Price 1 night single VT4,950 (US$46); double VT5,500 (US$51); 3 nights single VT11,250 (US$105); double VT12,500 (US$116), 7 nights single VT29,700 (US$277); double VT33,000 (US$308) + 10% tax.

Hideaway Island

The island is 9km from Vila by ferry which leaves from Iririki Wharf several times a day. It is protected and has a Marine Sanctuary in Merle Bay. Good swimming beach, a blue lagoon full of fish, a glass bottom boat, complimentary snorkelling equipment. The Club Nautica Diving School will give you lessons. There is a grass roofed bar and bistro serving lunch, snacks and refreshments, including beer, wine and champagne. Simple accommodation is available from A$46 (US$32). 2 bungalows, rooms with bunks and dormitory, fans, tea/coffee making. Children not allowed in dormitories. PO Box 1383 Port Vila, ph 25 770, fax 25 792 or Iririki Wharf Sales Office ph 25 830, fax 25 684. Spend a day or a week or as long as you wish.

Tanna

Tanna Beach Resort, PO Box 27, Tanna Island, ph/fax 68 610. On west side of the island, 3km from airstrip. 8 acres of tropical gardens, private beach. 12 bungalows up to 4 persons. Meet and greet at airport. Pool, restaurant, bar. Horse riding, snorkelling, croquet court, baby sitting and helicopter landing. Tours with guide available. Price garden bungalow VT7,000-9,000 (US$65-84); Ocean bungalow VT10,500 (US$98); Beach and suites VT14,000 (US$131). No hotel tax on Tanna.

White Grass Resort, Box 5, Tanna Island, ph/fax 68 688. Melanesian-style bungalows can accommodate 5, solar electricity and hot water. Bar/restaurant. Average price for 3 meals per day VT2,500 (US$23). Snorkelling, tours. Price single VT6,000 (US$56); double VT6,900 (US$64); triple VT7,200 (US$67); quad VT7,500 (US$70).

Budget

Four new guest houses have recently opened. Nina Guest House, Nikity Guest House, Uma Rocks and Paradise Bay. They are small bungalows with hot showers (except Paradise), kitchen and lovely views. If you don't want to cook, White Grass Plains and Tanna Beach Resort are not far away. Price on request from the Tourist Bureau or any tour operator.

Santo

Bokissa Island Resort, PO Box 261, Santo, ph/fax 36 855. Situated 6km off Santo in tropical rainforest. 12 bungalows. Fridge, coffee/tea making, fan, en suite. Pool, beach, restaurant, bar. Dive tours, instructors, game and reef fishing. Price single/double VT9,600 (US$90), 25% discount for 5 nights. Transfers airport-Bokissa-airport Adult VT3,500 (US$33). Child 12-15 VT1,750 (US$16) tax included.

Bougainville Resort, PO Box 116, Santo, ph 36 257, fax 36 647. 15 minutes from airport, 5 minutes from town. On island of Acre in landscaped gardens. 18 bungalows. Fan, continental breakfast, restaurant, pool. Diving agencies nearby. Transfers single VT1,800 (US$12) per person each way. Price single VT8,500 (US$79); double VT9,500 (US$89).

Lonnoc Beach Resort, PO Box 190, Santo, ph 36 835. 1km from Champagne Beach. Bungalows tea/coffee, linen. Restaurant, bar. For budget minded. Snorkelling, swimming at beach, live coral. Tours arranged. Price VT1,200 (US$11).

Ambryn

Milirest Guesthouse. 3 units. Restaurant. Price VT1,000 (US$9). House Guest 1 bungalow VT1,000 (US$9). There is now a 3 day/2 night tour. It includes pick up from Vila hotel, fly to Ambryn, local guide, bungalow accommodation. See custom dances, sand drawings and village life that hasn't changed since the first white man set foot on the island. Operates daily. Price 36,000VT (US351).

The 5 day/4 night tour is similar but a full day is taken to visit the volcanos in the centre of the island.

Ambae

Tausala Guesthouse. 3 units, self catering. Price VT1,000-1,500 (US$9-14).

Erromango

Metesons Guesthouse. 3 units. Restaurant. Price VT4,000 (US$37) including meals.

Malekula

Lakatoro Resthouse. 4 units (21 beds). Self catering. Price VT1,000 (US$9). *Norsup Resthouse*. 3 units. Self catering. Price VT1,000 (US$9).

Local Transport

Efate

Bus

Mini-buses have a frequent service but no timetable. Flag one down and say where you want to go. Fare VT70 to anywhere.

Taxis

All taxis are metered and the fares are reasonable. They are plentiful so don't ring for one or you will pay for the time from the depot.

Boat

Inter-island boats taking deck passengers are irregular. Cruise ships call quite often.

Car Hire

Driving is on the **right**. Cars, 4WD, jeeps, mopeds and bicycles are available for hire. Avis, Budget and Hertz all have offices in Vila.

Eating Out

Vanuatu is a gourmet's delight. There are so many first class restaurants that you will never sample them all. French, Melanesian, Polynesian, Indian, Chinese, Vietnamese, English and Japanese cuisines are all available, but try something you can't get at home. Coconut crab and flying fox are two specialties and a must. Both have a naturally rich, gamy flavour. Beef, seafood, fruit and vegetables are plentiful.

A full list of restaurants is available from the Information Centre in Vila. French and Australian wines are readily available. There is also a large selection of beers.

All the resorts have restaurants but here are a few you might like to try:

Chez Gilles & Brigitte. French. Seafood specialist. Open lunch & dinner. Closed Sunday.

El Gecko. Small bistro, reasonable prices. Open lunch, dinner closed Sunday.

La Cabane. Seafood specialties. Has boutique. Open 6.30-10pm daily.

Le Rendez-vous. French haute cuisine also fixed menu. Open lunch and dinner Mon-Sat.

L'Houstalet. French family restaurant, reasonable prices. Try Flying Fox. Open daily 6-11pm.

Ma Barker's. Specialises in steak and seafood. Reasonable prices. Open daily 7.30am-10pm.

Pisces. Italian and seafood. Open daily 5-10pm.

Rossi. Specialises in seafood and sandwiches. Take away. Open breakfast, lunch & dinner except Sat lunch Mon dinner.

Scooter's Beer & Burger Bar. Low prices for beer & wine. Burgers and delicacies eat in or take away. Open daily 9am- late.

Talimoru. Specialises in inexpensive lunch and dinner, 500VT including coffee. Shell of karva before meal in bar. Open daily 7.30am-11pm.

Vila Chaumieres. Romantic restaurant specialising in seafood and coconut crab. Open daily lunch 11.30am-2pm, dinner 6pm.

Erisu. Only Japanese in town. Open 6.30-11pm closed Sunday.

Bamboo Royal Chinese. Spicy food. Open daily 10am-1.30pm & 5.30pm-10pm.

Harbour View Chinese. Specialises in beef, seafood. Sunday lunch 'Jam-Cha'. Open daily 10am-2pm & 6pm-10pm.

Mondia. Vietnamese & Thai. Open daily 6pm-10.30pm.

Shopping

There is a wide choice of duty free items from jewellery to CDs. Purchases can be picked up two days before departure but are sealed until you leave the country.

There are a number of shops selling jewellery, handicrafts, souvenirs and clothes. They are mostly on Kumul Highway and the side streets.

The markets are open daily except Sunday. Local handicrafts, fruit and vegetables are the main products. The markets are in the town centre.

Don't overlook the supermarkets. *Better Price* has seven outlets and sells everything including hardware and second hand clothes. *Chew Store* does not sell fresh food but everything else you can think of. They also have international newspapers and magazines.

Here are more places to browse.

Afro Asia Arts. Duty free. Souvenirs, jewellery etc.

Cost Less. Real bargains from fashion to furniture.

Drug Store. Medicine, duty free perfume. You name it they've got it.

Gift Affair. Cards, porcelain, crystal, silverware etc.

Goodies. Gift shop and money exchange. Open Sun morning.

Kis Photo. Opposite Westpac Bank. Buy films and have them

developed.

Queenie Gift Shop. Clothes, manchester, unusual beaded handbags, etc.

Rococo Boutique. Imported fashions at reasonable prices.

Snoopy's. Books, magazines, maps, stationary etc.

Top Shots. 1 hour processing, laminating.

Vanuatu Optical Boutique. Only optometrist in town. Duty free prices.

Annabelle. Beauty salon.

La Vanuatu Beauty Centre. Top to toe beauty treatments.

Tiffany's. Duty Free. Top quality watches, jewellery, perfumes, etc.

Florabunda. The only florist. Gift baskets. Flowers sent world wide.

Cruising

Sailing is very popular, and there are boats for hire. There are always numerous boats, moored in the marina, which have sailed from other parts of the world. Everyone is catered for. The inexperienced can take cruises on manned ships and old sea dogs can charter a bareboat. Diving, fishing and snorkelling can all be arranged. Most boats are fully equipped, just ask when booking.

South Pacific Cruises, ph 25 020 have, a South Seas Adventure Cruise on the *Coongoola,* a large classic timber auxiliary sailing ketch. They visit caves, feed fish, swim, dive, view coral and hopefully see dolphins at play. They have morning and afternoon tea and a beach barbecue. Cruises run Tues-Sun. Scuba diving available on request.

Moorings Rainbow PO Box 8327, Symonds Street. Auckland, NZ, fax 64 9 378 0931. Cruising around Efate to Port Havanna recommended for the casual sailor, and north to Santo for the experienced. Bareboat with local guides. Professional skippers available. Yachts hold 2-6 persons.

Nautilus Scuba, PO Box 78, Port Vila, ph 22 398. Located on waterfront with swimming pool and barbecue facilities. They have fully trained instructors and dive guides available to dive with you. Dive boats are fully equipped with safety equipment. Full toilet and cabin facilities, refreshments. The boats are Catamarans, Diveboats or Fast Dive Cats. There is also a scuba school and shop with duty free prices.

Le Lagon has a package deal for divers. 8 days/7 nights with 6 dives. There is a Santo extension 4 days/3nights 4 dives to see wreck of the *President Coolridge.*

For big game fishing contact *Phantom Charters,* PO Box 961. Live-aboard MV *Mungana.* Day trips arranged.

Glass Bottom Boat, *Neptune II* has half day tours. You can view

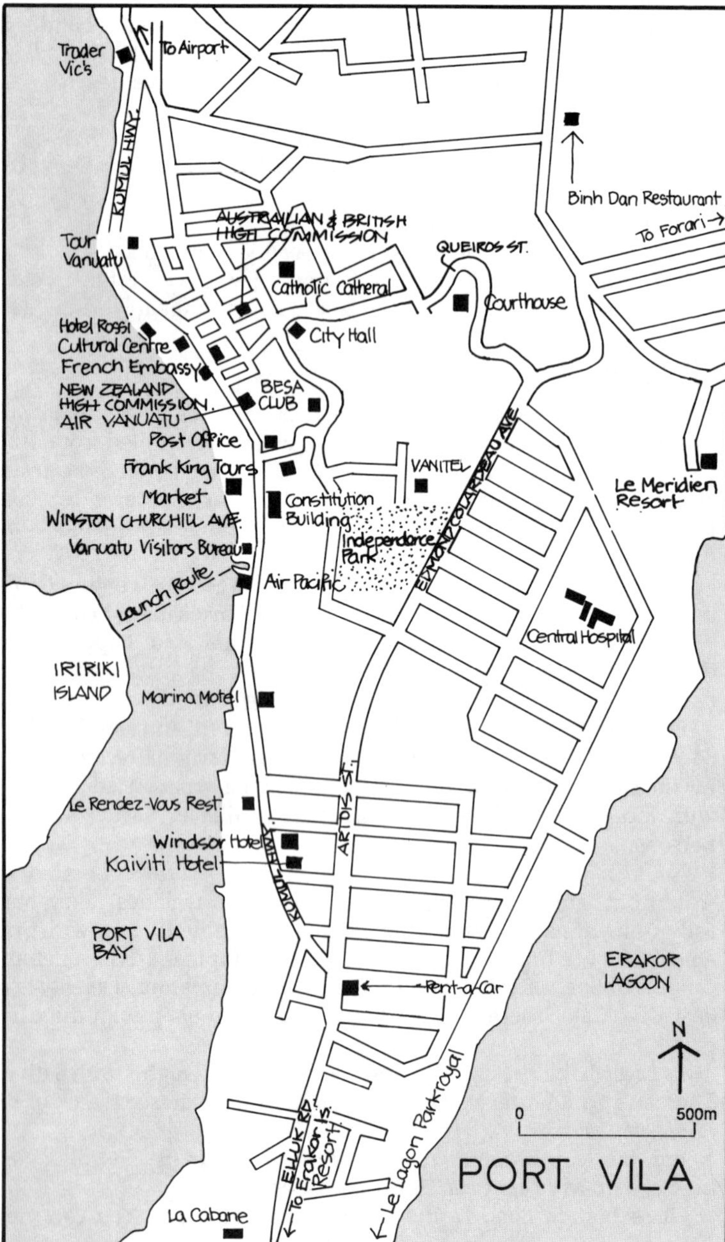

Trader Vic's
To Airport
KUMUL HWY.
AUSTRALIAN & BRITISH HIGH COMMISSION
Binh Dan Restaurant
To Forari
Tour Vanuatu
QUEIROS ST.
Catholic Catheral
Courthouse
Hotel Rossi
City Hall
Cultural Centre
French Embassy
NEW ZEALAND HIGH COMMISSION
BESA CLUB
AIR VANUATU
Post Office
Frank King Tours
VANITEL
Market
Le Meridien Resort
Constitution Building
WINSTON CHURCHILL AVE.
EDMOND COLARDEAU AVE
Independance Park
Vanuatu Visitors Bureau
Launch Route
Air Pacific
Central Hospital
IRIRIKI ISLAND
Marina Motel
ARTOIS ST.
Le Rendez-Vous Rest.
Windsor Hotel
Kaiviti Hotel
KUMUL HWY.
PORT VILA BAY
ERAKOR LAGOON
Rent-a-Car
N
0
500m
ELLUK RD.
To Erakor Is. Resort
Le Lagon Parkroyal
PORT VILA
La Cabane

coral, snorkel, swim and even hand feed fish. Leaves Port Vila seawall Mon-Fri 9am-11.30am and 2pm-4.30pm except cruise ship days. Sun pm only. Price 2,850VT (US$28).

Tiva, a 37ft Trimaran, has day and half day trips. It takes you to Efarfel beach and other places for swimming, snorkelling or relaxing. Lunch included on day trip, tea and coffee on all other departures. Operates daily 9am-5pm. 9am-11am and 2pm-4pm. Price 5,000VT (US$49) full day; 3,000VT (US$29) half day.

Sightseeing

Port Vila

It is advisable to take a half day bus tour to familiarise yourself with the layout of Port Vila. Any tour agency, such as Tour Vanuatu, will make bookings for you. If you are game, take the local bus.

The tour of Vila and environments takes in all the sights plus a visit to the Soap Factory. Refreshments are taken at Etau Malep Beach. Pick up from all hotels, minimum 2 passengers. Operates daily except Sat pm, Sun and cruise ship days. Time 9am-11am and 2pm-4pm. Price 2,000VT (US$18).

Les Cascades is for those interested in nature walks. It goes to Mele Village, Klems Hill Lookout and the Cascades waterfall. Refreshments with fresh local fruit are served. Operates 7 days except Sat pm. Times 9am-11am or 2pm-4.30pm. Price 2,000VT (US$18).

You do not need a tour to visit the **Cultural Centre** on Kumul Highway, west of the town centre. It is only a short walk. The Cultural Centre and museum is a must. There is a wonderful display of artefacts and photographs. They also have videos of Vanuatu customs.

For more culture, go to one of the evenings at an hotel. You can also experience dancing and a feast.

Efate

Hire a car or take a tour around the island of Efate. There are many pretty beaches, friendly people, colourful villages and tropical rainforests. See **Mele's Cascades** where the water flows all year. Visit **Havannah Harbour** where the US fleet was stationed during World War II. A short distance further north is **Siviri** village which has a cave where children beat the earth to light the inside! Don't be afraid to take any dirt road. Most lead to pretty beaches.

If you miss anything, it is possible to take a tour by air. Enquire at Information Centre.

The **Round the Island Tour** is well worth considering. You will see all the sights of Efate on this full day tour with a knowledgeable guide. The tour includes pick up from hotels, has morning tea and a swim at

Eton beach, lunch at a Melanesian restaurant and refreshments at beautiful Undine Bay. Take your camera, swimming gear, hat, sunglasses and suntan lotion. Operates daily except cruise days. Time 9am-4.30pm. Price 4,000VT.

A 15 minute **Helicopter Tour** of Vila costs 4,000VT per person.

Tanna

There are day trips to the island of Tanna but it is better to stay at least one night. The main attraction is **Yasur**, an active volcano. It is more interesting to go at dusk and watch the transformation as the light fades. You can drive to within a 15 minute walk to the crater rim where you can see the three vents of Yasur below. Several times during an hour it is not unusual to experience an eruption that shoots glowing ash and stones into the air. The earth trembles and moans and the smell of sulphur is overpowering. As night draws on, the natural show becomes more eerie. The vents appear like blood. The shocks can knock over photographers. If your guide tells you it's an easy climb, don't believe him. The soft ash pulls you back and you begin to wonder if you will ever reach the top.

Especially good in the dry season is a visit to the **White Grass Plains**, where the wild horses live. As they gallop across the earth, mains flying, they resemble phantom horses.

It is possible for your hotel to arrange a visit to a **Cargo Cult** custom village. The people still live and dress in the traditional way. It is interesting to meet and chat with the chief and be entertained by the children.

A one day tour starts at Vila hotels for a flight to Tanna's Lanakel Airport. The plane is met by a guide who will take visitors to the volcano, a custom village and a picnic lunch. Operates daily. Price 29,500VT (US$288).

A two day tour includes the wild horses, custom village, beachcombing and hot springs. You have a choice of accommodation. Price of tour 29,500VT (US$288) plus accommodation. Tanna Beach Resort 6,400VT (US$62) single, 7,200VT (US$70) double. White Grass Resort 6,000VT (US$58) single, 6,900VT (US$97) double, 7,200VT (US$70) triple. Meals 3,000-3,500VT (US$29) Tanna Beach per day. 2,500VT (US$24) White Grass. Children half price on transfers and tours.

The **Toka dance** is performed once a year between August and November on Tanna. Traditionally it marked the end of tribal war. Today it is performed to renew alliances between neighbouring villages.

The women start. Spectacularly dressed, they dance the Napen-Napen all night. When dawn breaks, an eerie silence pervades the huge dance ground. Everyone awaits the men's dance - the Toka.

The men dance all day then into the night. The next day, the host village performs the Nao and everyone exchanges gifts. A full day tour includes Port Vila transfers, return airfare, airport tax, Toka entrance fee, transfers and lunch. Price 29,000VT (US$283).

An overnight package costs the same plus accommodation.

Espiritu Santo

During World War II, James A. Michener, a lieutenant in the US army, was stationed on Santo. The place effected him so much that he wrote *Tales of the South Pacific* from which sprang the musical *South Pacific*. Michener would gaze across the sea to a volcanic island, often with its summit shrouded in cloud and dream of Bali Hai. This was the island of **Ambae** and it still beckons romantic souls.

Luganville, the second largest town in Vanuatu, has a slower pace than Vila. It is a country town with an interesting general store, mostly Chinese restaurants and scuba dive sights unequalled anywhere. The *President Coolidge*, 30,000 ton, sank in the harbour after striking a 'friendly' mine. It is still intact lying in 20-60m of water. Outside the channel, the destroyer USS *Tucker* sank after meeting a US mine. Dive tours can be taken to these vessels.

A place called **Million Dollar Point** is another amazing sight. It is where the US forces dumped their surplus goods. Coco cola and 7-Up bottles have become bonded by beach rock to machinery and other items. It stretches for 1km.

The small industries centre and the large experimental plantation and farm are of interest.

Year round 1-10 day guided history and nature walks are available.

There is a day trip from Vila. Fly to Luganville and be met by a local guide who will take you to Champagne Beach, the Blue Hole, Sarami Plantation and Million Dollar Point. The price includes picnic lunch, entrance fees and guide. Operates Mon-Sat. Price 29,100VT (US$284).

The two day trip from Vila has visits to Fanafo village, Sarami Plantation, American World War II hospital, Bali Hai Viewpoint, Blue Hole. Two breakfasts, one lunch. Minimum 2 persons. Operates Mon-Sat. Price 29,100VT (US$284) plus accommodation and dinner. Bungalows 2,000VT (US$18) single, 2,500VT (US$24) double. Bougainville Resort 8,500VT (US$83) single, 9,500 (US$93) double plus dinner.

For diving tours of the *President Coolridge* and USS *Tucker*, contact Aquamarine Santo, PO Box 1574, Port Vila, ph 26 537, fax 26 528, or your local travel agent.

Pentecost Island

Only on Saturdays in April and May in the Bunlap area of South Pentecost, can visitors experience the mind boggling Pentecost Land Dives. You can see this event on video but nothing can match the experience of being there.

The origin of the jump is obscure. According to legend, a young woman was repeatedly beaten by her husband, Tamalie. She ran into the jungle and climbed a coconut tree and hid in the uppermost foliage. It was some time before Tamalie found her and started to climb the tree. She threatened to jump. As Tamalie reached out for his wife, she dived to the ground. In a fit of grief or rage, Tamalie plunged after her to his death. He did not realise that his wife had tied vines to her ankle to break her fall.

To celebrate the event, the women of the village tied vines to their ankles and jumped from trees. As so often happens, the ritual changed. Now the men jump, but not from trees, from tall towers built around the trees. As many as 25 jumps may be performed in one day from the same tower. As the height of the jump increases, to as much as 35m, so does the tempo of the traditionally dressed men and women dancing and chanting around the tower. The atmosphere is electric and the experience unforgettable.

The jump is now associated with the rites of manhood and very young boys jump from the lower parts of the tower. Weeks before the jump, each diver must undertake rituals to purify himself and ward off evil spirits. If the rituals are not complete, the diver may be killed or injured. Men have been killed and there are frequent injuries. The jump is also associated with the yam harvest. As the vines pull taut, the diver's head should just graze the earth, fertilising the soil for that year's yam crop. There is a fee to watch this spectacular.

There is one guest house on Pentecost. Day trips, by air, are available from Vila, flying with *Vanair*. The trip includes a familiarisation lecture in the Cultural Centre, Vila, the night before departure, airfares, transfers, entrance and photography fees, lunch, refreshments, guides and a T-shirt. Price 40,000VT (US$390).

A sea package is for 4 day/4 night on a charter yacht. There is time for swimming, snorkelling, diving and fishing on the way. *Response* is a 42ft (14m) Lidgard Sloop with a Kiwi skipper. Price 40,000VT (US$390) per day plus 1,500VT (US$15) per day for food. *Galaxie* is a luxury 72ft (22m) ketch with American skipper. Price US$1,500 per day all inclusive except for alcoholic beverages.

Waterfall Village Tour for 3 days/2 nights. Pick up at Vila hotel, fly to Pentecost. You'll be met by your host Johnas Tabi who will take you to Hot Water then to Waterfall Village where lunch will be served. Explore the village in the afternoon. Dinner will be served at 6.30pm.

Next day Johnas will take you to meet Chief Raisis at the Custom Village. You will be greeted with a complementary shell of karva. You will go to the huge Custom Cave where the guide will tell you the legend. On to the Waterfall and yet another legend. A swim before lunch then back to the guest house for dinner. After breakfast on day 3, transfer back to the airport.

Operates Mon-Wed or Wed-Fri. Price 29,500VT (US$288). The 4 day/3night tour is as above but an extra day is spent at the Custom Village and a karva ceremony with chief Raisis. Operates Fri-Mon. Price 31,900VT (US$310).

Package Deals

There are many package deals available from most countries. These usually include air fares, accommodation, transfers and a tour. They can be taken with another island in the Vanuatu group or combined; Noumea and Vanuatu or Vanuatu and Fiji. Average price is from A$1050 (US$735) for 8 days/7 nights fly drive in Vanuatu to A$1753 (US$1227) island hopping in the Vanuatu group for 15 days/14 nights.

Sport and Recreation

Apart from the great variety of water sports - reef and wreck diving and deep-sea fishing- there are many more sports to play.

There are four excellent golf courses in Port Vila, plus tennis courts, fitness centres, jazzercise, cycling and squash. Visitors can follow the Hash House Harriers or go horse riding.

The annual picnic horse race day is a must. Enquire at the Information Centre for the date.

The Amateur Theatrical Society produces excellent stage shows. Other entertainment takes place at hotels. Karva drinking ceremonies are common everywhere.

Watch the notice boards outside supermarkets for up and coming events.

Tour Operators

Air Club Vila, ph 22514, for scenic adventure flights. 4000VT.

Talova Tours. Book through Aliat Wi, ph 25225, for all tours.

Tour Vanuatu, ph 22745 & 22733 in Vila; 36 110 on Santo. On Tanna in Lenakel Mon-Fri 8am-4.30pm, Sat 8-11am. All tours are available.

NOTES

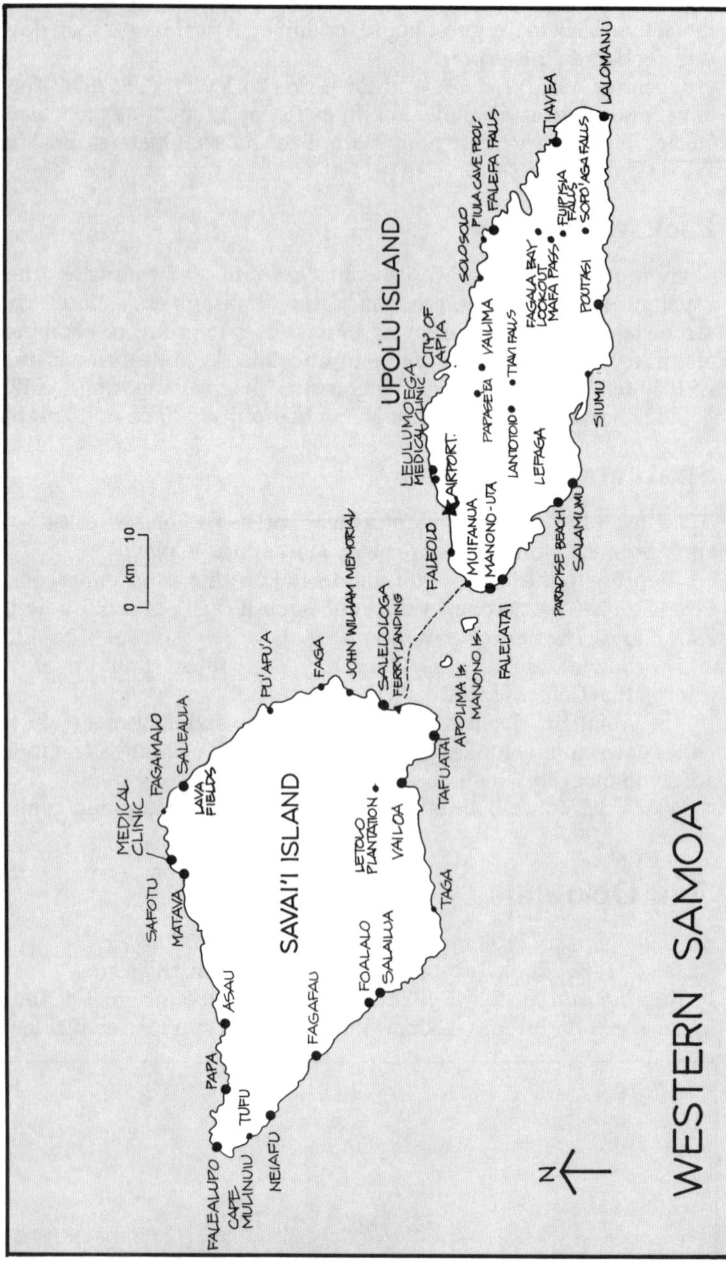
WESTERN SAMOA
N
0 km 10
SAVAI'I ISLAND
UPOLU ISLAND
FALEALUPO
CAPE MULINUIU
NEIAFU
TUFU
PAPA
ASAU
FAGAFAU
FOALALO
SALAILUA
SAFOTU
MATAVAI
MEDICAL CLINIC
FAGAMALO
SALEAULA
LAVA FIELDS
LETOLO PLANTATION
VAILOA
TAGA
TAFUATAI
PU'APU'A
FAGA
JOHN WILLIAM MEMORIAL
SALELOLOGA FERRY LANDING
APOLIMA IS.
MANONO IS.
FALEOLO
FALELATAI
MUIFANUA
MANONO-UTA
AIRPORT
PARADISE BEACH
SALAMUMU
LEULUMOEGA MEDICAL CLINIC
LEFAGA
LANTOTOID
PAPASE'EA
SIUMU
CITY OF APIA
VAILIMA
TIAVI FALLS
FAGALAI BAY LOOKOUT
MAFA PASS
POUTASI
SOLOSOLO
PIULA CAVE POOL
FALEFA FALLS
FUIPISIA FALLS
SOPO'AGA FALLS
TIAVEA
LALOMANU

THE REPUBLIC OF WESTERN SAMOA

Western Samoa is the largest and most westerly portion of the Samoan archipelago, a chain of volcanic islands. It lies 4216km south-west of Hawaii, 4355km east of Sydney, and 2903km north of New Zealand. It is also 1279km west of Suva and 129km east of Pago Pago.

Western Samoa covers an area of 2242 sq km, and consists of two main islands, Savi'i known as the 'Big Island' as it covers 1554 sq km and Upolu, 1114 sq km. Apia, the capital, is on Upolu where the seat of government and centre of commerce are located. There are also two smaller islands, Apolima and Manono, and five uninhabited islets. Agriculture is the main occupation with bananas, copra and cocoa the chief exports. In recent years there has been some industrial development.

The islands have long white sandy beaches and lush tropical hardwood forests with mountain peaks rising to 1835m. There is a 4-5km skirt of gently sloping fertile land to which is attached a fringe of coral reefs and lagoons. Western Samoa is everything you ever imagined a tropical island to be. It is no wonder that Robert Louis Stevenson spent the last four years of his life on Upolu and was buried, at his request, on the summit of Mt Vaea.

The poet Rupert Brooke found peace in the Samoan islands and wrote: "You lie on a mat in a cool Samoan hut and look out on the white sand under the high palms, and a gentle sea, and a black line of reef a mile out, with moonlight over everything. And then amongst it all are the loveliest people in the world, moving and dancing like gods and goddesses. It is sheer beauty, so pure it is difficult to breathe it in."

History

Early history is vague, although it is known that the islands were occupied by Polynesians.

In 1721 Jacob Roggeveen, a Dutch navigator, visited, followed by Frenchman Bougainville, who anchored in 1786 but did not land. The Frenchman who did land was La Pérouse, in 1786. He didn't stay long, though, as 12 of his crew were killed while searching for water on Tutuila. This place is still called Massacre Bay.

In 1791 the English ship *Pandora* came in search of mutineers from the *Bounty*. Then followed whalers, traders, escaped convicts from Australia and of course the missionaries.

The Rev John Williams of the London Missionary Society landed at

Savi'i in 1830 aboard the *Messenger of Peace*. By 1840, most Samoans had been converted. His son, John Williams Jr was the first copra trader in Samoa.

During the 19th century Britain, Germany and the USA had conflicting interests in the territory and administered it jointly from 1889-99. Ultimately the land was divided into two with Germany annexing Western Samoa and the USA exercising sovereignty over Eastern Samoa as a territory under naval control. During World War I the Germans were driven out by a New Zealand contingent who remained until 1920.

The Treaty of Versailles saw New Zealand receive a League of Nations mandate which lasted until 1946 when Western Samoa became a UN Trust territory. Steps were started in the 1950s for local autonomy and the change was gradual. In 1962 Western Samoa became an independent state within the Commonwealth.

His Highness Malietoa Tanumafili II became joint head of State with another traditional ruler who died soon after. Malietoa Tanumafili was then granted Head of State for life. The Prime Minister at independence was Fiame Mata Afa Mulinu'u. He lost power in 1971, regained it in 1973 then died in 1975. In 1976 the first Prime Minister not of royal blood, Tupuola Taisi Efi, was elected.

In 1974 an opposition came together and formed the Human Rights Protection Party (HRPP) and won the 1982 election with Va'ai Kolone becoming Prime Minister. Later that year he was replaced by Tupuola Efi who resigned a few months later when his budget was not accepted. The new HRPP leader was Tofilau Eti Alesan who resigned at the end of the 1982, and Va'ai Kolone returned to lead a government of independents (now known as Tupua Tamasese Efi) and formed the new Christian Democratic Party (CDP). At the February 1988 election there was a hung parliament with Tofilau Eti Alesana as Prime Minister.

Following the introduction of universal adult suffrage in 1990, Tofilau Eti Alesana was returned for three years. In 1991 Va'ai Kolone became leader of the opposition. Tofilau Eti Alesana made wholesale changes to his cabinet, and in May 1991 he brought in Fiame Naomi, the first woman to serve in the cabinet.

Climate

A tropical climate with temperatures ranging from 22C to 30C. May to November are the cooler months while December- April is the rainy season. Average annual rainfall is 300-700cm per year. Relative humidity averages 80% yearly and there is approximately 2500 hours of sunshine. Sea temperatures are ideal throughout the year.

Population

The 161,298 Samoan citizens are Polynesians whose life-style is based on the extended family and village. Most live in the 300 villages, each containing about 350 people. Indigenous Samoans account for 97% of the total population, whilst 2.4% comprises of residents of Samoan descent.

Language

Samoan is the national language but English is used in commercial and government businesses. Illiteracy is unknown and most Samoans are competent in English.

Here are a few words in Samoan. To help in pronunciation, note that 'go' is pronounced 'ng' and 't' as 'k'. The apostrophe indicates a glottal stop between syllables.

Hello.......................................talofa
Goodbye..................................tofa
Thank you...............................faàfetai
Please......................................faàmolemole
How are you?..........................faàpefea mai oe?
Where are you going?.............alu i fea?
Woman....................................fafine
Man..tamaloa
House.......................................fale
How much?..............................pe fia?
Kava bowl................................tanoa
Beach.......................................matafaga
Village.....................................nuu
Good luck................................soifua
Lei..ula
Good night..............................manuia le po
Boat...vaà
Blowhole..................................pupu
Very good................................lelei tele
Bad...leaga
Yes...ioe
No..leai

Public Holidays

January 1...........New Year's Day
January 2...........New Year
March/April....Good Friday, Saturday, Easter Monday

April 25............. Anzac Day
May 15.............. Samoan Mothers Day
June 1-3............. Independence Day
August 7........... Labour Day
October............. White Sunday, Monday
November 3..... Arbour Day
December 25.... Christmas Day
December 26.... Boxing Day.

Entry Regulations

A visa is not required but visitors must have a valid passport, a return or onward airline ticket, and a specific place of stay, before entry is permitted into Western Samoa for a stay of up to 30 days. For more than 30 days, an entry permit must be obtained. Refer to Western Samoan Overseas Missions for information on visas for each relevant country.

Customs

The duty free allowance is: 1 carton cigarettes or 50 cigars and one 40 or 750ml bottle of spirits. Prohibited imports are: firearms, ammunition, explosives, drugs and indecent publications of any kind.

It is against the law to import live animals, plants or products of that nature including fruits, seeds, soil, etc. without authority of the Director.

Departure Tax

There is a departure tax of WS$20 (about US$17), payable in local currency.

Embassies

Australia: High Commission, Tamaligi, ph 23 411.
Canada: No resident representative. Refer to Canadian High Commission in Canberra. ph 06 273 3844.
New Zealand: High Commission, Tamaligi, ph 21 404/21 711.
USA: American Embassy, John Williams Boulevard, ph 21 631.
UK: The Honorary British Consul, PO Box 2029, Apia Kruse, Va'ai ph 685 212 1895

Money

The Western Samoan currency is the 'Tala' for dollar and 'Sene' for cent (100 sene = WS$1). Most hotels and large stores will change notes and traveller's cheques. The Bank of Western Samoa, Pacific Commercial Bank and the Post Office Savings Bank are open during Mon-Fri 9.00am-3.00pm. Bank of Western Samoa is also open Sat 8.30am-11.30am.

Notes are in denominations of $2, $5, $10, $20, $50, $100, and coins are 1, 2, 5, 10, 20 and 50 senes and $1.

Approximate rates of exchange, which should be used as a guide only, are:

A$	=	WST1.90
Can$	=	WST1.79
NZ$	=	WST1.66
S$	=	WST1.74
UK£	=	WST3.72
US$	=	WST2.43

Communications

The Post Office is open Mon-Fri 9am-4pm. The Telegraph Office at the Post Office is open 24 hours a day. The main Post Office is in Apia with sub-branches in various districts.

IDD service is available and the country code is 685.

The main newspapers are the *Observer*, the *Samoa Times* and the *Samoa Weekly*.

Emergency Services

Fire, Ambulance, Police...........999.
National Hospital.....................21 212.

Miscellaneous

Time

Local time is GMT - 11.

Business Hours

Shops are open Mon-Fri 8am-noon, 1.30-4.30pm. Some shops stay open during the lunch hour.
Banks are open Mon-Fri 9am-3pm.

Electricity

90% of the populated area of Upolu is served by combined hydro-electric and diesel-electric installations. 95% of the island of Savai'i is served by wood fuel turbine and diesel engine installations.

The current is 240 V AC 50 cycles but can be converted to 110V in most hotels. Take an adaptor in case the plugs are a different shape.

Credit Cards

Most major cards are accepted in main hotels.

Medical Services

Western Samoa is free from most tropical diseases including malaria.

The Moto'otua National Hospital has medical services at a reasonable fee. There are also private clinics.

There are two private dental clinics: Leavai ph 20 172 and Soonalole ph 21 145.

Tipping

Tipping is unknown in Western Samoa and is discouraged. A small gift for excellent service would be appreciated.

Water

It is advisable to boil drinking water. Bottled water supplied by the Vaitele Spring Water and Aquarian Water Co is available from stores throughout the country at reasonable prices.

Insurance

It is advisable to be fully insured, with full medical cover.

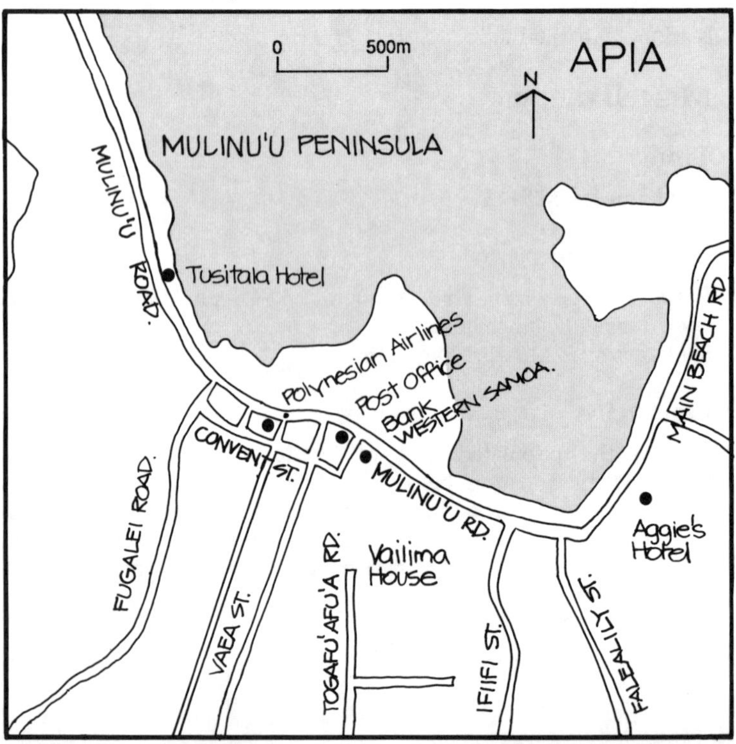

Travel Information

How to get there

By Air

Air Polynesia, Air Pacific, Air New Zealand, Hawaiian Air and Samoan Air operate international flights into Western Samoa through Faleolo International Airport.

Air Polynesia and Samoan Air operate flights from American Samoa into Fagalii Airport.

Domestic: Polynesian Airlines has daily flights into Fagalii Airstrip in Apia, and to the Maota Airstrip on the south-east of Savi'i.

Airports: The Faleolo International Airport is located 35km from Apia. The Fagalii Airport in Upolu is five minutes' drive from downtown Apia. The Maota Airstrip is situated on the south-eastern part of Savi'i.

By Sea

A few cruise ships call at Apia. Passenger/cargo ships sail from Pago Pago to Apia twice a week.

Tourist Information

Western Samoa Visitors Association, PO Box 2272, Apia, ph 20 180, fax 20 886.

Accommodation

First Class

Aggie Grey's, PO Box 67, Apia, ph 22 880, fax 23 626. On Beach Road, Apia Harbour, 10 minute walk to town, 35km from airport. Located Beach Road. Apia Harbour 10mins walk. A legendary hotel made famous by the late Aggie Grey and family. Robert Louis Stevenson lodged here. 154 rooms and fales with A/C, fan, fridge, en suite, tea/coffee making, iron and board. TV, hair dryer and mini bar in New Wing. Pool, safe deposit, money exchange, 2 bars, 2 restaurants, laundry, babysitting. Sunday BBQ with island music, Wednesday night Fiafia (island feast), complimentary afternoon tea, credit cards. Price single standard US$75, Fales US$95, New Wing US$115, Suites US$150, Twin/double standard US$85, Fales US$105, New Wing US$125, Suites US$160. Children 0-4yrs free, 4-11 half rate, 12 and up full rate. All rates + 10% tax. Meal plan: US$35 per person per day for breakfast, light lunch and dinner in dining room only.

Hotel Kitano Tusitala, PO Box 101, Sogi, Apia, ph 21 122, fax 23 652.

Located only a minute walk from town and close to Robert Louis Stevenson's home and grave. 'Tusitala' meaning teller of tales, was Stevenson's Samoan name. 94 rooms. A/C, private bath, tea/coffee making, fridge, phone, patio/terrace. Restaurants, bars, pool, tennis courts, laundry, room service during restaurant hours, 24hr reception, safety deposit boxes, parking, hairdresser, gift shop, taxi stand, baby sitting, tour desk. Deluxe rooms offer TV, in-house entertainment, mini-bar, hair dryer and alarm clocks. Samoan floor show and dancing Thursday nights, live band several nights. Price standard single US$75, double US$85, triple US$95. Deluxe single US$105, double US4118, triple US$128. Suite US$220. One child under 12 sharing with adults free. Meal plans available. All prices + 10% tax.

Coconuts Beach Club, PO Box 3684, Apia Resort, ph 24 849, fax 20 071, Apia fax 22 538. On south coast right on beach in Maninoa Village, a typical Samoan seaside village where life has changed very little in the last 100 years, 30 minute drive from Apia. 20 rooms and fales with A/C, bath/shower, private bathing pools, balcony, mini-fridge, coffee/tea making. Restaurant with seafood specialties, bar, French and Italian specialties, Californian and European wines. Watersports, windsurfing, snorkelling, fishing, sailboards, paddle boats and scuba diving with certified divemaster, 4WD jeeps for tours and rental. Airport transfers free. Price standard US$95-US$165, deluxe US$120-US$165, suites US$145-165, fale US$170-239 + 10% tax.

Standard

Hotel Teuila, PO Box 182, Apia, ph 23 959, fax 26 887. In centre of Municipal district opposite the University, 8 minutes from Fagalii Airport and golf course. Regular bus stop. 15 rooms with A/C, phone, fridge, tea/coffee making. Conference room with bar service, hair salon, restaurant, cocktail lounge. Your host, Jerome Grey sings for you nightly. Price single US$55, double US$85 including tax.

Traveller's Inn, PO Box 6605, Pesega, ph 26 055, fax 20 110. Opposite Morman temple. 18 standard single/double units, 9 self-contained, rest dormitory. Price single WS$12 (US$10), double WS$75 (US$64), triple WS$85 (US$72).

Budget

Samoan Outrigger Hotel, Box 4074, Apia, ph/fax 20 886. On Vatala Beach, 10 minutes walk from Apia. Bed and breakfast, communal kitchen, reading room, lounge and laundry, garden setting. Canoes and snorkelling equipment for hire. Price single WS$40 (US$34), double WS$60 (US$51), triple WS$90 (US$76).

Fales

Fagatele Beach Fales, PO Box 2272, Saleapaga, Lepa Aleipata. Brand new fales. Beautiful beach for swimming, snorkelling etc. 1½ hour drive from Apia. Price single WS$15 (US$13), double WS$30 (US$25), triple WS$45 (US$38).

Salani River Fales, Box 4962, Salani Village, ph 20 180, fax 20 886. 9 fales on bank of river Salani. Price single WS$10 (US$8), double WS$20 (US$17), triple WS$30 (US$25). Meals: breakfast WS$5 (US$4), lunch and dinner WS$7 (US$6).

Vavau Beach Fales, ph 20 954, (direct 26 267), fax 22 680. In Vavau village, on the south coast. 6 new luxury fales with self catering on beachfront. Price WS$20 (US$17) per person.

Savai'i Island

Standard

Savai'ian Hotel, Private bag, Lalomalava, ph 51 206, 51 295, 51 258. Lalomalava is 12km from ferry terminal. 6 self contained units A/C with cooking facilities, tea/coffee making, fridge, patio. Restaurant, bar. Canoeing, snorkelling, island tours, hire car. Price single WS$95 (US$45), double WS$115 (US$55), triple WS$135 (US$65). Children under 6 free, 6-12 half-rate. Breakfast WS$10, dinner WS$25. All rates include 10% tax.

Stevenson's at Manase, ph 58 219, fax 58 219 or 24166. At Manase, 45 minutes from Maota Airport and Ferry. 10 A/C rooms, 2 A/C VIP rooms, 10 fales, 10 tents. Electric oven, fridge. Restaurant, 2 bars, beach, pool. Canoes, dinghy and cruising boat for water sports. Tours, bush walks. Price single US$34, double US$40, triple US$45, suites US$70, fale US$16.50.

Safua Hotel, Private bag, Salelologa, ph 51 271, fax 51 272. At Lalomalava. 12 thatched fale units in garden setting. Bathrooms, screens and fans. Special feature Samoan culture. Price rooms with meals single 1-4 days US$66, double US$88. 4-10 days single US$55, double US77. American plan meals. Room only single US$44, double US$55 all including tax.

Fales

Satuiatua Beach Fales at Satuiatua, Palault 1 Sisifo. 11 fales hidden under giant pulu trees on beach, 3 common rooms, shop. Swimming, surfing. Price WS$35 with meals.

Tanu Beach Fales, Manase village. 10 beach fales for overnighters with common room for socialising. Price single WS$20 (US$17).

Local Transport

Air

Air Polynesian has daily flights from Fagalii airstrip in Apia to Maota Airstrip on Savi'i.

Buses

There are plenty of buses on Upolu. Ask the Western Samoan Visitors Bureau for schedules. On Savi'i there are public and privately owned buses, but there are no time tables. Visitors are advised to consult any policeman at the new market bus depot.

In Apia, airport buses are provided for passengers to Aggie Grey's and the Tusitala by P & F Schuster Tours for WS$3 (US$2.50) one way. Phone 23 014 for more information.

Taxis

Taxis are available on both islands. The fares are set by the government. Enquire at the Western Samoan Visitors Bureau for the average price of longer journeys. The minimum fare in the town area is WS$2 (US$1.70). The taxi fare from the airport into Apia town is WS$30 (US$25).

Cars

There are more than 1800km of road on the two islands, 396km of which are main roads and 260km are sealed. Driving is on the **right** hand side of the road and signs are in English. A small fee is required by the Ministry of Transport for a local licence. Visitors must have a current driving licence and be 25 years of age.

Apia Rentals, ph 24244; Avis, ph 20 486; Billie's, ph 20 561; Emka, ph 23 266; Funway Rentals, ph 22 045; G & J Rentals, ph 21 078; Hibiscus, ph 24 342; J & S Car Rental, ph 24 503; Mt Vaea, ph 20 620; P & K Filo, ph 23 014; Pavitt's-U-Drive, ph 21 766; Reliance Rentals, ph 21 828; Teuila rentals, ph 20 284.

Rates vary from WS$110 (US$93) depending on type of car and length of time. A deposit of WS$100-150 (US$85-127) is required. Vehicles can be delivered to your hotel or to the airport. Most include unlimited mileage with full tank.

There is a petrol station about 5km from the airport. Other stations are almost all in Apia. There are no service stations in remote areas. Cars must be returned with a full tank.

P & F Schuster, ph 23 014, have buses for charter 30/15 seater.

Apia Ricksha Ltd, ph 26 069, have three-wheeled vehicles for hire.

Deposit WS$200 (US$170), rate WS$60 (US$51) per day.

Tulei's Bike Rental, ph 24 145, have Yamahas for hire, deposit WS$200 (US$170), rate WS$50 (US$42), helmet WS$5 (US$4).

Savi'i

Savi'i Car Rental, ph 51 206, 51 295, fax 51 291. Suzuki 4WD WS$100 (US$85) per day tax included.

Ferries

Western Samoan Shipping Corporation operates daily ferry services between Upolu and Savi'i. One way fare WS$6 (US$5). It also operates a twice weekly service between Apia and American Samoa. One way fare WS$30 (US$25). Because of frequent schedule changes, it is advisable to contact the Shipping Corporation, ph 23 0935, 20 936, or the Visitors Bureau.

Mulinu'u Road, Apia

Eating Out

The main hotels provide dining rooms and cocktail bars for guests and visitors. Aggie Greys's and Kitano Tusitala hotels host a Samoan 'fiafia' night once a week. The Coconuts Beach Club, Maninoa has a 'fiafia' night each Saturday on the beach. This is an excellent way for visitors to experience the food and entertainment of Western Samoa.

The evening begins with a buffet supper including seafood such as lobster, crabs, fresh baked-fish in coconut cream and many other Pacific dishes. The Samoan stone oven (umu) yields roast sucking pigs, baked taro, taamu, breadfruit and a special Samoan delicacy - palusami (fresh spinach or young taro leaves backed with coconut cream and onions wrapped in banana leaves).

Entertainment includes the traditional dances and songs of Samoa. Guests will have the opportunity to view the graceful siva, the excitement of the Samoan slap dance, and the breath-taking fire dance performed with a special type of knife. The evening program finishes with popular music and dancing.

Tour operators will make arrangements with nearby villages to hold a 'fiafia' for cruise ship passengers or other groups upon request.

Hotels and Bars

Aggie Grey's Hotel .... *ph 22 880*
Kitano Tusitala Hotel .... *ph 21 122*
O Le Satapuala .... *ph 42 212*
Coconuts Beach Resort .... *ph 24 849*
The Beachcomber Bar .... *ph 21 248*
Margery Ta's Beer Garden .... *ph 25 395*
Otto's Reef Bar .... *ph 22 691*
Don't Drink the Water Cocktail Bar .... *ph 21 663*
Le Lalaga Bar .... *ph 20 673*
Mount Vaea Nightclub .... *ph 21 627*
Rainbow Springs Bar & Reception Centre .... *ph 21 254*
RSA Club .... *ph 20 171*
Love Boat Bar & Nightclub .... *ph 24 065*
Koreana Bar .... *ph 26 919*

Restaurants

Apia Inn (European) .... *ph 21 010*
Canton (Chinese) .... *ph 22 818*
Coconuts Beach Club .... *ph 24 849*
Le Godinet .... *ph 23 690*

Mandarin (Chinese) .... *ph 20 988*
The Golden Dragon (Chinese) .... *ph 20 988*
The Waterfront .... *ph 20 977*
The Treasure Garden (Chinese) .... *ph 22 568*
Wong Kee's (Chinese) .... *ph 22 988*
Stevensons (Tusitala Hotel) .... *ph 21 122*
Koreana Restaurant .... *ph 26 919*
Flavio's Cuisine (Italian) .... *ph 25 510*

Snack Bars & Coffee Shops

Aggie's Fale Snack .... *ph 22 880*
Apia Rainforest .... *ph 25 030*
Chester the Chicken .... *ph 20 029*
Coffee 'N' Things .... *ph 21 038*
Daphne's Coffee Shop .... *ph 22 400*
Giodano's Pizzaeta .... *ph 20 162*
Josie's Deli .... *ph 24 242*
Marie's Cafe .... *ph 23 554*
Seafood Gourmet .... *ph 24 625*
Kitano Tusitala Snack Bar .... *ph 21 122*
Mom's cafe (Savi'i wharf) .... *ph 51 111*
Le Tiara .... *ph 22 400*
Love Boat Snack Bar .... *ph 24 065*
Bamboo Snack Hut .... *ph 20 238/21 078*

Shopping

Duty Free shops are at Faleolo Airport, where there is a wide selection of international goods ranging from clothing, cigarettes, liquor, perfume and jewellery to electrical goods. South Pacific Duty Free is at the Clipper Arcade, Apia, where you can view and organise purchases to be picked up at the airport on departure.

The Philatelic Bureau on the ground floor of the Post Office has a wide selection of Samoan postal stamps, a prized collection of their award winning designs. The Treasury Department sells commemorative issues and mint sets of Samoan coins.

Local fashion and souvenirs can be obtained from hotel shops and the many boutiques in Apia at fairly reasonable prices.

Handicrafts

A wide variety of artefacts made by Samoan families for their personal use are very popular because of the beauty of the wood, fibres, quality of craftsmanship and the unique designs. Siapo (Tapa) cloth made from the mulberry bark and painted with native dyes is much sort after. Mats, hats and baskets are traditional crafts. Kava and food bowls are hand carved. Shell jewellery and brightly coloured printed fabrics are also popular. Best places to buy these items are the New Market, Aggie Grey's Gift Shop, Chan Mow's general store, Janet's Handicrafts and the Kava and Carvings.

Sightseeing

Upolu

The drive from Faleolo Airport to Apia is indeed a sight. James A. Michener called this 'the most beautiful drive in the South Pacific'.

Vailima Estate

This is a must. About a 5 minute drive from Apia on the cross island road stands Vailima, the former home of Robert Louis Stevenson. You may view the grounds but it is not possible to enter the house itself. When Stevenson died in 1894, Vailima became the official residence of the Head of State.

Stevenson's grave is on top of Mt Vaea and the walking track starts behind the estate next to the Botanical Gardens. The track is very slippery and good shoes should be worn. It takes several hours to reach the tomb of Tusitala (Teller of Tales) as the Samoans called Stevenson. On the tomb is the immortal 'requiem' carving:

Under the wide and starry sky,
Dig the grave and let me lie,
Glad did I live and gladly die,
and I laid me down with a will.

This be the verse you grave for me:
Here he lies where he longed to be;
Home is the sailor, home from the sea,
And the hunter home from the hill.

Stevenson's wife, Fanny, died in California in 1914. Her ashes were brought back to Samoa and buried at the foot of his grave with a bronze plaque bearing her Samoan name, Aolele, and Stevenson's words:

Teacher, tender comrade, wife,
A fellow-farer true through life,
Heart-whole and soul free,
The August Father gave to me.

Most tours continue on for a stop at Styles Clothing Factory and a winery, about another 10 minute drive. Another 20 minutes and you come to Tiavi Falls. Tours usually stop at the Coconuts Beach Club for a drink.

Palolo Deep Marine Reserve

The only marine reserve in the country, it was established in 1979 and is under the management of the Division of Environment and Conservation. It is very close to Apia and offers visitors the opportunity to view the exotic marine life.

Papaseea Sliding Rocks

Mother Nature has carved waterfalls over rocks with pools at the bottom. Ideal for children, it is on the outskirts of Apia and can be reached by bus or taxi. The name on the bus is 'Seesee'.

Piula Cave

Situated on the east coast road at Lufilufi, near the Piula Methodist College, and about 28km from Apia, the cave is in a grotto with a small freshwater pool, fed by an underground spring. Many take advantage of the pool for a refreshing dip.

Falefa Falls, Mafa Pass, Fuipisia Falls & Aleipata Area

A 64km drive along the east coast threads through some of the most beautiful scenery on the island. At the end of 29km are Falefa Falls. The drive continues over the Mafa Pass with a wonderful view of the shoreline before reaching Fuipisia Falls, a 548m waterfall.

The drive ends at the village of Amaile in the Aleipata district on the east side of Upolu.

O Le Pupu Pu'e National Park

This was Western Samoa's first National Park and it was declared such in 1978. It covers an area of 2,833 hectares extending from Mt Pu'e in the centre of the island to the south coast and coastal cliffs (o le pupu). It houses uncommon tropical vegetation and wild bird species. Togitogiga Reserve forms part of the park.

Togitogiga Falls

The falls and swimming area on the Mataloa River are managed and protected by the Division of Environment and Conservation. They are popular for picnics and a special area has fales and a rest area.

Savi'i

Attractions around the north coast include the idyllic villages of Falealupo and Papa, timber mills at Alelo, bathing pool at Saleaula, the Virgin's Grave, and large lava fields. On the south coast there are the blowholes at Cape Asuisui, Lovers Leap at Fagafau and the beautiful villages of Palauli, Sagone Fualalo and Fualuga.

Sightseeing is leisurely. It can either be taken in a mini-bus arranged by the hotel or guest house or by public bus. Taxis are few but arrangements can be made in advance.

Tours

Take a trip around the island of **Manono**, the legendary Bali Hai of Samoa with its beautiful clear waters. Go ashore on one of the beaches for lunch, or swim in one of the lagoons. You also pass the islands of Apolima and Nuulopa.

The boat leaves from Manono-uta, near Cape Lefatu on the west coast of Upolu.

St Anne's Church, Leulumoega, Upolu Island

Central Group Cocoa Plantation

About 23km inland from Apia is an interesting illustration of one of Western Samoa's chief agricultural products. It was here that "Lafi 7", the highest producing hybrid cocoa in the world was first developed.

Multifanua Coconut Plantation

This is the largest coconut plantation in the southern hemisphere and is 41km west of Apia. The tour passes through villages and gives the visitor a clear look at the lives of Samoans.

Lake Lanotoo

A crater lake with gold fish about 19km from Apia, Lake Lanotoo is difficult to reach on your own. Usually a guide can be arranged through hotels.

Tour Operators

There are plenty of tour operators in Western Samoa. Your hotel or the Visitor's Bureau can advise you and make bookings.

Following is a selection:

Upolu

Annie's Tours, ph 21 550, in Matautu.
Eco-Tour Samoa, ph 25 030, Apia Rainforest, Tauese.
Oceania Travel & Tours, ph 24 443, PO Box 1572, Apia.
Samoa Scenic Tours, ph 22 880, Aggie Grey's.
Beehive Travel, ph 24 987, Wendy Complex, Saleufi.
Island Hopper Vacations Samoa Ltd, ph 22 036, Wendts Complex.

Savi'i

Savi'i Travel, ph 51 206, Salelologa, Savi'i.
Vaisala Hotel Tours, ph 58 016, Savi'i.

Sport

Tennis

Public tennis courts built for the 1983 South Pacific Games are at Apia Park. Open daily from 8am-6pm. One tala per player for ½ hour is charged per court.

Private tennis courts at Chanel Collage, Moamoa, are open to visitors Monday, Wednesday, Saturday and Sunday. Reservations, ph 21 821.

Tennis courts at the Kitano Tusitala are for their guests only.

Squash

Apia squash courts are at Apia Wharf (after Seaside Inn at Matautu-tai). Tournaments are sponsored by the various business houses to commemorate a holiday or as a promotion for their business. Enquiries and bookings, ph 23 780 or 22 571.

Heem's Squash courts on the outskirts of Apia, ph 20 183.

Fitness Centres

Jazzercise and aerobic classes are held at Body Torque in Savalalo and Genesis Fitness Centre in Apia. Weight training is available at both Heem's Fitness Centre, ph 20 183, and Genesis Fitness Spectrum, ph 20 113, or contact the Visitors Bureau.

Golf

The Royal Samoan Country Club is close to Fagalii Airstrip. The 18 hole course is open to visitors at a green fee of WS$50 (US$42) including caddy fees. Golf clubs are available for hire. The men's official day is Saturday, women play Tuesdays.

Lawn Bowls

Lawn Bowls are played at the Apia Bowling Club, adjacent to the Hotel Kitano Tusitala, and at Apia Park sporting complex. Arrangements can be made through hotels, tour agents or the club secretary.

Hockey

The hockey season is August-December, and games are played at the Apia Park sporting complex.

Netball

This is the most popular sport with the ladies and is played all around the islands. The season is end of March to late May.

Rugby

The most celebrated sport in Samoa. Its season is February- July. An international 7-a-side Tournament is hosted by the Marist St Joseph's annually toward the end of February. Rugby league follows from July-November in the early evening at Apia Park.

Samoan Cricket (Kirikiti)

One of the most traditional sports and played in most villages. Season is April-June. The finals are one of the many sporting activities in the

Independence Celebrations in June or the Teuila Tourism Festival in September.

Soccer

Soccer is played from the end of June to early August in Apia Park.

Shooting

Western Samoan Shooting Association hosts local and international tournaments.

Swimming

There are swimming beaches all around the islands. Be careful of the undertow when the tide is going out at Vaiala beach.

Solosolo Beach is good for surfing but again, be careful of the undertow.

Mulinuu beach, 1km from the Kitano Tusitala Hotel, is very popular with locals and visitors.

Other beaches close to Apia: Saluafata, Lalomanu, Aufaga, Vavau, Tafatafa, Aganoa, Coconuts Beach Club, Mulivai, Saanapu, Salamumu and Lefaga.

Samoan Style Accommodation

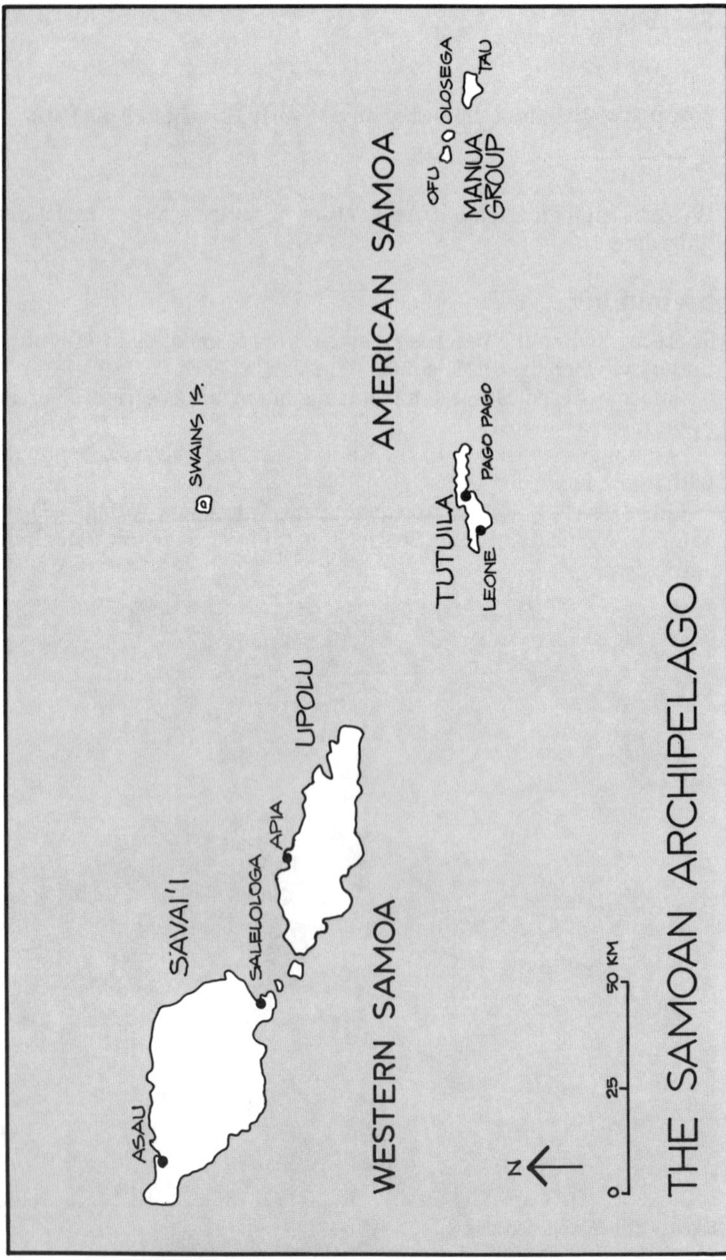
THE SAMOAN ARCHIPELAGO
WESTERN SAMOA
AMERICAN SAMOA
SAVAI'I
ASAU
SALELOLOGA
APIA
UPOLU
SWAINS IS.
TUTUILA
LEONE
PAGO PAGO
OFU
OLOSEGA
TAU
MANUA GROUP
N
0
25
50 KM

AMERICAN SAMOA

American Samoa is situated in the central South Pacific, 129km from Western Samoa. It comprises six inhabited islands: Tutuila, the largest with an area of 137 sq km, Aunuu, Manu'a Group (Ofu, Oloseag, Tau), Rose and Swain's.

The Manu'a Group are volcanic in origin and are dominated by high peaks. Rose is an uninhabited coral atoll to the east of the two island groups.

American Samoa, is 3700km south-west of Hawaii and is the only American territory south of the equator.

The main export is tuna fish. The capital is Pago Pago (pronounced Pango Pango), which is on the island of Tutuila.

History

Until 1899 when Germany annexed Western Samoa and the USA took Eastern Samoa, the history of Western Samoa is common to both.

The first administrators of American Samoa were naval personnel who ran the island like a military installation, sadly neglecting the welfare of the local Samoans.

In the mid-1930s Japan began to emerge as an international power giving the naval station at Tutuila a strategic importance. By 1940 the Samoan islands had become a staging and training area for the US Marine Corps. It was the sudden influx of Americans that gave the Samoans a taste of modern society. Some feel this was not for the better.

Fortunately for the Samoan people, the fighting during World War II did not reach Samoa. In 1945 the US Marines left as suddenly as they had arrived, and American Samoa returned to the quiet, peaceful way of life it had enjoyed before the war.

A constitution was drawn up in 1960 and revised in 1967. Today, American Samoa is an unincorporated territory of the USA. Its people are classified as Americans. The executive branch of the government is headed by a popularly elected Governor and Lieutenant Governor. American Samoa's Fono (legislature) is bicameral and the representatives are also elected. Senate members are chosen by the Samoan matai system - country councils - according to Samoan custom. The judicial branch consists of the High Court, the District Court and Village Courts. The Chief Justice, head of the judiciary, is appointed by the Secretary of the Interior.

Elections are held every even numbered year.

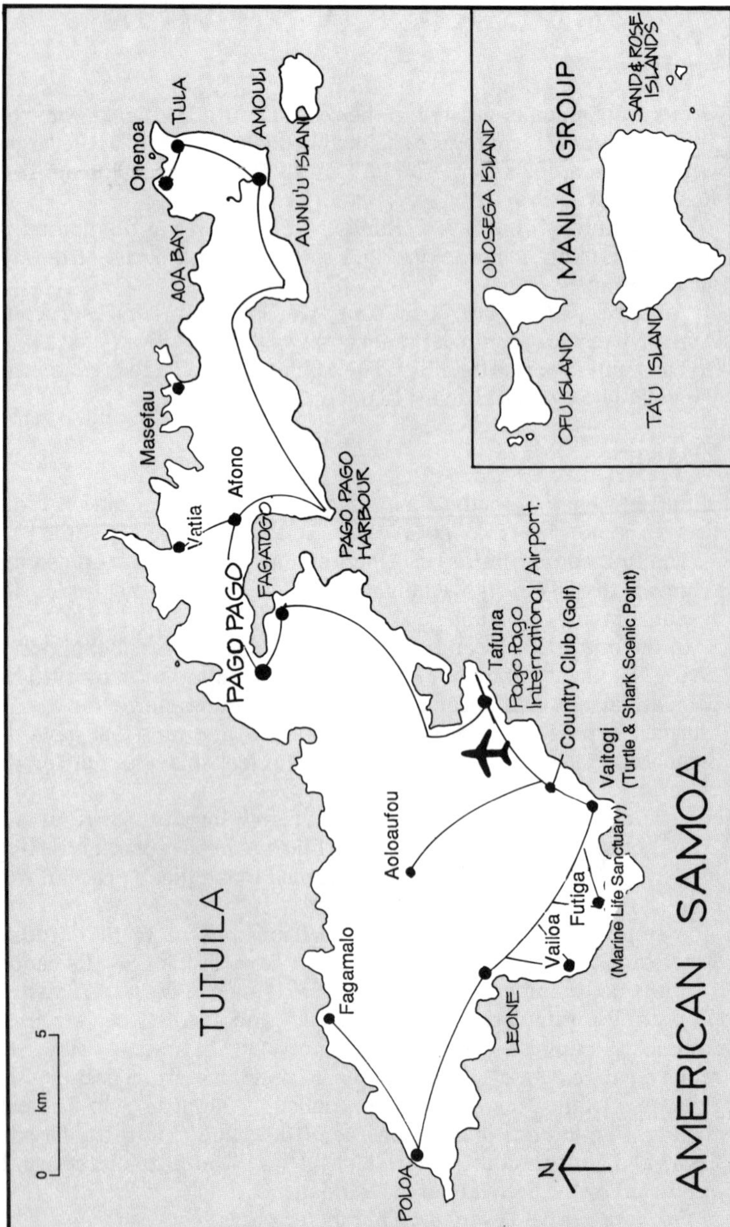
AMERICAN SAMOA
TUTUILA
0 km 5
N
POLOA
Fagamalo
LEONE
Vailoa
Futiga
(Marine Life Sanctuary)
Aoloaufou
Vaitogi
(Turtle & Shark Scenic Point)
Country Club (Golf)
Tafuna
Pago Pago International Airport.
PAGO PAGO
FAGATOGO
PAGO PAGO HARBOUR
Vatia
Afono
Masefau
AOA BAY
Onenoa
TULA
AMOULI
AUNU'U ISLAND
MANUA GROUP
OFU ISLAND
OLOSEGA ISLAND
TA'U ISLAND
SAND & ROSE ISLANDS

Climate

American Samoa's climate is typically tropical with temperatures seldom above 25C. Nights are balmy, and cooling tradewinds blow constantly. There are heavy rains but even in the rainy season, December-March, there are periods of sunshine each day. June-September is the best time of the year to visit.

Population

The population of American Samoa is about 52,000 of which 10,000 are Western Samoans and 3000 Tongans. Tutuila has 45,043, Manu's Group 1714 and Swain's Island 16! Because American Samoans are US nationals, they have free entry to the USA and about 60,000 live in Hawaii and California. They are US nationals, not citizens, so they cannot vote in a US Presidential election.

Nearly 70% of high school graduates leave Samoa within a year of graduation. Many have forgotten their own culture in their haste to become Americans but those left at home fiercely defend their origins.

Language

The official language is Samoan but most people speak English.

Public Holidays

January 1 ....New Year's Day
February ....President's Day
March/April...........Good Friday/ Easter Monday
April 17....................Flag Day
May ....Memorial Day
July 4 ....Independence Day
July 16 ....Mamu'a Flag Day
September ....Labour Day
October....................Columbus Day
October....................White Sunday
November 11 ....Veteran's Day
November ....Thanksgiving Day
December 25 ....Christmas Day.

American Samoa's Flag Day in April is a major event. There are gala traditional ceremonies, a Polynesian longboat race and a general re-enactment of the cession to the USA.

First week in May is Tourism Week and the Miss American Samoa Beauty Pageant.

The second Sunday in October is White Sunday. The children dress in white and take part in a procession to the church. They take the seats of honour and lead the service.

In October and November, when the moon and the tide are just right, a sea annelid (worm) called palolo emerges from the reef to begin its annual reproductive cycle. Samoans consider palolo a great delicacy and turn out in force with nets to scoop up the 'Caviar of the Pacific'. Many eat the creatures raw straight from the water. This is a great opportunity to join the natives and wade out to the reef with them.

October hosts the Moso'oi week festival and arts Fia Fia for the month.

The third week in December Christmas festivities begin.

Some public holidays have moveable dates. Check with the American Samoan Tourist Bureau.

Entry Regulations

A passport is required by all except US citizens and must be valid for at least 60 days beyond the date of departure. No visa required for stays of under 30 days, provided the visitor has confirmed accommodation and an on-going ticket.

Customs

Duty Free allowance: 200 cigarettes or 100 cigars, 2 bottles (fifths) of liquor, and a reasonable amount of perfume for your own use.

Departure allowance if going to the USA, 2 gallons of liquor and 2 cartons of cigarettes.

There is no departure tax.

Embassies

Australia: No representative. Refer to the High Commission in Western Samoa.

New Zealand: No representative. Refer to the High Commission in Western Samoa.

Canada: No representative. Refer to the High Commission in Wellington. NZ.

UK: No representative. Refer to the High Commission in Canberra, Australia.

Money

The currency of American Samoa is the US dollar. Approximate exchange rates are

A$	=	$0.77
Can$	=	$0.74
NZ$	=	$0.68
S$	=	$0.72
UK£	=	$1.53

Communications

International direct dialling telephone calls are available everywhere, and the country code 684.

The local COMSAT satellite station has many telephone channels to USA, Hawaii and New Zealand. Telegraph, telex and fax facilities available. COMSAT also provides TV and radio broadcasts.

The Post office in the Lumanai Building, Fagatogo, and is open 24 hours. There are branches in Leone and Faguita villages that are open Mon-Fri 8am-4pm, Sat 8.30am-noon.

Papers include the *Samoan Journal, Samoan News* and the *South Seas Star*. There is a Samoan and English radio station and TV station. Viewing is available until midnight.

Pago Pago Harbour

Miscellaneous

Time

Local time is GMT - 11.

Business Hours

Banks are open Mon-Fri 9am-3pm. Bank of Hawaii and America Samoa Bank in Fagatogo offer a special service window that is open until 4.30pm Friday. Bank of America Samoa Bank, Nu'uuli Branch is also open on Saturday 9am-noon.
Shops are open Mon-Fri 8am-5pm, Sat 8am-1pm.

Electricity

Electric current is 110/120V AC 60 cycles. Take an adaptor and check that your electrical equipment will work on the islands. You will probably need a converter.

Credit Cards

All are widely accepted.

Tipping

Although this is an American territory, tipping is not customary and is actually discouraged.

Medical

The Fagàlu Institution offers 24-hour medical and dental services. There is also full health care available at the LBJ Tropical Medical Centre. A nominal fee is charged for each visit.

Excellent medical, dental and pharmaceutical services are available 24 hours a day.

No vaccinations are required unless coming from an infected area.

NOTES

Water

Most visitors do not have trouble with the water. However, if you feel your stomach may not like the local water, mineral water is readily available.

Etiquette

When visiting a Samoan village, ask before taking photos, picking flowers or using the beach. Every Samoan thinks he owns the entire village. Permission is sure to be granted.

In a Samoan home, sit before talking or eating. It is considered to be impolite to stretch your legs out in front of you so try to fold them under.

Don't eat while walking through a village.

If you are invited to take kava with Samoans, spill a few drops on the floor or mat in front of you before drinking.

Every evening at dusk, each village stops for family prayers which last about 10 minutes. If you are walking through the village, stop and wait until the prayers are finished. You may be invited to join in the prayers; you are welcome to do so.

If driving through a village at this time, keep going.

It is considered to be thoughtful to be extra quiet on Sunday.

Pago Pago bay with the Rainmaker Hotel in the foreground and the mountain with the same name forming a backdrop

Emergency Phone Numbers

Police, Fire, Hospital - 911.

Insurance

It is advisable to take out a comprehensive insurance policy before leaving home.

Dress

Light and casual wear is the most appropriate, but remember to be well covered in the towns and villages.

Travel Information

How to get there

By Air

Hawaiian Air, Samoa Air and Polynesian Airlines provide regular services.

Hawaiian Air connects American Samoa with the USA via Hawaii, and once a week direct to/from Los Angeles.

Polynesian Air links American Samoa with Australia, New Zealand and Fiji via Apia in Western Samoa.

Samoa Air provides an inter-island service and also connections with Tonga and daily flights to Western Samoa.

Pago Pago International Airport is 10km from the town, and there is an airport bus.

Day Trip

It is possible to fly from Apia, in Western Samoa, to Pago Pago in the morning, tour the island and fly back to Apia in the late afternoon.

Sea

Several cruise ships call at Pago Pago. There are also a few cargo/passenger ships that call, but not on a regular basis. Enquire from the Tourist Centre.

Tourist Information

American Samoan Office of Tourism, PO Box 1147, Pago Pago, American Samoa 96799, ph (684) 633 1094, fax (684) 633 1091/1092/1093.

Accommodation

First Class

Rainmaker Hotel, PO Box 996, Pago Pago, ph 633 4241, fax 633 5959. 184 A/C rooms with phone in the main building plus several beach fales. Situated on Pago Pago Bay in shadow of Rainmaker Mountain. Coffee shop next to pool, snacks, restaurants, cocktail bar, colour TV to rent. Polynesian floorshow Friday nights. Private beach, snorkelling, scuba diving, sports-fishing, hiking. Price: Harbour wing single/double US$60-US$125. Beach front standard US$72, fale standard US$85, executive Suite US$150. A 50% deposit 30 days prior to arrival, final payment before date of booking.

Standard

Motu'o Fiaflaga Motel, PO Box 1554, Pago Pago, ph 633 7777 fax 633 4776. Within walking distance of town centre. 12 A/C rooms. Good for business or pleasure. Price: single US$50, double US$60.

Herb & Sia's Family Style Motel, PO Box 430, Pago Pago, ph 633 5413. Right in heart of Pago Pago shopping centre. 15 rooms island style with fridge, A/C. Price: rooms with shared bath single US$35, double US$45. With private bath single US$40, double US$45.

Apiolefaga Inn, PO Box 336, Pago Pago, ph 699 9124. 5 minutes from airport. 27 rooms with A/C, cooking facilities, fridge, bath/shower, TV lounge. Restaurant, bar. Price: single US$50, double US$60, triple US$65.

Budget

Barry's Bed & Breakfast, Afao (PO Box 5572, Pago Pago), ph 699 5113, fax 633 9111. East of airport. 4 rooms. Price: single US$35, double US$40.

Camping can be arranged with village chiefs.

People seeking inexpensive or more personal forms of accommodation should try 'Fale, Fale Ma Ti' (house, mat and tea). The host acts as unofficial authority on the islands, offering information on the Samoan way of life, customs and traditions. Prices vary from US$25-45 depending on the homes. Some are Western-style, others thatched roof fales. There is also space for campers. All have modern conveniences, and provisions are extra.

Visitors interested in FFT should make prior arrangements with the Office of Tourism, ph (684) 633 1094.

Manu'a

Standard

Vaoto Lodge on Ofu Island, Manu'a, c/- Vili Malae, Ofu, Manu'a, American, ph (684) 699 9628/655 1120. 10 rooms with private facilities. Own beach, fishing, scuba diving, snorkelling, swimming, hiking, camping and other water sports. Food and refreshments. Regular flights from Pago Pago with Samoan Air. Price: single US$35, double US$40, extra person US$10.

Fitiuta Lodge, PO Box 1858, Pago Pago, ph 633 1283/633 1284. Situated at Ta'u, Island of Manu'a. 8 rooms. Price: single US$25, double US$30.

Ta'u Motel, Ta'u, Island of Manu'a, Pago Pago 96799, ph 677 3155/3504, 699 9885. 9 rooms. Price: single US$30, double US$40.

Don & Ilaisa, Olosega, (PO Box 932, Pago Pago), ph 633 2304/655 1212. 6 rooms. Price: Single US$20, double US$35.

Local Transport

Bus

There is a service from the airport to the centre of Pago Pago.

Buses connect the town centre with outlying villages, but they are unscheduled. Flag one down and when you reach your destination, ask the driver when he will be returning.

Taxi

These are plentiful, and the fares are fixed by the government.

Ship

There is a service from Pago Pago to Manu'a Islands. Contact the Tourist Centre for schedules.

Twice a week, there is an inter-island boat between American Samoa and Western Samoa, and the trip takes about 8 hours.

Car

There are several car hire firms but they require the driver to be at least 21 years old, some want the driver to be 25. Driving is on the RIGHT hand side of the road.

Avis, ph 699 4408/9 & 699 2746, also at the airport; Pavitt's U Drive, ph 21 766; Royal Samoa Inc, ph 633 5884/2017 also at Rainmaker Hotel; Kathy's Tours & Travel, ph 633 1283/1284.

NOTES

Food and Entertainment

The snack bar and the restaurant at the Rainmaker Hotel offer a good variety including hamburgers and authentic Samoan food.

The restaurant at the Apiolefaga Inn is one of the best.

There are plenty of fast food outlets, and American, Chinese, Japanese, Mexican, Italian and Polynesian restaurants are dotted around the island. Following are some restaurants and snack bars.

Leloaloa

Ramona Lee Restaurant
Aggie's Refreshment Stand

Atu'u

Seoul Restaurant
S. Shalhout
Te'o Fuvai's Place
Kim Yung Chung, ph 644 2327
Lunch Wagon, ph 644 4115

Pago Pago

Paisano's Pizzeria at Pago Plaza
The Odyssey at Pago Plaza
Evalani's Cabaret
Pago Park Fast Food Outlet
Kims Restaurant, ph 633 4527
Pago Bay Restaurant, ph 633 2837

Malaloa

Korea House Restaurant
Korean BBQ

Fagatogo

Alamoana Recipe
Hot Pot Inc, ph 633 7053
Milovale's Drive In
Pele's Place
Pizza Time
Sadie's Restaurant
Te'os Kitchen
The Sweet Shop

Utulei

Ifo's Burger, ph 699 4588
Pago Pago Yacht Club
Panda Tea House

Fatumafuti

Chicken Out
Alamai-Samoa Fast Food

Nu'uuli

Little Sams
Pago Joe
Milovale's Drive-in
Le Tausala restaurant, ph 699 5128

Tafuna

Luisa's Laundromat & Snack Bar, ph 699 1882
C & K Yogurt & Hot Dogs
Airport Restaurant
Alafou Fast Food.

For an idea of price. Breakfast at the Pago Bay Restaurant costs from US$4.95 for eggs and bacon to US$8.95 for grilled fish. Hotcakes/waffles are US$2.95; Oatmeal US$2.50; Fruit Platter US$3.95; Toast with butter and jam US$1,50; Tea/coffee US$0.75; Fruit juice US$1.75.

Lunch - Appetisers from US$2.50 for a spring roll to US$7.95 for Sashimi; Soups from US$1.50 a cup; green salad US$2,95; Sandwiches & Burgers from US$5.50 to US$8.95.

Dinner - Appetisers, average, shrimp cocktail US$6.95. Soup and salad same as lunch. Main courses from US$8.95 for chicken curry to US$23 for sirloin steak. Seafood from US$15.95 for scampi to US$27.95 for lobster thermidor. Chinese soups from US$4.95 to US$10.23. From the wok US$7.95 for steamed chicken and green onion to US$12.95 for sweet and sour shrimp.

No matter where you go, steak is at a premium ranging from US$13.95 for stewed to US$28.95 for grilled T-bone.

Unexpectedly, seafood is also pricey. Sandwiches and burgers start at US$5.50. Beer battered fish and chips is one of the most affordable dishes, about US$6.95.

Tour operators can arrange Samoan Fiafias, which include kava drinking ceremonies and Samoan feasts. The food consists of roast sucking pig, breadfruit, taro and puiasami made from coconut cream wrapped in taro leaves and cooked in a umu (underground oven).

The Rainmaker Hotel has a good floor show on Friday nights. There are also live bands, BBQs, and an American Happy Hour which lasts from 4.30pm to 6.30pm.

Shopping

Pago Pago is a duty free port. The duty free shop at the Rainmaker Hotel has a plentiful supply of souvenirs and other goods.

For an authentic sampling of Samoan lifestyle a visit to the *handicraft centre* is a must. It is situated at the Old Age office at the south end of Pago Pago Park. It has the usual tapa cloth, shells, baskets, etc.

Samoa Rentals, PO Box 3482, Pago Pago, ph 688 1525, fax 688 2253, have everything you need for camping.

Pago Plaza Shopping Mall has many shops to choose from. It is close to Pago Pago Park at the east end of the city.

Sightseeing

Pago Pago Harbour is the crater of an extinct volcano. It was the setting for Somerset Maugham's short storey *Rain*, which featured Sadie Thompson. It was made into a classic Hollywood film starring Rita Hayworth.

Start your tour from the tourist office, and you will find most of the sightseeing within a very short distance.

The **Courthouse of American Samoa**, a stately, white two-storey building, cost US$46,000 and was completed in four years. It looks more like a southern mansion than a government building. It was used, during the Naval administration as offices for the Commandants, the Governor and the Attorney General. It has also been used by chiefs, leaders and representatives of the various villages as a meeting place.

The **Fono** (Legislature) building is close by. It demonstrates a successful blending of traditional architecture and modern materials. The **fale tele** (round meeting house) and the **fale afolau** (long oval-shaped residence) designs are incorporated in this comparatively new structure.

Jean P Haydon Museum was originally built as a naval commissary. Immediately in front of the museum entrance are Samoan fales used to teach and demonstrate local arts and crafts. Inside is a collection of artifacts and handicrafts, and items of cultural history.

Mt Alva is reached by taking the cable car/tramway that is a little further on from the museum. It crosses Pago Pago Bay on its way to the top of Mt Alva (488m) for wonderful views that are at their best early morning or late afternoon. The tramway is 1.5km long and has one of the world's longest non-supported cable spans. It operates every day except Sunday from 8am-4pm, and there is a small fee.

The **Governor's Residence** is close to the Rainmaker Hotel.

Afono Pass winds from one side of Tutuila to the other. There are several scenic points where Pago Pago Harbour and the north shore of the island can be viewed.

Blunt's Point, visible from the Rainmaker Hotel, was a gun emplacement during World War II.

Breaker's Point, Virgin Falls and **Leone Falls** are highly recommended scenic spots for the first-time visitor.

Fagaitua, farther along on the eastern side of the harbour, is where you will find the burial grounds of the ancient chiefs.

Vaitogi Village, past the airport when heading west, is a favourite with locals and visitors. According to legend, a young married couple who loved each other dearly, learned that the husband was destined for the feast of the cannibal King Malietoa Faiga. Fearing reprisals for their village, they set out for the island of Upolu. Their canoe was blown off course and they landed on the island of Tutuila where they were offered lodgings in the home of the generous chief Letuli of Ili'ili.

Later, when king Malietoa ceased practising cannibalism, the Letuli family offered to escort the couple back to their home. They refused, wanting to repay the chief and his family for their kindness.

Together they climbed a cliff in Vaitogi and jumped into the sea. Instantly, the husband turned into a shark and his wife became a turtle. The shark told the villagers, 'If you want us to appear on the surface of the sea, let the children stand on the cliff and sing'. The children still assemble on the cliff and sing, and it is said that a huge shark and turtle appear on the surface.

Massacre Bay, A'asu Village, still farther round to the north-west of the island, is where 11 members of a French Scientific Expedition were murdered in 1787. It so shocked the western world that it precluded those governments from establishing themselves on Tutuila until the late 19th century. French warships still return to A'asu to honour their fallen comrades. To reach the bay, you will have to turn right just after Apiolefaga Inn.

Fagelele Boys School and **Atauloma Girls School,** seen if you keep to the coast road, heading west towards Fagamalo, are considered to be worth visiting. Very handy for those staying at Barry's Bed and Breakfast.

Most of the sightseeing can be done by local bus.

Manu'a Island

The Act of Congress that established the National Park of American Samoa is special in a number of ways. Firstly, mindful of its responsibility to ensure the continuance of the traditional communal land system in American Samoa, Congress carefully crafted its legislation directing the National Park Service to manage parklands by means of long-term leases with each of the villages with lands in the park. There is no taking of lands by the government for national park purposes. In no other national park has Congress taken this unusual step.

Secondly, the park is comprised primarily of a largely undisturbed and uninhabited native climax rainforest of a type found nowhere else throughout the national park system. The rainforest provides natural habitat for at least 35 bird species, most of which are native resident breeders. There are also two species of native flying foxes. These large, soaring fruit bats are important pollinaters of rainforest plants.

The park is in three units of widely separated islands. Comprising nearly 9,000 acres, a thousand of which are off shore waters on the outer edge of coral reefs, the park has some of the most scenic island shoreline on earth. There are long white sandy beaches, sea cliffs, sheltered coves and islets spread over with lush green vegetation extending all the way to the ocean's edge.

Located on the islands of Ofu, Olosega and Ta'u are the villages of Ofu, Olosega, Sili, Fitiuta, Faleasao, Si'ufaga and Lume. The twin villages of Si'ulaga and Lume, also known as Ta'u village, were the site of Margaret Mead's anthropological study which resulted in her book *Coming of Age in Samoa*.

Ta'u is believed to be ancient Samoa. A great majority of original history, legends and stories make up the basis of oral traditions and formal ceremonies. They are based on incidents which occurred on Ta'u.

Whether the first Polynesians lived in Manu'a or Savai'i is a matter of conjecture. It is conceded that the Tuimanu (King of Manu'a) was one of the strongest and most powerful leaders of ancient Samoa and neighbouring islands. It is commonly believed that holders of the Tuimanu title held both supernatural and human powers.

A visit to Manu'a will reveal many fascinating living examples and tangible evidence of the ancient legends and stories of Samoa.

Activities on Manu's Islands are: water sports, snorkelling, scuba diving. Traditional village customs may be observed and visitors are encouraged to join in.

A restaurant has opened at Ofu Airport.

Sport and Recreation

Diving

Scuba diving and snorkelling with diving experts is popular. All equipment provided, night dives and reef dives. Contact *Dive Samoa,* PO Box 3927, Pago Pago, 96799, ph 633 2183.

Game Fishing

For those once-in-a-lifetime big and special catching moments, come to where the action is and join in the major Billfish and Shore Casting Tournaments. Contact *American Samoa Game Fishing Association,* PO Box 191, Pago Pago 96799, ph 633 4598.

Golf

The *Lava Lava Golf Course* offers club rentals, fully furnished Pro shop, Rent-a-carts, 18 holes, Club house restaurant. Open 7 days a week. Home of the American Samoan International Pro-Am Open.

Tennis

The American Samoa Tennis Association is very active and has popularised tennis among youngsters through free clinics. Regional ASTA now sponsors an Annual Junior Championship Tournament.

There are public tennis courts at Lions Park close to the airport.

Other sports are: swimming, sailing, rugby, cricket and rainforest trails.

Tour Operators

Kathy's Tours & Travel, PO Box 3244, Pago Pago 96799, ph 633 1283/84, fax 633 5714, for hotel bookings, tours, transfers, car rental.

Royal Samoa Travel, PO Box 3483, Pago Pago 96799, ph 633 5884, fax 633 1311. Transfers, excursions, sightseeing in island-style coaches with English-speaking guide.

CDI Travel & Tours, PO Box 3485, Pago Pago 96799, ph 633 5077, fax (684) 633 5714.

Pleasure Tours & Travel, PO Box 727, Pago Pago 96799, ph 699 2575.

Tropical Island Travel (TTT), PO Box 178, Pago Pago 96799, ph 633 5646, fax 633 5637.

TERRITORY OF THE WALLIS & FUTUNA ISLANDS

Known to the Polynesians as *Uvea*, which means consolation, Wallis and Futuna Islands are 250km apart and Wallis is surrounded by a lagoon that has an area of 95 sq km and a circumference of around 50km. Both islands are ringed by coral reefs.

Uvea is roughly 3000km south-west of Tahiti and 340km east of Samoa, and the two islands are vastly different in landscape. Wallis Island has a semi-desert centre with pandanus trees, while Futuna has volcanoes, the highest being Mt Puke (760m).

History

Wallis Island was discovered by Samuel Wallis in August 1767. On the same voyage, in his ship *The Dolphin*, he also discovered Tahiti.

Futuna Island was discovered in 1616 by Guillaume Schouten and Jacob Lemaire, who also discovered Tonga.

Wallis was not inhabited until the late 13th century when Tongans migrated, meanwhile some Samoans had settled on Futuna.

French Marist missionaries arrived in Uvea in 1837, and although they were extremely successful in their attempt to spread the faith, it was not without a cost. St Peter Chanel was a victim of cannibalism in Futuna, on April 28, 1841. He is now known as the "Apostle of Oceania".

Both islands became part of the French colony in 1942, and in 1958 the inhabitants chose to become an overseas French territory.

On Wallis, the old traditional ways of life are still valid with leadership held by the *Lavelua*, who is elected by a group of elders and assisted by a council of advisers.

Wallis and Futuna imports most of its foodstuffs, clothing, fuel and machinery, and exports only copra and handicrafts. Its main revenue comes from licensing of fishing rights to foreign countries, subsidies from the French Government, and levies imposed on the more than 11,000 expatriate workers in New Caledonia.

For travellers who want to get away from it all to an undiscovered tropical paradise, Wallis and Futuna could be the answer.

Climate

The weather for both islands is hot and humid, with an annual average of 27C. The rainy season is from November to April, and the dry season May to October.

Population

The latest statistics show that Wallis has a population of 8973, while Futuna has 4732, and that the total population has increased more than 60% during the last 30 years. Approximately 98% of the people are Polynesian, and all are Roman Catholic.

Language

The main language is French.

Public Holidays

All religious holidays are celebrated, as well as:

April 28	St Peter Chanel
May 3	Armistice
June 29	Sts Peter and Paul
July 14	National Day.

Entry Regulations

All visitors must have a valid passport, and a visa is required by all except nationals of EEC countries.

Vaccinations are not necessary unless visitors are from an infected area.

There is no departure tax.

Money

The currency of the islands is the French Pacific Franc (CFP), and approximate rates of exchange can be found in the French Polynesia chapter.

There is only one bank on Wallis, the Bank Wallis and Futuna.

Communications

Postal and telecommunication facilities are open from Monday to Saturday. The international telephone system is via satellite.

Miscellaneous

Local Time is GMT + 12 hours.

Electricity supply is 220 volts.

Credit cards - Visa is accepted in a very few businesses, the other cards not at all.

Tipping is not allowed in Wallis and Futuna.

Travel Information

How to get there

Air Caledonie International have flights Noumea/Wallis on Mondays, Tuesdays and Thursdays, and these connect with flights to Sydney, Brisbane, Papeete, Port Vila or Auckland.

Wallis Hiltifo airport is 5km from Matu-Utu, the capital, and Futuna Point Vele airstrip is 10km from Sigave.

Accommodation

There are two hotels on Wallis Island - *Dinh Francois* and *Hotel Albatros* - and they provide sufficient and comfortable accommodation for the number of people who visit.

Local Transport

There is no public transport, nor a taxi service on the island, but both hotels can arrange rental cars. There are 100km of roads on Wallis, 16km of which are sealed. Futuna had 20km of earthen roads.

Sightseeing

There is not a lot to see, Wallis and Futuna is more for relaxing and communing with nature.

Wallis Island

The north-eastern coast has some really beautiful and unspoiled beaches, and there are small villages and churches all around the island that are just waiting to be discovered.

For scenic beauty, it is worth taking a trip to Kikila and Lanutaua Lakes, but if you only want to stay around the main town area, you have to visit the king's palace and the cathedral.

Futuna Island

The island is home to the sanctuary of St Peter Chanel, and there is also a museum with relics of the missionary days.

Also recommended is a trip to the uninhabited sister island of Alofi.

INDEX OF MAPS

INDEX

General

Places and Attractions